THE MEANING IN DREAMS AND DREAMING

The Meaning in Dreams and Dreaming

The Jungian Viewpoint

MARIA F. MAHONEY

THE CITADEL PRESS

Secaucus, New Jersey

To a great man,

CARL G. JUNG,

whose invitation to undertake work
"of the highest importance,
although a highly difficult and ambitious task,"
I accepted

Sixth paperbound printing, 1980

ISBN 0-8065-0095-6

CONTENTS

6

ACKNOWLEDGMENTS

I wish to express my gratitude to the following publishers and institutions for permission to quote:

The Bollingen Foundation, New York, for the *Collected Works of C. G. Jung:* (1. Two Essays on Analytical Psychology; 2. Psychology and Religion; 3. The Psychogenesis of Mental Disease; 4. The Structure and Dynamics of the Psyche; 5. Symbols of Transformation; 6. Archetypes and the Collective Unconscious; 7. Essays on a Science of Mythology; 8. The Practice of Psychotherapy; 9. The Development of Personality; 10. The Interpretation of Nature and the Psyche: Synchronicity, an Acausal Connecting Principle); and for *Psyche and Symbol,* edited by Violet de Laszlo; *The Hero With a Thousand Faces,* by Joseph C. Campbell; *Man and Time,* "Art and Time," by Erich Neumann (Eranos Yearbook 3); *Change,* by Hellmut Wilhelm; *Man and Time,* "Transformations of Science in Our Age," by Max Knoll (Eranos Yearbook 3).

Yale University Press, New Haven, Conn., for *The Psychology of Jung,* by Jolande Jacobi.

Routledge & Kegan Paul, Ltd., London, for *New Developments in Analytical Psychology,* by Dr. Michael Fordham; and *An Experiment in Depth,* by P. W. Martin.

Tavistock Publications, London, for two selections from *The Journal of Analytical Psychology,* "Cybernetics and Analytical Psychology," by Anthony Storr (Vol. I, No. I) and "Analysis of Patients Who Meet the Problems of the First Half of Life in the Second," by Dr. I. Jay Dunn. (Vol. VI, I).

Pantheon Books, Inc., New York, for *The Leopard,* by Giuseppe di Lampedusa.

The Belknap Press of Harvard University Press for *On Knowing,* by Jerome Bruner.

Barnes & Noble, Inc., New York, for *The Lost Language of Symbolism,* by Harold Bayley. (U.S. and its possessions, and the Philippine Islands.) And to Ernest Benn, Ltd., London, for remaining world rights.

Harcourt, Brace and World, Inc., New York, for *Exploring Inner Space,* by Jane Dunlap.

Beacon Press, Boston, for *Science and the Modern Mind,* edited by Gerald Holton.

The Julian Press, Inc., New York, for *Depth Psychology and Modern Man,* by Dr. Ira Progoff.

Harper & Row, Inc., New York, for *The Future of Man,* by Pierre Teilhard de Chardin.

Andover-Newton Theological School, for The Cutter Lecture, 1959, delivered by Dr. C. A. Meier, Zurich, Switzerland.

McGraw-Hill, New York, for *Encyclopedia of Science and Technology*, Vol. 8.

Houghton Mifflin Co., Boston, for *The Human Use of Human Beings*, by Norbert Wiener.

Basic Books, Inc., New York, for *Prelogical Experience: An Inquiry into Dreams and Other Creative Processes*, by Edward S. Tauber, M.D. and Maurice R. Green, M.D.

The Viking Press, New York, for *The Masks of God*, by Joseph C. Campbell; and *The Biology of the Spirit*, by Edmund W. Sinnott.

In addition, I am indebted to the following for permissions to quote from articles in *Spring*, the publication of the Analytical Psychology Club of New York: Dr. Eugen Boehler, of Zurich, Switzerland; Mrs. Aniela Jaffe, of Zurich; Dr. Jolande Jacobi, of Zurich; Dr. Edward C. Whitmont, of New York City; Dr. Eleanor Bertine of New York City; Dr. Eugene A. Henley, of New York City; Dr. Erich Neumann, of Tel Aviv; Dr. James Kirsch, of Los Angeles, California. Also to Dr. I. Jay Dunn, of Los Angeles, for permission to quote from his article.

For permission to quote from addresses before the Guild of Pastoral Psychology, London, England, I am indebted to the following: Dr. Gerhard Adler, London; Barbara Hannah, Zurich; and Dr. Edward F. Griffith, London, England.

Finally, I wish to express my appreciation to Dr. Carl Alfred Meier, of Zurich; to Jeannie Hughes, of Ossippee and Boston; to Christiana Morgan of Cambridge and Rowley; and to Bertha Klausner of New York City, to each of whom I am uniquely indebted and but for whom this book could not have been written.

                                                                M. F. M.

INTRODUCTION

Of the three major schools of psychological theory, the Freudian, Adlerian and Jungian, only that of the late Dr. Carl Gustave Jung, the renowned depth psychologist of Zurich, Switzerland, has developed techniques of dream interpretation primarily intended for non-neurotic, *normal* persons. Early in the course of his half-century of practice, Dr. Jung recognized that the benefits of the information and guidance emanating from the unconscious psyche through the interpretation of dreams, which is part of the therapeutic treatment of those ill with neuroses or psychoses, had, obviously, just as invaluable meaning to the non-neurotic.

I learned this at first-hand some years ago when those two most fateful of arbiters, Time and Chance, led me to the acquaintance of Miss Jeannie Hughes, a warm friend of Dr. Jung's, who lent me one of his early books, *The Integration of the Personality*. It dealt with a series of about four hundred dreams of an erudite scholar (not a bit neurotic) who had consulted a Zurich psychologist about his profuse dreams which, because of their strange contents, he sensed were profoundly meaningful experiences. The psychologist recognized their archetypal nature and referred the record of the dreams to Dr. Jung. Subsequently, they were made the subject of the book referred to.

The effect on me of reading that book was electric. As if on cue, a single baffling dream I had had more than a year previously rocketed into recall. So impressive had it been at the time I dreamt it that I had been unaccountably moved to write it down but, as I could make nothing whatever out of it, it finally receded into the limbo of the forgotten. Now it returned, but not alone, for it marked the start of a rush of dreams nightly, as though they had long been waiting in the wings to come through.

Understandably, I wanted to know the meaning of these dreams, if any, and under the unforgettable tutelage of patient,

steel-minded Miss Hughes, began the task of studying Jung's
Analytical Psychology and unravelling the meaning of the
dreams. That was in New York City. But as my life took me
from one to another place, I continued learning more: at the
Jung Institut in Zurich, in California, in Boston, and in Cambridge, under the polished expertise of Mrs. Christiana Morgan,
good friend and wise woman.

If one thing more than any other might have eased my task,
especially at the beginning, I believe it would be the information
I have put together in this volume. Nowhere is there available a
single volume devoted exclusively to presenting the information
about dreams and their interpretation according to the principles
Jung laid down, although, to be sure, there abound innumerable
essays, chapters, pamphlets and articles on the subject, scattered
throughout Jung's own works and in the publications of Jungian
psychologists throughout the world.

In fact, I mentioned the need for such a book to Dr. C. A.
Meier when he was serving as Director of the C. G. Jung Institut, right after he had finished delivering a lecture on dreams
and their interpretation. It was an excellent address, and I exclaimed, "Why don't you write a book expanding what you've
said? Wouldn't it be extremely useful as an introduction to Jung
and his approach to dreams and their interpretation?"

"Absolutely!" agreed Dr. Meier, beaming in the manner of a
man just struck by a very good idea. "Why don't you do it? *You*
write it!"

And so I have.

Granted, this or any other book can give no more than the
necessary intellectual presentation of the subject; and that is only
a part of what is actually required. The rest comes out of the personal experience of the dream and its interpretation—something
that has to be experienced subjectively, as Jung himself emphasizes: "On paper, the interpretation of a dream may look arbitrary,
muddled, spurious; but the same thing in reality can be a little
drama of unsurpassed realism. To *experience* a dream and its in-

terpretation is very different from having a tepid rehash set before you on paper. Everything about this [dream interpretation] is, in the deepest sense, *experience:* the entire theory [Jung's method of interpretation] even when it puts on the most abstract airs, is *the direct outcome of something experienced.*"

I bear witness, as this book testifies, to the truth of Jung's statement. Jung's method of interpretation is empirical; it works, and you know it works because you, yourself, feel, experience, live, unforgettable, stunning truths. Like any major human experience, say, for example, falling in love, nothing you ever read quite tells you what it is like; only when it really happens to you do you know the living experience of it. Then you feel as though a living nerve had been touched in the depths of your being. After that, when you read about falling in love, not only do you know what the writer is writing about, you also know if the writer knows what he is writing about.

That is how it is with the interpretation of your dreams. Through this art (for it is an art as well as a technique which can be learned), you may enter into a living relationship with your own unconscious, out of which your own unique life-line is determined.

MARIA F. MAHONEY

Springfield, Massachusetts
February, 1966

CHAPTER ONE

Do Dreams Have a Practical Meaning?

The analysis of dreams is an art,
a technique, a science of psychological life;
it is not a game but a practical method of
inestimable value to those who learn its
language.
   C. G. JUNG

THE DREAM EXPERIENCE

More than a third of our lives is passed in sleeping and dreaming. For the majority of people the nightly mystery of dreams is a sealed book. Only what occurs in waking life is assumed to be "real." By that we mean as real as any of the ordinary occurrences of daily life, such commonplace events as answering the telephone, driving to the station, swimming in the lake, or such uncommon events as an accident, an unexpected inheritance, falling in love or out of it. The senses provide evidence which conclusively substantiates real experiences.

But, how about the inner kind? Are the following experiences less real?

On January 25, 1960, every newspaper in Boston, Massachusetts, ran front-page stories about Clinton H. Elliott, 66, a sandhog on a new tunnel being constructed under Boston Harbor who was killed instantly when a towering crane inexplicably buckled and crashed to earth less than half an hour after safety engineers had completed their routine check of every bit of equipment on the project. All had been as it should be. Then, this shocking catastrophe. Moreover, certain aspects of the tragedy defied rational explanation. For one thing, the massive arm of steel that stretched several stories skyward had collapsed and crashed, not according to the laws of gravity, but *against* them! The arm had swung up and around, defying its own mechanism, coming down on the side opposite from its normal course. Another strange thing: Elliott had been on the point of leaving the spot, since his shift was over, when he was called at that very instant to answer the telephone in the work shack on the construction site. He was walking toward the shack when the accident happened.

"Well," you might conclude, "one of those things. Unfortunate, but that's how it is on a construction job. Sudden death is not uncommon. A certain percentage is expected in hazardous work of this kind." True enough; but there remains still one more extraordinary circumstance. Elliott had been forewarned of his death several weeks beforehand.

About six weeks before, he had dreamed of his mother who had died when he was a small boy in Maryland. In the dream she told him he would die by July 27th. Elliott had told his wife of his forthcoming death. He believed the warning, he had good reason to. Some years before, he had predicted his sister would die within six weeks, because he had dreamed it. She did. Now, with his own death foretold, Elliott went around tidying up his affairs. He called on all his friends, fellow sandhogs, and the officials of his union to bid them farewell. He spent hours with his oldest son, also a sandhog on the same job, talking over his approaching death and other matters he wished to confide. He discussed with other members of his family, his wife and two other sons and four daughters, his wishes for their welfare after he had gone. He even told his wife his choice of a funeral home.

His family took him seriously because they remembered vividly that Elliott had foretold his sister's death, but understandably, some of his fellow workers and union officials were skeptical.

The secretary of Local 88 of the Tunnel Workers' Union reported to newsmen: "I told him he was crazy to believe a dream. But he was so serious it made us all uneasy. I tried to laugh him out of it but it was no use."

This is one example of what dreams do, cited here not because it is out of the ordinary. Quite the contrary. Dreams warning of death, accidents and other disasters are relatively common experiences. So are dreams touching all the other kinds of events which encompass the human experience.

Another widely publicized dream made a different sort of impact, several years ago. A well-to-do man named Chafin died in North Carolina leaving a duly witnessed will giving all of the family property to one of his four sons. The will was executed in due course. Needless to say, the three disinherited sons had quite different feelings about the disposition of their father's estate from the one who inherited all of it. But nothing could be done since the only testament that could be relied upon to indicate the beneficiary was the legally valid instrument produced by the heir. Four years after the will was executed, one of the disinherited sons had a dream. His father appeared to him and told him to look in an old overcoat pocket for another will. The father's old coat was found at the home of one of the other disinherited sons. In the stitched-up pocket was a paper. On it was a reference to a page in the family Bible. The Bible was opened and there was a second will, in the father's script, leaving the property to his four sons in equal shares.

Thoroughly documented, this incident and the will were finally accepted by the court of Davie County, North Carolina, without contest.[1]

The *practical* value of these dreams is obvious. In one, justice triumphed over the grave itself. In the other, something less tangible but undeniably as valuable was given to Elliott, namely, the strongest kind of psychological support to enable him to meet death with dignity and composure.

If one particular condition, more than any other, is conspicuous for its rarity in our nuclear age, we nominate that of a tranquil mind, especially when man contemplates his end. For most men, Hegel's assessment of the human plight is frighteningly accurate: we pass through life as men on shipboard, moving in a direction opposite to that of the ship's course; the ship sails north, we walk south, ignoring the fact that the ultimate destination cannot be circumvented. All the more extraordinary Elliott's tranquil mind, then; how uncommon, how enviable! What was his secret?

Something more than mere acquiescence to his fate. Elliott's serenity clearly accords with the positive attitude he held toward his dreams. He heeded them. He knew they offered precious information, useful to him. He was, in short, very well knit together; his inner-world activities were wholesomely integrated with his outer-world experience; his actions in the external world reflected the direction and advice given him by his dreams. He must have felt possessed of an incomparable guide, and so he was.

Now here's a dream reported as news in *Time* magazine.[2]

"The automatic elevator stops with a jolt. The doors slide open, but instead of the accustomed exit the passenger faces only a blank wall. His fingers stab at buttons; nothing happens. Finally, he presses the alarm signal and a starter's gruff voice inquires from below: 'What's the matter?' The passenger explains that he wants to get off on the 25th floor. 'There is no 25th floor in this building,' comes the voice over the loudspeaker. The passenger explains that, nonsense, he has worked here for years. He gives his name. 'Never heard of you,' says the loudspeaker. 'Easy,' the passenger tells himself. "They are just trying to frighten me.' But time passes and nothing changes. In that endless moment, the variously pleading and angry exchanges over the loudspeaker are the passenger's only communication with the outside world. Finally, even that ceases; the man below says that he cannot waste any more time. 'Wait! Please!' cries the passenger in panic. 'Keep on talking to me!' But the loudspeaker clicks into silence. Hours, days or ages go by. The passenger cowers in a corner of his steel box, staring at the shining metal grille through which the voice once spoke. The grille must be worshipped; perhaps the voice will be heard again. "

"This is not a story from Kafka," comments *Time*, "but a recent dream remembered in precise detail by a successful New Yorker (one wife, three children, fair income, no analyst), who works with every outward appearance of contentment in one of Manhattan's new midtown office buildings. The dream serves as a perfect allegory of an era notoriously stamped as the Age of Anxiety."

Now what can be the point of such a dream? Does it have *any* meaning? Concealed within it, could there be some distortion of wish-fulfillment? Or some practical purpose, as in the first two dreams?

Curiously enough, this dream of *Angst* is not only a perfect allegory for our age, as *Time* remarked; it is also typical of the nightly dreams of innumerable dreamers the world over, as the records of many analysts all too painfully reveal. Note the similar pattern of personal disaster in this dream from the collection of a New York Jungian analyst, Dr. Eugene Henley. As the dreamer related it, he is on the ground floor of his office building in New York, in the marble-lined lobby of its solid structure which towers high into the sky. Suddenly the building begins to tremble and sway. Perhaps it is going to collapse? Everybody is rushing out. He darts about; tries to enter the elevator. But somebody shouts to him, "Beat it!" He runs to the street just before the building falls. Now all the buildings are swaying; they totter and crash. The whole city topples into ruins.

Dr. Henley's interpretation of this dream will be found in Chapter 15, "Prospective Dreams." For the moment let us focus on the phenomenon of the dream itself.

How eerie the experience of dreams really is! Time without count, dreams force the dreamer to *escape* into waking life, heart pounding, pulse racing, emotions churning. The possibility that heart attacks during sleep may be caused by terrifying dreams has not been overlooked by many doctors knowledgeable in the field of sleep physiology. Where do they come from, these nocturnal visitations? How do dreams happen? What does science know about them, if anything: their origin, their meanings, their purpose?

The answers are positive, they are enlightening, and they are amazing. In the past fifteen years tremendous progress has been made by medical scientists studying sleep. Their physiological findings combined with the insights provided by depth psychology has greatly contributed to the current high level of understanding about the phenomena of dreams. To be sure, dream *interpretation*, an art and technique predating Homer, continues to lag, having barely begun to emerge from years of obscurity as a meaningful study, and at that, primarily from the impetus provided by psychiatry. We will return to this topic further on. First:

THE PHYSIOLOGICAL STORY

One of the most exciting accounts in the annals of medicine has been imprinting itself on EEG [3] (electroencephalograph) tapes during the past decade, hovered over by the highly technical segment of medical science involved with the physiology of sleep. An incredible number of gaps in our knowledge of sleep and dreaming have been filled, but none more significant and far-reaching than this: *the importance of dreams to the dreamer's physical health has been incontrovertibly established.*

Thousands of men and women have been tested under controlled conditions in sleep laboratories at such centers as the University of Chicago,[4] New York University, Cornell, Duke and others. Volunteers with electrodes clamped to their skulls have slept night after night, while their brainwaves, charted on the EEG machines, have traced out the answers to questions long sought by scientists.

Now we know that nightly we experience four stages of sleep, from light to deep; basic sleep rhythms of approximately 80 to 90 minutes in adults are the rule. Muscular tensions associated with transitions from one sleep stage to another are distinctly measure-able; muscles slacken just prior to the beginning of the dream period, and chànges in respiration, circulation, pulse and heartbeat, indicating stress, tension and emotion, can be recorded.

What is more, *everyone* dreams, with the exception of infants under six months of age and the very drunk. In both these cases the level of consciousness is too feeble to record.

An average of three dreams each night occurs, about an hour's dreaming time all told, during which we shift our arms and legs, while our shoulders and hips seek new positions on the bed and our heads find a fresh expanse on the pillow. Then, with rare ex-ceptions, at the close of the 80–90 minute cycle, sleep lightens as it approaches Stage 1. The slow rolling motions of our eyes change to very fast darting movements (Rapid Eye Movements they are called, abbreviated to REMs among sleep researchers), which signal the start of a dream. As long as the dream is in progress we lie quite still, although our eyes follow intently the action of the inner drama. It is exactly as if we watched a real scene in waking life. In fact, our entire nervous system does react as though we were actually involved in the real thing. Luckily, there also exists some inner mechanism preventing the dreamer from acting bodily; in other words, some part of us seems to know that what we are watching *is* a dream and we can stay in bed. We do see a partial breakdown of this protective mechanism in cases of sleepwalking and, to some extent, in sleeptalking. Not much is known about this inhibiting monitor as yet, and it remains on the agenda of continuing research.

What is perhaps the most astonishing evidence [5] brought forth in the last five years is the fact that men have penile erections be-ginning with the typical muscle slackness to be noted a few sec-onds before REMs indicate a dream is about to start. The erec-tions generally continue throughout the REM period, however long that may be. The tumescence gradually diminishes as the sleeper moves out of the REM state. There can be no doubt some fundamental biological mechanism possibly incorporating sexuality, but as yet not in the least understood—is at work.

Because dreaming is universal and is now proven to be absolutely vital to the functioning of the human organism, as we shall soon see, intensive research is currently afoot, based on the hypothesis that there exists a "third state" [6] on a par with the two known states of waking and sleeping. It is in the "third state" that dreaming occurs and brain activation often mounts to a point above that of the waking state, although bodily motor impulses are suppressed, except in cases of somnambulism.

Scientists have determined that sleep deprivation can lead to serious physiological and psychological disturbances. The discovery that dream deprivation can have the same consequences, is another scientifically established fact. In sleep deprivation, disturbances ranging from irritability to belligerence, marked increase in appetite, and hallucinations have appeared as typical symptoms. Torture and the refined brutality known in present-day warfare as "brain-washing" make effective use of this knowledge by keeping a person awake for long periods, permitting only broken and irregular periods of sleep, and, in the final sophisticated twist, placing the prisoner in solitary confinement during the process, so that pathological distortions of the personality to the point of psychosis can result.

Deprived of sleep for a night or several nights, a person seems to need to "catch up" on sleep. He also *needs to make up for dreaming time he has lost.* Moreover, the need to dream is so strong in the human organism that all normal rules about sleeping and waking are thrust aside so that the need can be served. This is the fascinating story accrued through research of sleep scientists, which we can do no more than sketch here, since we would be going too far afield from our main subject. The full account is told brilliantly in a recent book by Norman MacKenzie, *Dreams and Dreaming*, which we strongly recommend.

In brief summary: the first dream deprivation experiments began only a short while ago, in 1959, under the direction of two physiologists long connected with research in sleep, Dr. William Dement and Dr. Charles Fisher, the latter having discovered the phenomenon of penile erections accompanying REM. Using the EEG machine to detect REMs, planned interruptions of REM sleep were undertaken. Control nights were arranged in which sleepers were disturbed just as frequently in their non-REM periods. The results, first published in *Science* in 1960, reported that sleepers deprived of dreaming, or REM time, showed increasingly severe strain; anxiety, irritation, a noticeable increase in appetite, and, finally, at extremes of periods of dream deprivation, psychotic symptoms appeared in some cases. Left undisturbed following a night or period of dream deprivation, sleepers increased their REM periods substantially in the effort to make up for lost dream time.

One striking experiment covering a period of 15 nights illustrates what generally happens when a sleeper is deprived of normal REM periods. In this experiment the sleeper was prevented from having his REM periods in the laboratory and was watched day and night to insure he was not getting "bootleg" sleep while he was not in the laboratory. The chart showing the jiggling saw-tooth brain-wave markings on the EEG, his muscle relaxation, respiration, pulse and so forth, started off normally enough. On successive nights, however, as his REM sleep periods were interrupted at their start by awakening him, an increasing number of awakenings became necessary. Then, REM periods began to crowd out the normal sleeping states; it was evident the sleeper was trying to make up for dream time lost on previous nights. He became more difficult to awaken; even the use of the drug Dexedrine to help awaken him and keep him awake, became ineffective. By the 15th night his need to dream was so strong that REM sleep began as soon as the sleeper's head touched the pillow, something *never* seen in adults under normal circumstances. In the first two hours, twenty awakenings to keep him out of REM sleep were necessary; but by 4:00 A.M., thirty-six awakenings were required. His situation became desperate. As

Dr. Dement described it, "The experiment had to be halted because it became absolutely impossible to awaken the subject and interrupt the dream periods. Eye movements could be temporarily halted by struggling with the subject, hoisting him upright, shouting in his ear, etc. . . . but as soon as the stimulation ceased, the eye movements resumed. The only way dreaming could be stopped was to drag the subject out of bed, walk him around until he was awake, and then keep him awake." [7]

On the following night the sleeper was permitted to sleep undisturbed; he quickly began to make up for lost time. He plunged straight into REM sleep, and throughout the night registered long REM periods, totalling over 60%, or nearly four times as much as usual, of his sleep time.

The need to dream is obviously so urgent that all normal ways of sleeping and waking will be broken in order to have normal dream time; that is the plateau from which further research takes off. There is the possibility that the complex biochemical process producing the condition known as REM sleep may be so vital that in its absence we would die. In actual experiments, the ultimate limit is reached at that point where psychotic symptoms begin to show up when dream deprivation goes beyond the point of tolerance of the sleeper. Consequently the question whether the subject really would die remains open. But, and this has a significant bearing on the matter, *cats* have died in experimental laboratories when deprived of their REM sleep for more than twenty days. Even in a decorticated cat, that is, a cat from which the cerbral cortex has been removed, REM, or dreaming, sleep continues, as the pioneer work conducted by Professor M. Jouvet and his colleagues at the University of Lyons has demonstrated. Apparently, some very primitive area of the brain seems to be involved in the biological mechanism of the body, commanding both sleep and the phenomena of dreams. This, among other considerations, supports the present trend toward accepting the hypothesis of the "third state" as normal, indeed imperative, for the well-being of the human organism.

Many unanswered questions remain, of course, continuing to be the subjects of active investigation. For example: What is the link between REM sleep and dreaming? What about recall? What *has* been established about recall is, the ability to recall dreams is greatest *during* the REM period, a recall rate of about 83%, while sleepers awakened outside the REM period show extremely different results. In the majority of cases there is no recall at all, and in others a fragmentary recall. Still others, who insist they are non-dreamers but are highly visual (about 15% of all adults) claim they have been "thinking," not dreaming, when aroused from REM periods. The question of whether dreams are recalled accurately has yet to be conclusively proven; in fact, the methods used by different experiments and the way the experimenter defines "dream" and "recall" have to be uniformly established before the authoritative criterion can be set up in this area.

Too, there is the question of dreams being "lost" when they cannot be recollected. Does some part of the brain "remember"? Many real-life experiences supposedly forgotten have been recovered to consciousness under special circumstances, as in analysis or hypnosis. Does this hold for dreams as well?

The speed with which dreams are forgotten is another open question, and so is the condensation of time characteristic of dream events. Dream recall drops rapidly soon after awakening from an REM period when it is at its highest level. Then the dreamer can give a report of his dream approximating the length of time elapsing since his dream state began, up to a ceiling time of approximately five minutes. After that, the length of the dream recall does not increase with the actual duration of the dream. The dream might have lasted thirty minutes or so, as the REMs indicate, but the dreamer will be able to recall no more than he could after five minutes of dreaming.

As for the time condensation typical of dream action, the movies appear to best demonstrate the kind of time scale operative in dreams. On film we can see a boy growing to manhood, embarking on a long sea-voyage, the events of a day, week, years or lifetime, in a few minutes to two or three hours. Our time sense is one of the most curious of our faculties. (Since we deal with it at length later on in the chapter on Consciousness we will not elaborate further here except to call attention to well-known variations.) How time drags when we are bored or waiting for someone late for an appointment. By contrast, how swiftly time melts away when we are enjoying ourselves or are deeply interested in a project at which we are working.

Summing up the physiological story: the conclusions are that some fundamental biological mechanism is operative in man, as the REM periods prove with their freight of dreams and the penile erections accompanying the process in men (what happens to women is as yet totally unexplored). *Everyone dreams*, with the exceptions previously mentioned. *Every night we dream:* from 15% to 25% of the average good night's sleep is spent dreaming.

The rock-bottom riddle physiologists may never be able to answer is, *Why* do we dream?

With that query we enter the domain of psychology, and find such a profusion of answers we will need to remind ourselves from time to time that all three schools of psychology have successes and failures, and whatever abyss of opinion separates them, they all come together in agreement that there exists a dynamic interplay between inner forces and outer fate.

THE PSYCHOLOGICAL STORY

Freud, Jung and Adler constitute the triumvirate which illumines the field of depth psychology as the sun does the sky. There are lesser luminaries whose contributions have been impressive, but their roles are as satellites to the eminent three.

The majority of educated people today are aware that these three psychiatrists made discoveries about the human psyche in the early decades of this century. Probably less well-known is that the three men each developed different methods for exploring the psyche and each had an impressive following. The Freudian school practices Psychoanalysis; the Jungians are exponents of Analytical Psychology; the Adlerians, of Individual Psychology.

Each school places great emphasis on dreams, and dream interpretation plays an important part in the treatment of pathological symptoms. As a consequence, the notion exists that bothering with dreams is for the neurotic.

What is little known is that one of the three, Carl Gustav Jung,[8] the renowned Swiss medical psychiatrist who broke with Freud in 1913, recognized even then that dreams are as pertinent to the normal individual as they are to the neurotic whose cure is facilitated through dream interpretation. Jung used dream information to deliberately foster growth of personality in persons not at all ill, in the conventional sense of the term—that is to say, no more ill than the New Yorker whose dream of *Angst* depicts an inner emotional state as completely off-the-ground, up-in-the-air, facing a blank wall, overwhelmed by awareness of helplessness and waiting for a voice from below. Beckett's "Waiting for Godot" dramatizes the identical situation as the three uneasy derelicts in the play portray what seems to be a hopeless dead end. There reverberates, unspoken, the age-old human cry, "Help! Someone help! I have come to the end of my rope!"

At just such critical impasses in life, Jung discovered that often help *does come* from the profoundest depths of the psyche in dreams.

He says this flatly, drawing upon the undeviatingly empirical experience of his life's work, as his writings, numbering more than twenty volumes in English translations at present, report. Thousands upon thousands of dreams over the past half century have been exhaustively analyzed by Jung and his colleagues in Zurich and elsewhere around the world. Jung estimated that he dealt with more than eighty thousand dreams in the course of his practice. This immense body of documented research by Jung and Jungian scholars is a topographical map of the inner world of dreams, visions, fantasies, "active imagination" and all else heaved up from the ever-bubbling contents of the psyche.

Jung declares:

1. Dreams are an indispensable tool for self-knowledge.

2. Dreams are *not* "nothing but a dream." They are *not* freaks of nature, the accidental by-products of sleep. Dreams intend to advise, correct, punish, comfort, heal and warn the normal dreamer just as much as they do the neurotic. (Can this be the reason that dream deprivation causes such intense anxiety, as physiologists have noted?)

3. *Communication* is the prime purpose of the dream; its goal is to achieve psychic equilibrium through the principle of Compensation. (See Chapter Nine.) The clearest statement about the inner state of the dreamer is condensed in the dream's imagery, and unerringly pointed, often with shattering accuracy, at blind spots in the dreamer's awareness of himself in some situation in his waking life.

4. As a natural phenomenon occurring spontaneously, the dream cannot be produced by an act of will or intellect nor influenced by consciousness to tell a different story than it does, any more than consciousness can affect any other natural phenomenon, such as thunder, gravity, or organic growth.

5. The dream speaks in images, a pictorial, sensual language, non-verbal, pre-logical. But the dream is saying what it means; there is no "latent meaning" beneath a "manifest façade," as the Freudians have it. If we cannot understand the dream it is because our interpretative powers are lacking, and not because we fail to penetrate its camouflage.

6. Far from being "sleep-protecting," as the Freudian viewpoint holds, exactly the opposite is true. The unconscious launches a dream to *wake up* the dreamer, literally awaken him to some aspect of his conscious life or personal attitudes about which he is sound asleep.

7. "Wish-fulfillment" is not the criterion for interpreting the dream, as orthodox Freudians maintain. There are indeed wish-fulfilling dreams. In addition, there are hunger dreams, anxiety dreams, fever dreams, dreams presenting transcendent truths,

philosophical pronouncements or homely good advice, nonsense dreams, wild fantasies and mysterious flotsam from long-ago memories, plans, anticipations, irrational experiences, telepathic visions, precognitions and other things so strange to the understanding as to defy interpretation.

8. Practised attention to dreams can detect the pattern to be in one of the following categories:

1. Compensatory or Complementary
2. Reductive
3. Reactive
4. Prospective
5. Somatic
6. Telepathic
7. Deep-level "big" dreams, i.e., archetypal dreams
8. Miscellaneous dreams which elude classification; hypnagogic visions (phenomena similar to dreams, except that the dreamer is not asleep but awake when they occur); visions; mystic states, including ecstasy; "active imaginations" (deliberately induced visionary states for penetrating the subliminal fantasy level). These latter are frequently employed in the process of "individuation" (which is a later development of personality), though they are neither advisable nor possible for the uninitiated without professional guidance.

The foregoing are a few of the tenets of the Jungian viewpoint which stand at the head of a long list of differences between it and other psychological schools. We shall not go into these differences in depth—that would require another book by itself—but the matter of differences will arise in forthcoming chapters, particularly among readers who have learned something about psychologies other than Jung's. Consequently, there is an important statement to make in connection with them before dropping the subject entirely. That is, the majority of Jungian differences contradicts the premises of other theories, but comes in conflict most noticeably with the predominant psychological method current in the United States, the Freudian. It is largely because the Freudian method is overwhelmingly prevalent in psychiatric practise in this country—and is the psychology included in the curricula of the majority of colleges and universities proffering courses in the subject—and because it has become the leading *leitmotif* of critical analysis of works of literature and art, that comparatively little is known of the Jungian viewpoint.

How little-known was spotlighted recently on a television program with the dolorous title, "Is the Whole World Sick?" [9] A panel of distinguished psychologists and psychiatrists, an American, a Canadian, a Nigerian, an Englishman and a Vietnamese among them, were discussing the topic. The American, a well-known Freudian practising in New York City, made a sweeping assertion about dream interpretation in the orthodox Freudian vein. Whereupon the Englishman, Dr. William Sargant, matter-of-factly interrupted, "But that very much depends on whether your patient is dreaming in Freudian or Jungian terms, you know! Jungians dream differently from Freudians; at least in England they do."

Sargant's comment is deeply significant for dreamers who fit in one but not the other demesne and who want to understand their own dreams. Jung's observation bears on this question. He said, "Apart from Freud's views I also had before my eyes the growth of the views of Adler. In this way I found myself in the thick of the conflict from the very beginning and was forced to regard not only the existing opinions but my own as well as relative, or rather, as expressions of a certain psychological type." [10]

Your psychological type: You come to bedrock when you know this and it is the living nerve of self-knowledge towards which your dreams will impel you. The superficial and the thoughtless may imagine they know themselves through-and-through, that there are no surprises in themselves. The reflective are not let off so easily. Who has not looked back and felt he was a stranger to the actions he knows he has perpetrated? But—*that is what you are!* And that is what your dreams show you. *That* is knowledge about yourself.

Self-knowledge isn't simple, for we are complex inhabitants of many worlds, within and without. We are at once animal, yet we have the ability to think; we are sentient creatures related to the apes and, at the same time, carriers of a transcendent spirit which makes us capable of a nobility creditable to the divine. We are all this and much much more, passing through a mysterious space-time continuum, swathed in a conglomerate of words and other pre-logical, non-verbal symbols which stringently condition the perceptions upon which all our mental processes depend. We are, in short, psycho-physical organisms, conscious, intermittently, of our existence in what seems many times *not* to be the best of all possible worlds. But *here* is where we find ourselves and can search for our identity, the mirror-image of self-knowledge.

Dreams help peel away illusions about yourself and bare the truth, but there won't be a splendid climax in which you at long last arrive at a clear-cut confrontation of the "psychological type" you know is the real you. What does develop is your recognition of an *emerging personality*, ever-growing, expanding, non-static and viable, whose outlines are muffled within the structure of your dreams. It is this true self Jung points to: "Behind a man's actions there stands neither public opinion nor moral code, but the personality of which he is still unconscious." [11]

THE CASE FOR UNDERSTANDING DREAMS

Knowledge of the inner world of the psyche, just because it exists to the extent it does today, makes its own *a priori* case for the understanding of dreams, just as the new math is now an imperative for the schoolboy. Going further for incentives, if there were no other, the appalling statistics on the state of our collective mental health should serve. Comparing what is known about the power of the unconscious to influence human life and what we see happening all about us, it is not going too far to say that anyone unenlightened about his own psychic processes is dangerously under-educated. Taking into account the fact that we have a built-in device for producing all the enlightenment we can handle, in the form of dreams, there appears to be nothing to keep us in the dark but ourselves.

Moreover, we have come into as favorable an intellectual climate for learning *about* dreams as from them. As history proves, knowledge waxes or wanes against the intellectual climate of its times; some knowledge comes "ahead of its time," as the saying goes. Galileo is the classic example, muttering under his breath, "But the earth moves, nonetheless," as he tottered in disgrace from the tribunal where he publicly recanted his discovery that the earth, not the sun, moved. For that matter, forty years after Newton had proven his law of gravitation he was still being authoritatively refuted in some of the best schools of England. Galileo was in his grave more than a century before his heretical equations found the times receptive enough to be insinuated into mathematical formulae that are the basis of today's experimental quantum physics. Now it is physics, the most exquisite of sciences, which has subtly but unmistakably influenced the growing general acceptance of knowledge *irrationally arrived at*, as dreams provide. Since we deal with physics and its correlation with Jungian psychology in a later chapter, we will go no further into the connection at this point.

Actually, dreams as the carriers of tidings have been rediscovered in this century, not discovered. The reader introducing himself to the subject of dream interpretation with this work would be amazed at, as well as enlightened by, the importance dreams have had over the centuries. A papyrus scroll detailing the secrets of dream interpretation, now at the British Museum, dates back to about 1790 B.C., about the period when Abraham of the Old Testament left Ur for the desert. Dreams lost their prestige only relatively recently, in the 18th and 19th centuries, with the rise of the natural sciences. Their return to prominence began with

Freud's insistence, at the turn of the century, that they were "the royal road to the unconscious." Since then, a great outpouring of knowledge about the powerhouse of drives, motivations, needs and responses, which are the materials of the deep psyche, has come to light. You are given food for thought when you reflect that, outside of medical psychiatry and depth psychology, the available knowledge has been quickly seized upon and utilized by two great forces in our culture, namely, Madison Avenue and the military.

Employing psychologists as "motivational research" experts, Madison Avenue has distinguished itself by its use of knowledge about the deep psyche: how to image such a basic drive as ego-affirmation, for example. We are regaled by their equations in ads of sleek, powerful, tiger-type automobiles and platinum-blonde furs—instant status symbols—and by deodorants that make you popular to be near, hair tonics that promise to incite maidens to attack, filter-tip cigarettes smoked only by the most virile, outdoorsy-type males, and such. Meanwhile, a sizeable percentage of the population of this nation continues to suffer from a gross denial of the vital images of ego-affirmation which are necessary to the attainment of first-class citizenship; hence the plight of the Negroes today and for more than a century.

The military have been equally as high-minded, as one instance alone will indicate. Sidney Hook, writing in "The Ends and Content of Education" [12] has pointed out that brainwashed American prisoners of war numbered one third of the entire number in Korea. The figure astounded this writer: *One third!* Meaning: the techniques that can result in the disequilibrium of the psyche comparable to bodily deformity or genetic mutation from exposure to atomic radiation have been so perfected they can be, and are, utilized like a new weapon. And this fact presents us "with the most deadly predicament since [man] climbed down from the trees," thinks Arthur Koestler.[13]

There are many ways to look at Madison Avenue's ploys with images. In one way it's a kind of brain-washing, but on the other hand, it helps keep the economy going strong. But the military use of brainwashing as a weapon—that's something else again. However dimly, it is possible to discern that some great issue larger than himself rides on the individual *conscious of his identity*—for example, the G.I.'s who were subjected to brainwashing in the Korean conflict but did *not* succumb. Somehow, from somewhere, by osmosis, by education, out of the climate in which he developed, that man had imaged in him the precious essence an individual is, as the idea is imbedded in the political and social philosophies dominant in the Western world and on which our civilization has risen and stands. Imaged interiorly in his psyche, exteriorized in his belief, the *idea* of the free individual could not be broken, though his body might be. The "deadly predicament" of which Koestler speaks is the contest shaping up in the immediate decade or so ahead, between the forces of collectivization and those who authentically mirror the ideas and ideals cherished by free men. The men caught in the ordeal of brainwashing will have had the most painful first-hand opportunity to come to self-knowledge on the matter of their beliefs. There remains the vast majority untested on this point: the outcome remains to be seen.

One additional consideration. As has been said, the gap between specialists and laymen in every discipline is enormous, and it grows daily. In the intimate area of self-knowledge, self-interest must be the ignition for the intelligent layman to become as well-informed as self-education can make him. The knowledge of unconscious processes, including the understanding of dreams, cannot any longer remain the exclusive preserve of professionals any more than personal hygiene is reserved for an elect.

Jung, when asked whether his viewpoints were reserved for specialists or an intellectual elite, answered:

"There are two distinct things. The use of psychic *therapy* [italics mine] is reserved for medical specialists, not everyone can fool around with that; but what you call the 'explanation' reaches a lot more people than I would have thought possible myself. I am very optimistic. The people do follow it. In the French part of Switzerland . . . [a] first edition was sold out in three months. Who reads it? Not the professors!" [14]

1. J. B. Rhine, *The Reach of the Mind* (New York: William Sloane Associates, Inc., Apollo Editions, 1960), pp. 184-85.

2. *Time*, March 31, 1961, p. 44.

3. The electroencephalograph machine, shortened to EEG by those who work with it, can record the very weak electric currents generated continuously by the brain through electrodes placed on the scalp. Amplified up to a million times, these impulses are fed into the machine and automatic pens trace variations in the signals onto a slow-moving drum of graph paper. The German scientist Dr. Hans Berger, of the University of Jena, was the first to demonstrate, some 40 years ago, that the patterns given off by the brain while sleeping, at rest, or responding to stimuli, had characteristic rhythms. Since then, the EEG and readings from it have been greatly refined. Today, a trained interpreter can read tracings that might be as long as 700 yards for one night's brain activity, and detect from it how the brain is working and whether some of its vital functions are impaired.

4. In 1957 Professor Nathan Kleitman and Dr. William Dement published "Cyclic Variations in EEG During Sleep and Their Relation to Eye Movement, Body Motility and Dreaming" (*Electronceph. clin. Neurophysiology*). This was followed by Dement's "The Effect of Dream Deprivation" in *Science* (July 10, 1960, p. 1705). These are the first scientific papers on research on sleep and dreaming conducted as scientific experiments under laboratory conditions. Professor Kleitman had, however, published his internationally recognized definitive work *Sleep and Wakefulness* in 1939, while on the faculty of the University of Chicago. A new edition, revised and updated, was published in 1963 and includes a superlative bibliography, listing some 4337 books and scholarly articles on the nature and problems of sleep, indicating the scope of the investigations currently in progress.

5. In 1964, at Mt. Sinai Hospital in New York, Dr. Charles Fisher, a collaborator with Dr. William Dement in earlier researches, devised the equipment and conducted the experiments producing the evidence of penile erections throughout REM sleep. Although Dr. Fisher has been controverted by others, he maintains, "There is approximately as much erection during the night as there is dreaming."

6. A large part of the life of infants is thought to be spent in the "third state." Long before the child has full development of his brain or control of conscious behavior, he, too, experiences REM sleep, as EEG research verifies.

7. Norman MacKenzie, *Dreams and Dreaming* (New York, The Vanguard Press), p. 268.

8. Died June 6, 1961, Kusnacht, Switzerland.

9. "Open End," David Susskind, Moderator, Channel 13, WNTA-TV, June 11, 1961.

10. C. G. Jung, *Two Essays on Analytical Psychology* (New York: Pantheon Books, 1953), p. 116.

11. C. G. Jung, *Psychology and Religion* (New York: Pantheon Books, 1958), p. 258.

12. *Daedalus*, Winter, 1959.

13. Arthur Koestler, *The Lotus and the Robot* (New York: The Macmillan Company, 1961).

14. *Spring*, 1960.

CHAPTER TWO

The Jungian Semantics

*The psyche is the world's pivot: not
only is it the one great condition for the
existence of a world at all, it is also an
intervention in the existing natural order,
and no one can say with certainty where
this intervention will finally end.*
  C. G. JUNG [1]

The first step for the reader new to Jung's work is to grasp the
semantics of the Jungian frame of reference. His concepts need
to be understood as he defined them, else we shall be at sea in the
coming chapters.

The sections that follow in this chapter define the concepts on
Some readers might find it agreeable to turn first to the chapters
directly concerned with the dream and techniques of interpretation, and then return to this section. In all likelihood this section
will be continually referred to in any case, until you have mastered the conceptual framework, and particularly when you
make your first attempts to interpret your own dreams. As your
acquaintance improves you will see the necessity for understanding exactly what is meant when, for example, references are made
to: Anima, Animus, Shadow, Persona, the Four Functions,
Archetypal image, and other terms which are exclusively Jungian. For one thing, these concepts describe specific images appearing in dreams. They will appear in *your* dreams. We mean this
literally.

The sections that follow in this chapter define the ground on which Analytical Psychology is based. Psyche, libido, will, complexes; consciousness, the unconscious, personal and collective. Each is dealt with separately.

THE PSYCHE

By *psyche* Jung means the totality of consciousness *and* the unconscious combined. Each sphere supplements the other but each is opposed in its properties.

Jung postulates the psyche as a *self-regulating system*, an extremely important concept to remember. On this he bases the principle of *compensation* which underlies most dream phenomena to be discussed separately later.

Technically speaking, self-regulation of the psyche means recovery and renewal of its mechanism. This occurs through the interplay of simultaneous coefficient functions strikingly similar to the "regulating circuit" device used in automation, described in *Cybernetics* by Nobel-prize mathematician Norbert Wiener, builder of the great Mark series of electronic computers at the Massachusetts Institute of Technology. What happens in the psychic processes is likened to the feedback of servo-mechanisms homeostatically arranged to create their own dynamic equilibrium.[2]

In Jung's formulation, the psyche utilizes the principles of thermodynamics and quantum physics, the difference being that where physics deals in *amounts* of energy, that is to say, in *quanta* which can be measured and expressed mathematically, Jung's psychology deals in *intensities* of energy, that is, in *qualities*. Freud's hypothesis, by contrast, posits a fixed quantity of libido in a hydraulic conversion process: "Express it here and it must be withdrawn from there," a formula that is a "kind of first-order nonsense," in the opinion of Jerome Bruner, professor of psychology at Harvard.[3]

More specifically, the similarity of cybernetics [4] to the psychic processes in the matter of self-regulation shows two directions, both of which *make up* for something lacking in the consciousness of the dreamer. One is *complementary*, understood as *adding to;* the second is *compensatory*, in the sense of *balancing*.

Jung postulates: When the balance between the conscious and the unconscious is disturbed and a one-sided development of the personality results through the repression of inherent functional potentialities, *the unconscious automatically attempts to correct the imbalance*. Dreams are one such corrective effort. Illness may be another; psychosomatic ailments are widespread and proliferating. At bottom, complexes, neuroses, and even psychoses are actually graduated extremes of psychic imbalance which disclose *a strong unconscious counterposition to the conscious direction of the individual*. So powerful is this submerged will that the conscious will of the individual is displaced. Such imbalance "almost universally," in Jung's exact words, occurs whenever an extreme one-sided tendency dominates the conscious life which is invariably typified by the predominant *function* of the individual.

The sense of the term "function in the foregoing accords with Jung's definition of the basic four psychological functions, one of which is early chosen by each individual and developed as his primary mode for adapting externally. The concept is important in Jung's psychology and is dealt with in detail in a subsequent chapter. Here it is sufficient to note that the *psychological type* of each personality is markedly conditioned by his *predominant function*, whether this be *thinking, feeling, sensation* or *intuition*.

LIBIDO

The psyche has been presented in terms that might just as well describe a computer: as though it were a motored, self-regulating dynamo. In that case we must look for its power. Nothing whatever moves or functions without power and the power of the psyche, *psychic energy*, is *libido*.

In the Jungian sense *libido* is the energy of the psyche power-ing *all* of man's drives. These are seen to be many more than the single drive of sexuality, to which Freud has actually attributed all that man has wrought throughout history. To Freud *libido* is the synonym for sexual energy.

Libido is not, of course, an actual substance, some sort of super-volatile lymph circulating along with your blood, or released by the endocrine glands, any more than *thought* is a materially dis-cernible substance. *Libido* is but a word, a concept, an abstrac-tion; "pure hypotheses," says Jung, "no more concretely con-ceivable than the energy known to the world of physics. . . ." But who will now question the wonders of the concept of energy which supports the manifold structure of physics as a science? Who can forget that formulations constructed on the hypotheses of quantum physics were valid enough to result in a detonation at Hiroshima that killed an estimated 150,000 people at one blow?

Libido, psychic energy, is your birthright; like Bergson's *élan vital*, it is an individual endowment. Freud's penetrating analysis of the libidinal gradient from infancy to adulthood is borne out in the physico-sexual development of the human's various physiological functions through their continual changes: infancy, pre-puberty, puberty, adult state. Libido invested in these auton-omous currents is not at your disposal. The physical plant oper-ates without consulting you: blood circulates, digestion proceeds, the heart beats, the brain works, and so forth. In this process the largest quantity of libido at your disposal is utilized. Up to this point the Freudian and Jungian view about libido coincides. Now the Jungian formulations take their own turn, beginning with the recognition that, of the remaining *libido*, a relatively small por-tion is at the service of your:

WILL

Will is a function of your consciousness. But the quantity that is yours is not free and clear for the obvious reason that your "will" is never securely your possession, like the nose on your face, nor firmly entrenched in your intermittent consciousness. "Will" can be and very frequently is affected, and sometimes adversely so, by quite a number of things, among them, most importantly:

COMPLEXES [5]

Everyone has complexes, ranging from mild foibles, such as incorrigible tardiness, or punctilious punctuality, all the way to crippling compulsions. Many "wills" are diminished by the strength of desires, passions, and vices. Consider dieters who cannot diet, smokers who cannot give up cigarettes, gamblers who cannot quit, and so on. "Wills" are not uncommonly rendered ineffectual by the invasion of strong emotions, to which everyone is vulnerable. These differ from the pathological variety only in intensity and duration; in fact, it is doubtful that even the most rational being has not, during the course of life, experienced a pathological invasion of overpowering emotion.

Finally, the remaining libido flows to the Four Functions, dealt with later. Their importance is equal to that of the Will. Your predominant function characterizes your psychological type.

CONSCIOUSNESS

Consciousness [6] is associated with your ego-complex, which serves as center of reference for the sphere of consciousness, sustained by memory. Consciousness is essential for experiencing the external world at all, and that experience enters the total psychic organism each individual represents through his ego-complex.

We did not include the definition of the ego-complex in the section on complexes because of its unique status and its identification with consciousness. In colloquial terms, we can readily recognize the ego-complex because it answers to our name, age, height, weight, occupation, social security number and wears our

Persona (about which more further on). Technically, Jung defines it as that complex to which all conscious, and some unconscious contents, are referable. Furthermore, it is distinctive as a persisting or recurrent sense of continuity of an individual in relation to time, space and causality.

As for consciousness, we have a great deal more to say about it than mere definition, because the average person is so identified with his ego-waking-self that only with the utmost difficulty can the limitations of that ego-self penetrate meaningfully enough to comprehend the phenomenon of consciousness.

Consciousness, overlaying the personal and collective unconscious (both of which are possessed of the power to intervene in the functioning of consciousness), is a peculiar condition. Its peculiarity consists principally in the fact that it is an *intermittent* phenomenon. One fifth, one third, even one half of human life, may be spent in an unconscious condition. During infancy, early youth, in sleep at night and for hours during waking life, a decidedly uneven state of consciousness is yours. You may be lost in thought, in fantasy, in work, or in other ways in which you are in varying degrees *un*conscious. Moreover, very few contents can be simultaneously contained in consciousness at any given moment; the rest is unconscious. You get only a succession of conscious moments at best while the greater part is dark and enormous and continuous. Consciousness [7] seems like a slit through which you peer, seeing only flashes of existence as you flow through the space-time continuum. And, as is evident to the most casual observer, a wide divergence in *capacity* for consciousness exists between one person and the next. Persons are not equal in their *recollections* of what conscious life is and has been. What you can factually and honestly recall to consciousness depends a good deal on what data your memories of your experiences supply. If your memory is faulty, then other people, or photos, or memorabilia, may assist, or under hypnosis, the remembrance of experiences in conscious life can be returned to you. In such ways a fairly accurate representation of "consciousness" for you over a period of years can be constructed. But only a minuscule part of the whole story of yourself will have been determined and that pretty questionable on many counts as well as purely subjective. The fact that consciousness constitutes but a very tiny dot on the surface of the entire psychic entity you actually are is extraordinarily difficult to comprehend. What amounts to legerdemain of the mind is required to keep your mental footing among the confusing evidences of a natural order whose secrets have barely begun to be deciphered.

Your perceptions are a function of your consciousness which, through its sensory apparatus, continually gives you mental pictures of the world which you *assume* to be the facts. When you see a bed of yellow roses what takes place within you is this: the little camera called the "eye" picks up on its retina electromagnetic waves of a certain length radiating from the roses which effect changes in a criss-cross of nerves leading to the corticals of your brain. Molecular or atomic changes at those centers then image yellow roses. In the case of red roses, electromagnetic waves of a different length impinge on the visual organs which are so constituted that they sort out the disparities in waves to present the correct colors and forms. If the brain corticals in charge of this transformation were impaired or missing you would not be able to detect color at all, or some colors, as in the case of the color-blind, or those who continually mistake blue for green or *vice versa*.

Similar transformations take place with sound. The tolling of a bell starts oscillations of waves causing an alteration in the positional arrangement of brain particles or tensions acting on those particles: *then* you hear. In fact *all* the senses operate in a similar fashion. Now, if we reverse this idea, we skirt the perimeter of metaphysics, the exercise-yard of speculative minds since the Greeks coined the word and distilled the severely rational science of physics out of it. For now you see that some individual "you," somewhere, and some time, with your precious speck of consciousness, has been and still is mighty important for *whatever exists objectively* to be *real*-ized, that is, to be concretized and externalized. This is the essential meaning of the quotation from Jung which introduces this chapter, and it is profoundly significant to ponder its ramifications: "The psyche is the world's pivot: not only is it the one great condition for the existence of a world at all, it is also an intervention in the existing natural order, and no one can say with certainty where this intervention will finally end." [8]

Nor can physics, devoted to determining the *objective* nature of the universe as it exists independently of any human observer, diminish the *significance of the subjective* for the simple reason that some trace of subjectivity must always taint even its most esoteric calculations, a discovery that came as a by-product of the development of microphysics.[9]

Since physics is the crowned queen of sciences, and what is more to the point here, the opposite number to Jung's psychology as I have pointed out earlier in this chapter, her definition of what an individual is has a place in this account. Let us bear in mind that an individual is a carrier of consciousness, via an immensely complicated apparatus of perceptions, and now return to the discussion of colors. Physics, devoted as it is to determining the nature of the universe objectively and independent of the existence of any human observer, provides explanations about how color happens: electromagnetic waves of different lengths react through the eye-organs to register differently in the corticals. These explanations could be made to a blind man so that he could grasp intellectually the nature of color. But one thing couldn't be explained, and you could say this elusive something is the very essence of color: that is, the *redness* or *blueness* of the colors. These have literally got to be seen to be appreciated and the *eye and brain together*, the physical *and* psychical combined, have to function nearly simultaneously for the viewer to *see* red, blue, or any other color.

Now, is it known whether the color is *in* the object? Or, in the seer, the subject?

No, it is not known!

The same can be said for sound, taste, and the other senses. "It's all in the mind," the cliché goes, and it may be perfectly true. The brain, though it cannot create sensory appearances outside the individual, is nevertheless indispensable in whatever processes cause them to register *in* the individual. A hint of the scope of the brain's incredible powers can be judged by contrast with the marvelous computers described by Norbert Wiener.[10] Wiener suggests that it is entirely plausible in theory, even at this early stage of electronic development, that the organic pattern constituting a human being could be transmitted by telegraph, technical difficulties for avoiding the death of tissues and cells in the transmission process chiefly standing in the way of the accomplishment at present. Yet the fact remains, computers would still have far to go to overtake the fantastic potential of the human brain. You could easily conclude that point may not be so far off, at that, on pondering David Hawkins' blueprint for creating a *Machina Cogitans* of the human type; that is, a cogitating mind-type machine which he describes in an article, "Design for a Mind," [11] which makes not only credible but eerie reading.

Naturally, science has not failed to take cognizance of the correspondence between what happens *subjectively within* the individual when phenomena *objectively outward* come within the focus of attention. The red rose in the arbor registers inside the brain-pan behind the seeing eye. These are *two* facts but a third most important one must now be added. The two events accompany one another, running, so to speak, on parallel tracks in *time*. Time, therefore, is also of the essence, as much as the red rose and the registering brain.

Now, time has more aspects than we have space to enumerate here, and since Einstein, time as a *dimension* has been so exhaustively experimented with that outer-space research now includes calculations for traveling in time running backwards, and in slow-speed time. Both these concepts involve highly sophisticated mathematical formulae too remote from our present subject to describe here. But time as a *dimension*, what the physicist regards as the time continuum,[12] holds pertinence for us, although obliquely, because of the physicist's definition of the individual; the phenomenon of consciousness under discussion here occurs in the human entity we term "an individual."

As described by the renowned Sir Arthur Eddington, "An individual is a four-dimensional object of greatly elongated form; in ordinary language we say that he has considerable extension in time and insignificant extension in space. Practically, he is represented by a line, his track through the world." [13] Clear so far. But Sir Arthur adds cryptically, "*The 'track' of the observer is that observer himself.*"

What, we can well ask ourselves, is he saying?

To better envision Sir Arthur's description, imagine this mental construct: In Times Square in New York City high above the street there is an enormous illuminated advertising sign. Thousands of electric light bulbs in row after row make up its rectangular shape. Something interesting happens on this sign: some of the light bulbs are extinguished in patterns, creating dark figures like animated cartoons. These appear in the shapes of girls, boys, heroes, heroines, faithful Fido, wicked Tomcat, creating a delightful variety of characters who flit onto the sign, appearing at one side and moving across it as they tell their little tale, viewed by millions of eyes strolling the Great White Way, till they disappear from view on the opposite side.

Let's suppose that that sign is a replica of the time continuum and you, one individual, observe a figure entering the time continuum from the left. It is *you*, running, hopping, pirouetting, taking off your hat, bowing, whirling and waltzing as you move toward the right, leaving "tracks" all the way across the sign until you disappear off the other side. Now, Sir Arthur says, "The track of the observer is that observer himself." May we infer, then, that the *observer*, you, the individual, is the *physical* you? And that the image on the time continuum is, perhaps, the *psychical* you? Some sort of mental emanation projected outwardly?

No! Sir Arthur sets you straight at once! You are mistaken if you have in mind *two* distinct entities, one physical and one psychical, for *physically* the track would *be* the object, the observing individual, extended in time. In other words, from the time you, the figure *observed* as an animated object, entered the hypothetical time continuum, your "track" would extend from beginning to end *continuously* without leaving a space empty before or behind as you moved across the field of observation until you disappeared into infinity at the other end. At the same time, you the *observer*, are identical in every respect with that track you are observing.[14]

The conundrum man is, existentially and psychologically, eludes definition. As for various philosophical pronouncements on the nature of man, his purposes and destiny, Henry Adams has aptly observed, "Each succeeds in making out a case for himself but none succeeds in disproving the others." But one thing is clear: psychology and physics stand at the metaphysical intersection where parallel lines meet in infinity and where, presumably, the weighty question of the Scholastics may be answered, namely, "Has the universe an existence per se, or does it exist only in the mind of man?"

In any case, granting that relatively little is known about the condition described as "consciousness," a number of facts are known. Consciousness starts in infancy. Unconsciousness is *a priori*, the first state, the *condition prior to consciousness*. Consciousness grows *out* of it, and this Jungian concept, we emphasize, is a contradiction of the Freudian idea which has it just the other way around, deriving the unconscious from the conscious on the rational lines of conceiving it to be a necessary sort of trash-bin for the storing of repressed, sexually-toned, incompatible, pleasure-seeking Id wishes of the ego-self which accumulate from infancy on through adulthood. But consciousness is patently nonexistent in infancy and for many years of early childhood, during which children with rare exceptions are largely unaware of their "I" or conscious of being separate individuals.

Consciousness normally appears sometime between six and ten [15] and from then on it is a matter of *developing* the degree of consciousness. Throughout life consciousness continues to be a condition requiring considerable effort to maintain with any degree of consistency, let alone increase, as you would, for example, if you could interpret your dreams, thus *adding to* your consciousness what was unconscious to you before.

One final comment: a commonplace assumption about consciousness is that when a man is *thinking* he is most conscious. Not so, as the section on Thinking, one of the Four Functions, will clarify. However, a superior consciousness is often distinctive for its ability to engage in "directed thinking," a quite different cerebral activity than its polar opposite, "associative thinking," which is the running stream of subliminal imagery synthesizing impressions, unformed ideas and wishes, instinctive, unthinking urges as automatic as reflexes, into which we sink the moment the focus of our attention relaxes.

"Directed thinking" perhaps even more than the opposable thumb of man's ancestors, has been responsible for the human's striking evolutionary success; in truth *the history of human consciousness is the history of masculine development, aided by his capacity for directed thinking.*

THE UNCONSCIOUS

Jung identifies two levels of the unconscious: a Personal Unconscious and the Collective Unconscious.

Defining the unconscious both benefits and suffers from Jung's insistence that it be understood at the outset that what *can* be said about the unconscious is what the conscious says about it. The benefit comes from recognizing the paradox immediately; the definition suffers because you are in effect left without one. But the situation parallels that existing in experimental quantum physics, to which Jung's psychology stands in the relation of a complementary science: i.e., the psyche that is the *object* of observation is at the same time its *subject*, namely, the means by which you make the observation.

What Jung emphasizes is, it is always *as if* in the realm of the unconscious, for unconscious means exactly what the word states: *not*-conscious. When something is not-conscious to you it is not known.

THE PERSONAL UNCONSCIOUS

All the things that could just as well be conscious are contained in the personal unconscious. Dream imagery from the "subjective level" (Chapter Four) emanates here, things of definitely personal origin, individual acquisitions through personal experience or products of instinctive processes, things that have been forgotten or repressed, complexes, and creative potentials. This "area" obviously will vary from one individual to the next. Some people are just more conscious of what things there are for man to be conscious about; others are, frankly, blanks, which is tantamount to saying, some are better endowed than others from the start.

We are, of course, individually unconscious of an enormous range of things, as is our western civilization as a whole. For example, gross unconsciousness is the rule about many psychic processes which in other cultures are very much in the consciousness of their peoples. In India and China, for instance, levels of psychic development correlated to the physiological centers of the body are minutely detailed in the system of *chakras;* this is conscious knowledge, well known for centuries to the educated. Primitive peoples or country folk living close to nature often have an extraordinary consciousness of things about which city people have no awareness whatever: cycles of nature in the seasons, weather changes, animal life, plant lore and other useful knowledge.

Some complexes originate from the personal unconscious; others from the deep, or collective, unconscious. We all have complexes of one kind or another, but only those with sufficient tension or energy to form partial personalities, with their own willpower and a sort of ego of their own, would be powerful enough to interfere with your conscious will, or, in the other direction, with your physiological processes, i.e., upset digestion or breathing, cause the pulse to race or heart to palpitate, and so forth.

Dream imagery from the level of the personal unconscious is purely subjective, directly related to conscious life, as you will note in Chapter Four.

Important to know: such imagery can be interpreted *only* by the dreamer, even in an analysis; his subjective associations to the dream imagery, what he thinks they mean, take precedence over any "meaning" an analyst could proffer. This is not so about imagery from the deep, or collective, unconscious. *Archetypal* imagery emerges from the collective unconscious and, it should be noted, the average layman is unequipped with the necessary knowledge to understand their appearance, let alone interpret their symbolism. *Archetypes* are one of the most important intuitive and controversial concepts of Jung's psychology. As they are dealt with extensively in the chapter on *Archetypes,* and also in the chapter on *Imagery: Language of the Dream,* we will say no more about them here.

THE COLLECTIVE UNCONSCIOUS

If the consciousness of every living person could be eliminated, there would remain the collective unconscious; that is Jung's graphic description of the nether world of the instincts underlying civilized man's thin skin of consciousness.

Deeper than the personal unconscious is the collective unconscious, which cannot be explored directly. All that can be dealt with are contents which of themselves arbitrarily appear in consciousness through dreams and in other ways.

Jung conceives the collective unconscious to be that level where individual distinctions are non-existent; all of mankind at this level is fused into one common humanity, the individual mind also merges with the unconscious mind of the race. The human mind is seen to be basically uniform in structure, just as the body has anatomical uniformity; babies born today are not different from babies born to the Neanderthals: they have two eyes, two ears, one nose, one heart, and so forth, although qualitative differences can be marked in the skeletal development and brain potential, which are in the nature of improvements.

"Our mind has its history just as our body has it history," Jung says. "Millions of people do not know they have a thymus, but they have it. They do not know that in certain parts of their anatomy they belong to the species of the fishes, and yet it is so. Our unconscious mind, like our body, is also a storehouse of relics and memories of the past. Though a child is not born conscious, his mind is not a perfect blank. The child is born with a definite human brain; it is a finished structure; it will work in a modern way; this brain has its history built up over the course of millions of years, exactly as the body bears witness to its long history.[16]

In its nine month gestation period the human foetus repeats the evolutionary process—from the single living cell all the way up to the primate exhibiting the biological and neurophysiological pattern of *Homo sapiens*.

In the previous section we mentioned the archetypal imagery peculiar to the collective unconscious. We will elaborate: the collective unconscious is the archaic matrix of primordial images which go below and before language. Man at that stage was still pre-logical, non-verbal, capable only of expressing nuances of feelings, perceptions and awarenesses of external phenomena in grunts of onomatopoeic sound. Here began the myth-making mind, pointed to by Ernest Cassirer in his definitive work, *Language and Myth*. Cassirer traces the development of language from the archetypal basic image, demonstrating how, as language developed, differentiation became sharper, as if the words separated to some degree from the basic images. *But the images remain what they are,* nonetheless, because they are themselves, consisting of themselves. These basic images are what Jung calls archetypes, as Plato and Aristotle long ago perceived.

The missing link in the story of the evolution of the human mind was, as Jung recognized, the extraordinary imagery erupting in some of his patients' dreams which could not possibly be contents of that individual's consciousness or of his personal unconscious. He saw that it bore an unmistakable resemblance to mythological motifs which have been the content of age-old myths, legends and fairy tales, in every culture in the history of the human race. In short, beneath our known personalities and the level of the personal unconscious, our myth-making minds are still operating, spinning out the ingredients of our own personal myths.

In their excellent book, *Prelogical Experience*, two distinguished Freudians, Drs. Edward S. Tauber and Maurice R. Green, point to the evidence of the myth-making mind in their joint investigations:

> "A glance at the role that the image-making faculty has played in man's cultural history and creative experience . . . strengthens the impression that it is fallacious to identify prelogical processes with infancy, a chronological condition. *Prelogical thinking is part of the basic endowment of man throughout life operating continuously.* . . . This type of thinking is not something that existed in infancy and is then dragged inertly through later life, contaminating adult experience. . . . It is out of the well-springs of prelogical thinking that ordered logical thinking can finally emerge. Thus dream material relating to primitive thought and feeling can, and often does, relate to the present and even to the foreseeable future, and not necessarily to infancy . . ." [17]

The phenomenon of archaic symbols and mythological motifs in the dreams of patients in the widest variety of circumstances in life led Jung to his definition of the collective unconscious, by the same logic as Plato's. Plato records, as you may recall, that in his great vision of looking into a cave and seeing shadows dancing on the walls, he did not see the actual figures. However, the shadows on the walls are neither more nor less genuine than the figures which cast them.

Unquestionably, those who have not experienced archetypal dreams, or who have not recognized them if they did have them, must find the idea of archetypes rather myth-like itself. The concept has been extremely controversial, and because it is concerned with things admittedly out of the range of ordinary experience—or *awareness* of the experience—the matter has been thought to be most abstruse. For these reasons we go into an explanation of archetypes from a number of angles in the chapter which follows. Moreover, the chapter provides excellent examples, bringing archetypal dreams out of the realm of the recondite onto the level of every-day reality in the lives of countless individuals who have, like this writer, experienced the movements of archetypes unmistakably.

1. C. G. Jung, *The Structure and Dynamics of the Psyche* (New York: Pantheon Books, 1960), p. 217.

2. A rash of popular literature directing readers to easy success, popularity, riches, peace-of-mind, etc., is now published based on the principles of cybernetics. How to condition one's own mind with its built-in mechanism for imaging, is essentially the advice and instruction given. The neurophysiologists have discovered that the human mechanism can indeed find its own dynamic equilibrium. Curiously enough, neurophysiology today employs many of the terms of electronics: scansion, reverberating circuits, etc.

3. Jerome Bruner, *On Knowing* (Cambridge, Mass.: The Belknap Press of Harvard University Press, 1962), p. 24.

4. Anthony Storr, "Cybernetics and Analytical Psychology," *Journal of Analytical Psychology*, I:1, 93. This Jungian psychologist of London relates: "The body is regulated in such a way that the optimum conditions for the life of the individual may be maintained by a system of negative feedbacks which, when a change in the internal environment occurs in one direction, tend to encourage a change in the opposite direction, i.e., the regulation of calcium metabolism, of the heart rate and blood pressure, of the hydrogen-ion concentration of the blood, and others. The life of the body is thus

conceived as proceeding along a middle course between pairs of opposites; neither too hot nor too cold; neither osteoporotic nor calcified; neither hypertensive nor hypotensive. A self-regulating system, in fact, in which excesses in any direction are barred; or if not barred, at least dearly paid for in illness, discomfort or death. . . . [Norbert] Wiener points out that, 'The conditions under which life, especially healthy life, can continue in the higher animals, are quite narrow. A variation of one-half degree centigrade in the body temperature is generally a sign of illness, and a permanent variation of five degrees is scarcely consistent with life. In short, our inner economy must contain an assembly of thermostats, automatic hydrogen-ion concentration controls, governors, and the like, which would be adequate for a great chemical plant. These are what we know collectively as our homeostat mechanism.' "

5. Complexes, in the Jungian definition, are entities sometimes consisting of a great number of elements clustered around a nucleus: the original disturbance point. Around this point more elements continue to gather, in the course of time assimilating other elements, i.e., libido, like a hungry human being who tries to swallow whatever is near him. Complexes have a certain autonomy of action, often like a second will. Investigation has disclosed that many complexes have the qualities of a personality and a fully-developed, very strong complex may have the qualities of an "*alter ego*." This means, of course, that within that individual another ego, apart from what he recognizes to be his conscious self, lives its own life, interfering with his conscious life at the slightest provocation.

6. C. G. Jung, *The Structure and Dynamics of the Psyche* (New York: Pantheon Books, 1960), pp. 110–11. Jung's formal description of consciousness is this: "Consciousness is an interval in a continuous psychic process; it is probably a climax requiring a special physiological effort, therefore it disappears again for a period each day. The psychic process underlying consciousness is, so far as we are concerned, automatic, and its coming and going are unknown to us. We only know that the nervous system, and particularly its centers, condition and express the psychic function, and that these inherited structures start functioning in every new individual exactly as they have always done. Only the climax of this activity appears in our consciousness, which is periodically extinguished."

7. *Ibid.*, pp. 175–76. "Not without justice we connect consciousness, by analogy, with the sense functions," says Jung, "from the physiology of which the whole idea of a 'threshold' is derived. The sound frequencies perceptible to the human ear range from 20 to 20,000 vibrations per second; the wave lengths of light visible to the eye range from 7,700 to 3,900 angstrom-units. This analogy makes it conceivable that there is a lower as well as an upper threshold for

psychic events and that consciousness, the perceptual system par excellence, may therefore be compared with the perceptible scale of sound or light, having like them a lower and upper limit. Maybe this comparison could be extended to the psyche in general which would not be an impossibility if there were 'psychoid' processes at both ends of the psychic scale. In accordance with the principle *'natura no facit saltus'* such an hypothesis would not be altogether out of place."

8. *Ibid.*, p. 217.

9. Max Knoll, *Man and Time* (New York: Pantheon Books, 1957), pp. 228–30. "In experimental quantum physics only one of two properties ascribed to a particle, either an energetic one such as its impulse, or a space-time property such as its position, can be measured exactly at one time. The reason for this is that such measurements can be undertaken only with the help of additional particles or light quanta, and that a reaction between the 'observing' and the 'observed' particle cannot be avoided. Thus, even experimentally, in the exact measurements of instantaneous energy and space-time quantities, an analogous condition of uncertainty appears."

10. Norbert Wiener, *The Human Use of Human Beings* (Garden City, N.Y.: Doubleday & Co., 1954), pp. 102–3.

11. David Hawkins, "Design for a Mind," *Daedalus*, Summer, 1963.

12. *"Continuum"* encompasses the force and metric fields of nature, the gravitational and electromagnetic force fields at present known and yet to be known. In some manner at present unknown, the heaving, broken earth crust that is no more than five miles thick at places where mountains are the highest and oceans are deepest, and at other places only a few hundred yards through, supports the life of numerous diversified creatures in millions of species and variant forms which are shot through and through and thus sustained by the continuum. Energy-trading in known force fields and psychobiological forces both have their part.

13. Sir Arthur Eddington, *Space, Time and Gravitation* (New York: Harper & Brothers, 1959), p. 57.

14. *See* E. W. Dunne, *An Experiment with Time* (New York: The Macmillan Company, 1927), pp. 109–11, for an exceptional exposition of the paradox posed by the Relativists.

15. The ability to conceptualize, a concomitant of consciousness, begins to appear around the age of three, normally.

16. C. G. Jung, Privately published lectures, author's collection.

17. Maurice R. Green, M.D., and Edward S. Tauber, M.D., *Prelogical Experience: An Inquiry into Dreams and Other Creative Processes* (New York: Basic Books, 1959), p. 33.

CHAPTER THREE

Archetypes and Symbols

*Certainly they do not exist, any
more than a botanical system exists in
nature! But will anyone deny the existence
of natural plant families on that account?
Or will anyone deny the occurrence
and continual repetition of certain
morphological and functional similarities?
It is much the same thing in principle
with the typical figures of the unconscious,
the archetypes. They are forms
existing* a priori, *or biological norms
of psychic activity.*

C. G. JUNG AND C. KERENYI [1]

GENERAL COMMENTS

In the preceding chapter we touched upon the skepticism which is ordinarily the reaction of those who have not personally experienced, or recognized their experience of, archetypal imagery in dreams. It is hard to believe, and it will be even harder to believe that the archetypes Jung has termed the *Shadow*, the *Anima*, and the *Animus*, are personified nightly in the dreams of innumerable thousands of persons, right now, whether or not they know it.

We mention these three first because they are the initial archetypal figures every dreamer will encounter as he penetrates his own unconscious; there are a good many others, too, but we shall not deal with them in this work, excepting as they appear in the archetypal dreams cited in a later chapter. Understanding of their emergence and symbolic significance is beyond the capacity of the majority of untrained laymen, however well-read. Also, a certain amount of danger is associated with their disturbance of the psyche; the depths of the collective unconscious are stirring when they appear, and even those familiar with the movements of their own inner realm can be seized anew with the awe, fright, apprehension or reverence that these symbols invariably arouse. Therefore, professional guidance is, excepting for the rare few, wisdom itself when strange archetypal imagery appears.

The *Shadow*, a figure of the same sex as the dreamer, is generally the first to make its appearance; then the *Anima*, a feminine figure in the dreams of men, or the *Animus*, a male figure or figures in the dreams of women. We emphasize right here: these archetypal figures are *not* merely concepts devised by Jung to fit a theory. They have not been invented! These images were found existing in the dreams of many thousands of persons whose dreams came under the observation of Jung during more than a half-century of practice as a medical psychiatrist and depth psychologist.[2]

The Shadow, Anima and Animus are thoroughly discussed in separate sections which follow. They are brought to your attention now because they are the first of the archetypes whose activities you yourself will be able to detect in your dreams, when you know how to recognize them. They can, and will, appear in inner dramas of such dynamism, stirring you emotionally so realistically, that you will never again dismiss dreams as a "nothing but" experience. Then, too, you are reading this book, presumably, because you want to know things you can directly and personally relate to yourself, without undertaking to become an accomplished scholar in all the many studies bordering on dream interpretation. Such knowledge may very well come later, as you will see—and all the sooner when you discern the motif of your *own myth* in the process of being lived out. That enlightenment, however, comes after the individual's thorough acquaintance with his Shadow, and Anima or Animus, as the case may be, through the appearance of other archetypal symbols.

A clear understanding of Jung's use of the term "symbol" is essential. It is totally at variance with the Freudian usage, which accords fixed meanings to dream imagery and calls the images "symbols." More accurately, these would be "signs," not "symbols," though, more often than not, what are actually "signs" *are* spoken of as "symbols" outside the field of psychology.

A true "symbol" according to Jung, expresses unconscious contents not yet known, as yet unconscious, not yet formulated in language. It is still prelogical and nonverbal, and it presents an inner situation that is, in effect, a conjunction of opposites.

The word "symbol" stems from the Greek *symbolon*, combining two root words: *sym*, meaning "together," or "with," and *bolon*, meaning "that which has been thrown together."

Originally, *symbolon* meant the halves of a stick or coin retained by two parties as signs of a pledge. Thus, "symbol" was equivalent to a tally, referring to a piece of an object which, when restored to, or thrown together with its missing half, formed a whole object. The Jungian "symbol," therefore, leads to the missing part of the whole man, that part of him still unconscious, still in the process of becoming. Once your consciousness *knows* what a symbol means, it is no longer a symbol but a content of your consciousness; it is no longer alive and pregnant with unknown meaning for you. By "alive" we mean having power and influence over you, such as, for instance, the Christian cross or the Black Stone of Mecca have over believers.

As the previous chapter on dreams has already related, the intention of the dream is to communicate, to bring to conscious attention, in effect, to enlarge consciousness by adding to it what had been unconscious and therefore unknown by throwing up that which constitutes "the missing part of the whole." These are the purposes of the symbol in the pictorial language of the dream.

To return to the discussion of archetypes: suspicion of their existence has flirted through mankind's thinking since Aristotle and Plato. Jung's assertion that, from the beginning "there can be no empirical knowledge that is not already caught and limited by an *a priori* structure of cognition," has been a reaffirmation, on the level of depth psychology, of discernments made ages ago and recurrently through the years. St. Augustine, for instance, pointed to *typos*, as the generic category of inner, self-existent *form* as well as *meaning*, underlying all visible, external phenomena. Kant later pointed out that myth, art, language and science are really symbols of concealed forces which serve as *organs* of reality. Through them, through their expression, what is objectively (i.e., objective reality) may be apprehended by the subjective intellect and thus rendered visible. Cassirer, pointed to the *basic image*, identical with Jung's archetype, at the root of the development of language. And another modern philosopher, Susanne K. Langer, in her major work, *Philosophy in a New Key*, observes, "A mind that works primarily with meanings must have organs that supply it primarily with forms."

Philosophical speculation may still provoke pros and cons in the future as much as they have in the past, leaving in suspension George Bishop Berkeley's ironic question, "Ideas then are sensible and their archetypes insensible?" [3] But times have moved on. No time in history has witnessed such a burgeoning of knowledge in all fields such as we know at the present. There is grave concern about imbalance between scientific technological knowledge and the humanistic studies, and about the isolation of the layman from useful knowledge which is so peculiarly in the province of specialists. Nonetheless, many disparate studies are knitting together at their borders, their exclusive findings substantiating each other and binding all disciplines into one cohesive corpus of knowledge, as the following sections amply demonstrate.

ARCHETYPES: BIOLOGICAL BASE

The lowest possible level of life is protoplasm. The botanist and geneticist Edmund W. Sinnott has discovered protoplasm to be: ". . . not a substance but a *system possessing a pattern* which so regulates the course of the changes that go on within it that a specific form of activity tends to result. . . . There is inherent in the living system a self-regulating quality that keeps it directed toward a definite norm of course and the growth and activity of the organism takes place in conformity to it." [4]

Sinnott's discovery of the self-regulating activity *within* the formless, protinaceous blob of matter that is the very earliest beginning of life complements Jung's discovery of the *self-regulation of the psyche*.

More corroboration of psychological truths follows from other biologists who stride with seven-league boots into secrets of nature first penetrated by Mendel's proof of genetic mutation. The Nobel-prize-winning English scientists Crick and Watson have conclusively determined that *the same chemical bases*, four in number, are responsible for all living things existing on earth, about two millions of species in all. The differences among species depends on the natural order in which the four chemical bases are arranged in the DNA molecule (the substance out of which heredity-transmitting genes are made), which consists of a double helix, two chains of atoms arranged in a spiral-staircase structure.[5]

There is a *pattern innate*, or *primordial image*, beginning with *protoplasm*. The molecule affirms this fact and it is reaffirmed in the species *Homo sapiens* by the visible evidence that man develops from the embryo not as a tiger, or bird or frog—although for a clearly discernible period the embryo swims about as a tadpole in the amniotic fluid—but as a human being with human qualities, capable of specifically human activities. That potential was already present in the germ plasm containing at the outset the *primordial image*, the *pattern innate*, of a human.

ARCHETYPES AND INSTINCT

As *primordial images* archetypes are tantamount to instinct though not identical, the distinction being that instinct *and* image are separate but meet and fuse into *one*, as Sinnott described the pattern above.

Jung graphically illustrates this fusion in his analogy of the leaf-cutting ant: "Every instinct bears in itself the pattern of its situation. Always it fulfills an image and the image has fixed qualities. The instinct of the leaf-cutting ant fulfills the image of ant, tree, leaf, cutting, transport and the little ant garden of fungi.[6]

Instincts and archetypes share in common the fact of being essentially *collective*, that is, universal and regularly occurring. On the physical side, his instincts compel man to the human mode of existence; on the psychical side, the archetypes operate as organs forcing human ways of perceiving and apprehending, the latter also in specifically human patterns.[7]

One of the most dramatic accounts of archetypally determined characteristics is provided by mathematician Norbert Wiener. His exposition of the phenomenon of speech, the distinctive achievement of man "built into the brain itself," is so extraordinarily fascinating, it is given here in its entirety.

> "Why is it that chimpanzees cannot be forced to talk, and that human children cannot be forced not to? The animal psychologists have not been able to keep from wondering why a chimpanzee brought up in a human family and subject to the impact of human speech until the age of one or two, does not accept language as a mode of expression and itself burst into baby talk. Fortunately, or unfortunately as the case may be, most chimpanzees, in fact all that have as yet been observed, persist in being good chimpanzees and do not become quasi-human morons. . . . The failure so far is not a matter of sheer bulk of intelligence for there are defective human animals whose brains would shame a chimpanzee. It just does not belong to the nature of the beast to speak or to want to speak. . . .
>
> "Speech is such a peculiarly human activity that it is not even approached by man's closest relatives and his most ac-

tive imitators. A few sounds emitted by chimpanzees have, it is true, a great deal of emotional content, but they have not the fineness or clear and repeated accuracy of organization needed to make them into a code much more accurate than the yowlings of a cat. Moreover (and this differentiates them still more from human speech), at times they belong to the chimpanzee as an unlearned inborn manifestation, rather than as the learned behavior of a member of a given social community.

"The fact that speech belongs in general to man as man, but that a particular form of speech belongs to man as a member of a particular social community is most remarkable. In the first place, taking the whole wide range of man as we know him today, it is safe to say that there is no community of individuals, not mutilated by an auditory or a mental defect, which does not have its own mode of speech. In the second place, all modes of speech are learned, and not withstanding the attempts of the 19th century to formulate a genetic evolutionistic theory of languages, there is not the slightest general reason to postulate any single native form of speech from which all the present forms are originated. It is quite clear that if left alone, babies will make attempts at speech. These attempts, however, show their own inclinations to utter something, and do not follow any existing form of language. It is almost equally clear that if a community of children were left out of contact with the language of their seniors through the critical speech-forming years, they would emerge with something which, crude as it might be, would be unmistakably a language. . . . We merely state the fundamental facts by saying that in man, unlike the apes, the impulse to use some sort of language is overwhelming; but that the particular language used is a matter which has to be learned in each special case. It apparently is built into the brain itself that we are to have a preoccupation with codes and with the sounds of speech and that the preoccupation with codes can be extended

from those dealing with speech to those that concern themselves with visual stimuli. However, there is not one fragment of these codes which is born into us as a pre-estab-
lished ritual, like the courting dances of many birds, or the
system by which ants recognize and exclude intruders into
the nest. The gift of speech . . . is strictly a psychological
impulse and it is not the gift of speech, but the gift of the
power of speech. In other words, the block preventing
young chimpanzees from learning to talk is a block which
concerns the semantic and not the phonetic stage of language. The chimpanzee has simply no built-in mechanism
which leads it to translate the sounds it hears into the basis
around which to unite its own ideas or into a complex mode
of behavior. Of the first of these statements we cannot be
sure because we have no direct way of observing it. The
second is simply a noticeable empirical fact. It may have its
limitations, but that there is such a built-in mechanism in
man is perfectly clear." [8]

ARCHETYPES: IDEAS

Awareness of *images beheld* in lightning bursts of intuitive
comprehension is a well-known phenomenon among scientists,
whom I single out because it is generally taken for granted that
the writer, poet, artist, composer or other creative worker has a
Muse, an irresistible inner-something that sees, hears, or "knows."
"It's all as simple as can be," explained one humorist about an
artist, "He paints the things you cannot see." But Robert Louis
Stevenson credited his Brownies who "do my work for me when
I am fast asleep"; and Charles Dickens wrote of his gifts, "Some
beneficent power shows it all to me and tempts me to be interested, and I don't invent, really do not, but see it and write it
down." Milton, Wagner, Blake, Emerson, Sand, the Brontës,
Spitteler, Dante—the roll is endless—attest to the inner eye and
the *images beheld*.

Among the scientists the physicists are most articulate about the inner faculty of "comprehending-without-intellection," of "intuiting," of "instant knowing," a phenomenon preceding some of the greatest scientific discoveries of the present age. Nobel physicist Wolfgang Pauli has described the process known to himself and fellow physicists as intrinsic to their field and declared the archetypal image to be at the root of the phenomenon. Robert Mayer, who was not a physicist but a ship's doctor on a routine trip, has described his part in the "beholding" of one of the greatest ideas of the 19th century, the conservation of energy. August Kekule, whose development of the principles of the molecular structure of organic compounds and the discovery of the molecular structure of benzene rank among the greatest in the development of organic chemistry, has also described his moment of inner "seeing."

Physicist Pauli says: "Many physicists have recently emphasized the fact that intuition and direction of attention play a considerable role in the development of the concepts and ideas, generally far transcending mere experience, that are necessary for the erection of a system of natural laws (that is, a scientific theory). From the standpoint of this not purely empiristic conception . . . arises the question, What is the nature of the bridge between the sense perceptions and the concepts?

"All logical thinkers have arrived at the conclusion that pure logic is fundamentally incapable of constructing such a link. . . . When modern psychology brings proof to show that all understanding is a long-drawn-out process initiated by processes in the unconscious long before the content of consciousness can be rationally formulated, it has directed attention again to the preconscious, archaic level of cognition. On this level the place of clear concepts is taken by images with strong emotional content, *not thought out but beheld*, as it were, while being painted. . . . Inasmuch as these images are an 'expression of a dimly suspected but still unknown state of affairs' they can be termed symbolical, in accordance with the definition of the symbol proposed by Jung. As ordering operators and image-formers in this world of symbolical images, the archetypes thus function as the sought-for bridge between the sense perceptions and the ideas and are, accordingly, a necessary presupposition even for evolving a scientific theory of nature. . . ." [9]

Dr. Max Knoll, another physicist, writing on "Transformations of Science in Our Age," [10] says, "What is not so universally recognized (though often postulated) is the existence of a special 'intuitive' function, a faculty of 'inner vision,' which one might designate somewhat more accurately as a non-sensory perception of pre-existent 'ideas' in the Platonic sense, or of inherited archetypes in the Jungian sense, or of a previously unconscious content. . . . Particularly in quantum physics, however, the fact that an idea (for example an atomic model) suddenly emerges full-blown does call for the existence of a special intuitive function. The content of this idea is best described in qualitative, subjective, timeless, nonspatial and dynamic terms, in contrast to its subsequent systematic development by the thinking function, which is best presented in the form of quantitative, objective and space-time terms, e.g., calculations or rational deductions. Always unmistakable are the suddenness and activity of the intuitive event, and its tendency to occur in a state of relaxation, and after a protracted 'period' of meditation. A further characteristic (contrasting with the logical act which merely 'deduces,' but analogous to the act of observation) is the 'simultaneous' recognition of relatively complex, composite structures as a meaningful whole. . . ."

Pauli's and Knoll's descriptions of the process itself are impressively corroborated by Mayer and Kekule in their almost naïve accounts of their discoveries.

Writing to a friend in 1844, Mayer confides:

"I am far from having hatched out the theory at my writing desk. . . . Now if one wants to be clear on matters of physiology, some knowledge of physical processes is essential, unless one prefers to work at things from the metaphysical side which I find infinitely disgusting. I therefore held fast to physics and stuck to the subject with such fondness that, although many may laugh at me for this, I paid but little attention to that remote quarter of the globe in which we were, preferring to remain on board where I could work without intermission and where I passed many an hour as though *inspired,* the like of which I cannot remember either before or since. *Some flashes of thought that passed through me* while in the roads of Surabaya were at once assiduously followed up, and in their turn led to fresh subjects. Those times have passed, but the quiet examination of *that which then came to the surface* in me has taught me that it is a truth which cannot only be subjectively felt but objectively proven. It remains to be seen whether this can be accomplished by a man so little versed in physics as I am." [11]

As for August Kekule, addressing an audience gathered in his honor on the 25th anniversary of his momentous discoveries in 1890, he related how he had taken a late bus to ride across the city of London where he was visiting. On the bus, "I fell into a reverie, and lo, the atoms were gamboling before my eyes! Whenever hitherto these diminutive beings had appeared to me, they had always been in motion; but up to that time I had never been able to discern the nature of their motion. Now, however, I saw how, frequently, two smaller atoms united to form a pair; how a larger one embraced the two smaller ones; how still larger ones kept hold of three or even four of the smaller; whilst the whole kept whirling in a giddy dance. I saw how the larger ones formed a chain, dragging the smaller ones after them but only at the ends of the chain. I saw what our past master, Kopp, my highly honored teacher and friend, has depicted with such charm in his 'Molekular-Welt'; but I saw it long before him. The cry of the conductor, 'Clapham Road!', awakened me from my dreaming; but I spent a part of the night in putting on paper at least sketches of these dream forms. This was the origin of 'Structural Theory.' "

Of his second great discovery, the benzene theory, Kekule says: "I resided in elegant bachelor quarters on the main thoroughfare in Ghent. My study, however, faced a narrow side-alley and no daylight penetrated it. For the chemist who spends his day in the laboratory this mattered little. I was sitting writing at my textbook but the work did not progress: my thoughts were elsewhere. I turned my chair to the fire and dozed. Again the atoms were gamboling before my eyes. This time the smaller groups kept modestly in the background. My mental (inner) eye, rendered more acute by repeated visions of this kind, could now distinguish larger structures of manifold conformation; long rows, sometimes more closely fitted together all twining and twisting in snake-like motion. But look! What was that? One of the snakes had seized hold of its own tail and the form whirled mockingly before my eyes. As if by a flash of lightning I awoke, and this time also I spent the rest of the night in working out the consequences of the hypotheses. . . ." [12]

Volumes are required to do justice to the subject of archetypes, and even then, as historian Arnold Toynbee surmises, it may take a century or more before they are widely understood or integrated into the body of knowledge which serves to orient man to his situation in the cosmos. The Archetypes warrant intensive study of more than the abbreviated highlights provided above, which must on mature reflection raise many questions in thoughtful minds collateral to those they answer. But the painstaking, lengthy documentation necessary for a full explication requires that the serious scholar turn to Jung's own *Collected Works*.

1. *Essays on a Science of Mythology* (New York: Pantheon Books, 1949), p. 219.

2. C. G. Jung, *The Archetypes and the Collective Unconscious* (New York: Pantheon Books, 1959), pp. 183–4. "Since for years I have been observing and investigating the products of the unconscious in the widest sense of the word, namely dreams, fantasies, visions, and delusions of the insane, I have not been able to avoid recognizing certain regularities, that is, *types*. There are *types of situations* and *types of figures* that repeat themselves frequently and have a corresponding meaning. I therefore employ the term 'motif'

to designate these repetitions. Thus, there are not only *typical dreams* but *typical motifs* in . . . dreams." (Italics mine.)

3. George Bishop Berkeley, "Three Dialogues between Hylas and Philonous," *Readings in Philosophy* (New York: Barnes & Noble, Inc., 1950), p. 110.

4. Edmund W. Sinnott, *Matter, Mind and Man* (New York: Harper & Brothers, 1955), Vol. XI, World Perspective Series. (Italics mine.) *See also* Sinnott, *The Biology of the Spirit* (New York: The Viking Press, 1955), p. 64.

5. Ruth Moore, *The Coil of Life* (New York: Alfred A. Knopf, 1961).

6. Jung, *The Structure and Dynamics of the Psyche*, pp. 200–1. Freud also arrived in the vicinity of Jung's concept of the archetypes although semantics obscures their agreement. Thus Freud, on the unconscious, says, "An instinct can never become an object of consciousness, *only the idea that represents the instinct* can. Moreover, even in the unconscious an instinct cannot be represented otherwise than by an idea." But Jung exposes the limitations in Freud's premise: "Exactly *who* has the idea of the instinct in the *un*conscious state? For *un*conscious ideation is a contradiction-in-terms." (Italics mine.)

7. Michael Fordham, M.D., *New Developments in Analytical Psychology* (London: Routledge and Kegan Paul, 1957), pp. 14–15. Dr. Fordham, M.R.C.P., F.B.Ps.S., English analyst, cites the discovery of innate reflexes lying at the base of the neuro-endocrine system, pointing to near-proof of neural patterns of instinctive behavior. The brain at present shows that the hierarchy of the nervous system implicates the *whole sensory system in any perceptual act*, implying *a body image as present* even if not consciously involved in the localized area subject to experiment.

Curiously enough, the "body image," posited as implicit, receives extraordinary support from surgeons whose amputees continue to have sensations ranging from pleasant tingling to excruciating pain in a limb no longer there. Surgeons have known for 400 years that this is so. *Time* magazine, August 11, 1961, reports the methods of Dr. Allen Russek, New York University Rehabilitation Center, pioneering in exercises to exorcise phantom pain. An account is given of an electrician who lost his left arm and suffered massive scarring, who "felt that his phantom left arm was doubled up behind him, that the hand was numb, and that every now and then electric shocks coursed up and down the arm, with sparks snapping off his fingertips." Before fitting an artificial arm, Dr. Russek had the right-handed patient exercise his phantom arm by standing in front of a blackboard, closing his eyes, and practicing writing with his nonexistent left hand! The mental effort worked through the nerve stumps and nearby

muscles; after months of phantom writing the electrician said he had
brought the phantom arm around in front of his body and could
raise it over his head. More tangibly, scar tissue that had been painfully contracted was stretched so that extensive grafting became unnecessary.

8. Wiener, *op. cit.*, pp. 82–85.

9. C. G. Jung and W. Pauli, "The Influence of Archetypal Ideas
on the Scientific Theories of Kepler," *The Interpretation of Nature
and the Psyche* (New York: Pantheon Books, 1955), pp. 151–153.
(Italics mine.)

10. Max Knoll, *op. cit.*, pp. 270–271.

11. Letter from Robert Mayer to Wilhelm Griesinger, June 16,
1844, pub. Kleinere Schriften und Briefe, Stuttgart, 1893; *Two
Essays on Analytical Psychology* (New York: Pantheon Books,
1953), p. 66ff.

12. Quoted in Ira Progoff, *Depth Psychology and Modern Man*
(New York: Julian Press, 1959), pp. 215–18.

CHAPTER FOUR

You See You In Your Dreams

HOW THE DREAM WORKS

With this chapter we take up the most fascinating phase of the study of dreams: how you learn to detect *you* in the imagery of your dreams. That is, things about you of which you are not conscious but which your unconscious thrusts toward your awareness in dreams.

The (1) Four Functions: Thinking, Feeling, Sensation and Intuition, (2) the Persona, (3) the Shadow, (4) the Anima and (5) the Animus, and (6) Complexes, involved in the psychic mechanisms of (7) Projection and (8) Compensation, in the normal self-regulating processes of the psyche, are not only concepts defined by Jung; they are also actual components of the psyche imaged in dreams, usually as personifications.

In the chapter on the psyche we referred to the extraordinary parallel between cybernetics and the self-regulating system of the psyche. The former automatically performs through the interplay of active components in regulating circuits; the psyche similarly seeks dynamic equilibrium between conscious life and its unconscious functions, through the mysterious interplay of the psychic components named above. These may be outwardly expressed through the will, or conscious intention, or through projections, the autonomous, unconscious mechanism of the psyche.

The prodigious outpouring of imagery unique to dreams will reveal, when interpreted and understood, those unsuspected kinships between "facts long known but wrongly believed to be strangers to one another," of which the mathematician Henri Poincaré speaks in *Science and Method.* Dreams broadly declare:

1. Something positively or negatively relevant to the components mentioned above, as *compensation for the conscious situation of the dreamer at the time of the dream*

2. *Projections* made by the dreamer into the milieu, as well as blind spots about attitude, character, personality, in short, about things of which the dreamer is unconscious, but about which he should and could be conscious

3. *Progression* or *Regression* of libido, as the case may be, and which invariably indicates a critical juncture or painful impasse in the conscious situation of the dreamer

4. *Preliminary ground-plans of future activities and potentialities for development,* sometimes intimated in dreams long in advance of the time of the actual events

5. *Continuing guide-lines* for the individual's unique development, as long as he lives. In the Jungian view, to maintain close touch with your unconscious is vitally important; indeed, the very point and purpose of understanding dreams is to benefit from their counsel or warnings, and thus to develop the personality to the utmost of its potential.

The form of the dream is dramatic; in fact, the earliest Greek dramas drew their plots from the structure of dreams. The striking similarity to stage plays in the majority of dreams goes like this:

(*1*) *Statement of* DRAMATIS PERSONAE. *Time and place are stated.*

The dream begins with a statement in, of course, pictorial analogies. It may be quite simple, as, "I am in a street; it is dark." Or, more complex, as, "I am walking with a friend, John, in the park. At a crossing—we have to be very careful, the traffic is very heavy—we unexpectedly run into Mrs. Smith."

(*2*) *Exposition. The plot shapes up.*

A conflict or crisis begins to form. In this phase, the dream picks up action leading into a set of complications. As, "I. am in a street; it is dark. In the distance a car appears, approaching rapidly. It is being driven very erratically. I think, 'The driver must be drunk!' "

(*3*) *Culmination. The equivalent of a second-act curtain evolves.*

Now something either good or bad is going to happen to re-solve the deadlock in the action. For example: "Suddenly I see that *I* am in the car, I myself am the driver. But I am not drunk, only strangely insecure, as if without a steering wheel. I cannot control the fast-moving car. I am terrified. There is a wall di-rectly ahead. The car is heading for it."

(*4*) *"Lysis" or Solution.*

The dream resolves the crisis one way or another: either the car does smash into the wall, injuring or destroying the driver, or alternately, at the very last moment a metamorphosis, or tran-scendence, or other rationally-inconceivable solution, rescues the driver. As: the driver at the instant of crashing into the wall, miraculously grabs onto a trailing vine hanging providentially over the wall, and swings to safety.

(*5*) *Unresolved Crisis.*

Sometimes the crisis is not resolved in the dream. The emotion becomes so intense the dreamer wakes up, leaving the dilemma hanging in mid-air. In such a case, *the solution is left up to the dreamer's consciousness to work out,* a knotty problem demand-ing the utmost conscious effort on the dreamer's part.

Here is an example of the latter type of dream-ending. A woman deeply devoted to her two grown unmarried sons was their constant companion. The trio mutually enjoyed each other's companionship; they were inseparable. Outwardly, this appeared to be an idyllic relationship. Why shouldn't a mother enjoy the delightful vivacious society of two gifted, enterprising young men? How lucky, especially for a widow who necessarily is cut off from many social activities open to married couples? Then she dreamt the following:

All three were driving through a beautiful strange countryside in the sons' red Volkswagen. She was in the back seat as usual, thoroughly enjoying the outing, as usual. Suddenly she noticed the car was no longer on the road. Somehow, it had gone off into a forest; the road was bumpy now, and then, all at once, the car plunged into a stream. The stream, she observed, widened into a turbulent river just ahead. Rocks and hidden potholes were endangering the car, which still seemed to be going forward with the older son at the wheel. But actually, it could not go forward, nor could it turn back. Now, the wheels were spinning freely round and round without making progress. The water was rising, and soon would fill the interior of the car. It was only a question of time before the car must founder.

The woman awakened at this critical juncture, distraught, the crisis unresolved. But she knew enough about depth psychology to recognize immediately what the dream more than hinted: she and her sons were being carried along in a state of *"participation mystique"* i.e., unconscious identification; they violated their individual values. They leaned too much upon one another unconsciously. She, in the "back seat," was being carried along in life on the sons' libido, not her own; she was not using her own talent and will and effort to work out her own destiny and personal development.

The dream did not tell her what to do; it merely pictured the situation *as the unconscious viewed it,* leaving it up to her consciousness to take action, or not, *if she chose.*

Rarely does the unconscious take over the prerogative of the conscious ego, namely, choice, will, decision. When the unconscious resolves a situation it is often a matter of such one-sidedness in the personality that a cataclysm results rather than a solution, as is obvious in the instances of psycho-somatic illnesses, complexes of a compulsive nature, neuroses and psychoses.

Another dream of this type, told to us recently goes like this:

The dreamer, a young man just over the mid-point of 35, dreams he is flying an old-fashioned, open-cockpit airplane. Suddenly he realizes he is unable to land it, he doesn't know how, nor does he know how to keep on flying it, either. Terrified, he awakens.

By type, the dreamer is an intuitive-intellectual whose current life-problem demands a realistic coming-to-terms with very ordinary day-to-day facts of life. For more than a year he was unable to conclusively end an emotional real-life situation which he had long-since outgrown. Although the problem was an extremely complicated one that we cannot digress to discuss here we want to call attention to the conclusion, which is similar to the first dream. *The unconscious leaves it up to the dreamer;* unsaid, but tacitly assumed, is the idea that consciousness *can* deal with the problem, if it *wills.* Which is not to say that the solution chosen may not be difficult, painful, even agonizing. The main thing is, *life virtually stops* in such situations. Rather, the vital sense of being alive, of being in the current of life, zestfully participating in it, is in suspension, as is the case with this young man, up in the air in an outmoded aircraft which he feels unable to bring down-to-earth, where life must be lived. At the same time, there is a hint of menace in the alternative: he also feels he cannot keep it flying.

IMAGERY: THE LANGUAGE OF THE DREAM

Dream imagery literally means everything in and about a dream: personifications, picturizations of places, landscapes, ani-

mals, peculiar atmospheres or moods, tools, weapons, conveyances, typical motifs, and even the emotions gripping the dreamer
during the dream and at the moment of waking. These latter
often persist for hours, and an open question is, whether the
changing moods we notice from one day to another may not be
the residue of our nightly inner dramas, the resolutions of which
we capture only fragmentarily, if at all.

Of imagery, Jung says, "The dream speaks to us in images, that
is, in a pictorial and sensual language. It communicates the
thoughts, judgments, perceptions, directions and tendencies
which have been unconscious because of repression or through
mere ignorance." [1]

Ironically, although communication is the purpose of the
dream, the Sphinx never guarded her secret more jealously than
the average dream its meaning. Yet dreams can be stunningly
lucid, uncannily knowing, prescient to the point of omniscience.
How did the dream know Elliott was going to die? Where the
Chafin will was to be found? What is going to happen in the
future, as Telepathic Dreams relate?

Moreover, the dream does not lie, deceive, distort or disguise,
in the Freudian sense of having a "latent meaning" beneath a
"manifest façade." Without question, the language of the dream is
archaic, obscure, absurd, shocking, exasperating, ambiguous, sexual and frustrating; if it only spoke plain English we would all be
very much better off indeed. But we are confronted with the
necessity of making our way back to understanding the pre-
logical, non-verbal language of our remotest beginnings; because
we cannot even claim that the rudiments of human perception
and onomatopoeic sounds started with our remotest animal beginnings the philologist is only relatively better off than the rest of
us.

Because the dream is a natural phenomenon appearing at its
own pleasure (no cause that will produce the effect of a particular dream is known) interpreting dreams works in reverse—
from the effect (the dream imagery) backward to the probable

cause (the conscious situation of the dreamer at the time of the dream). These two factors will either compensate or complement each other; the former means to make up for something missing, the latter means to add to, enlarge or complete.

Dream imagery may arise from either the subjective level, which is the equivalent of the personal unconscious, or from the objective level, the collective, or deep, unconscious.

There are five factors creating or stirring up imagery, plainly related to the subjective level which can more or less easily be traced to waking life. They are: (1) "remnants-of-the-day." (2) somatic stimuli, (3) physical environment, (4) psychological factors of a relationship, and (5) the time factor. In addition, there are such peculiarities about imagery, which must also be considered as dream factors, as: (6) contamination, (7) condensation, (8) multiplication, and (9) repetition. The latter group will arbitrarily influence imagery from either the subjective or objective level. One further distinction remains: (10) imagery from the objective level must be distinguished from that of the subjective. From the deep unconscious, the objective level, archetypal imagery can emerge spontaneously—imagery which is not likely to be comprehended unless special training or professional guidance provides the necessary background. Creative ideas, sudden erupting intuitions, lightning insights—like an omniscient "knowing" —can also shoot up from this level, some of them presented in powerful dream imagery. And finally, from the objective level also emerge those dreams imaging new aspects of the dreamer's personality never before supected, but holding forth the seed ideas of future development of his personality.

FORMS OF DREAM IMAGERY

As a stimulus to your recognition of imagery in your own dreams the following list suggests the typical forms you will soon recognize as dream contents. Fixed "symbolism" is nonexistent in the Jungian formulation.[2] Typical motifs and typical symbols can be recognized, however, as already stated in the section on symbols.

1. PERSONIFICATIONS. You yourself, as you actually are at the time of the dream (your ego-self); or as a child, or in youth, or older than you are now, can appear. Also other persons, known or unknown to you, may appear; so may monsters, giants, dwarfs; creatures half animal, bird or reptile; angels, fairies, and so on. *Personification always means the unconscious has begun to stir of its own accord. The actions of such figures often foretell future activities of the dreamer.*

2. PLACES. Your current home, or a strange house, castle, cave, dungeon, cloister, bordello, or other setting may be chosen by the dream in ways demolishing space-time. Frequently the condition of your consciousness in a situation current in your life may thus be pictured, or a transitional stage in the development of your personality, as, for example, a ruin under reconstruction.

3. ANIMALS. Pictured in dreams, pets, or strange animals helpful in showing the dreamer the way out of dilemmas which appear utterly insoluble, are reminiscent of the helpful animals abounding in folk and fairy tales. They symbolize the help that can come to mankind from the deepest layers of his being, from instinctual animal-life. Animals live their lives true to nature, and it is as if their appearance reminds the dreamer to rely on nature, his basic instinct, which can lead him out of an impasse.

Among the archetypal and recurrent animal images, the *serpent* occupies a unique and ambivalent niche. In some aspects the serpent is the symbol of supreme wisdom; the Soter serpent heals, and in the Ophitic tradition, the serpent is identified with the Redeemer, Saviour of mankind. On the other hand, the serpent is the well-known tempter to evil, the devil himself, enticing the first man and woman to eat of the tree of knowledge of good and evil. To know what is good and what is evil is the equivalent of being *wholly conscious,* for only the conscious can distinguish between good and evil. Paradise, in this light, is *un*consciousness, which the old folk saying "Ignorance is bliss" baldly recognizes.

The horse is another universal symbol of libido, libido in the Jungian sense, not the Freudian sense of sexuality only.

Dreams frequently image the present-day form of horse as power, which is exactly what libido is, power, in the form of an automobile, taxi, bus, truck, train or plane. These all have *horsepower*.

Driving his own car can mean that the dreamer has full charge of his own energies, he himself is directing the course of his own experiences; someone else at the wheel can mean the opposite, that is, the direction of his life-force, his libido, has been taken over by some one or some thing, as the dream images the situation.

How strangely evocative the image-making faculty is can be inferred by the following report of a hallucination produced in experimenting with LSD-25. A writer describes the psychotic-like effect of taking the drug, which transformed her into a horse:

"Immediately I became a magnificent feminine Pegasus of the purest white. . . . My glistening white mane and tail had a silky quality. I had huge wings of snow-white feathers laid in perfect symmetry, dainty shell-pink nostrils, and large liquid-blue eyes. My opalescent hoofs were of iridescent mother-of-pearl. Awareness of my beauty made me intensely happy, the emotion again completely uncontaminated by egotism." [3]

4. PECULIAR ATMOSPHERES OR MOODS. Eerie or tranquil; frightening or blissful; awesome or commonplace; joyous or anxious—these states of feeling are considered to be imagery also. So too is the emotion registering at the instant of waking which often colors the mood of the dreamer for hours afterward.

5. TOOLS, WEAPONS, CONVEYANCES. Bus, train, auto, plane, ship; sword, knife, utensils, ladders, stairs—the tremendous gamut of objects extending man's five senses and his ability to act, move, do and achieve are very important, particularly with regard to their condition. Are they new and plainly effective, or outmoded, rusted, or otherwise in less than good condition, less than serviceable for the best interests of the dreamer?

And while an automobile driven by the dreamer, or in which

he may be riding as a passenger, may be construed as the ancient libido symbol of the horse in modern dress, a public conveyance such as a train or bus means something quite different. As a motivating force, the values and mores of society, the collective as opposed to the individual, are controlling the dreamer. If the dream imagery presents the dreamer's conscious attitudes in such a way as to warn him he is encased in armor, or in the clutches of a tyrant, or being taken along in a conveyance crowded with faceless, nameless numbers of people, the message could be that the dreamer has not wrought his own principles but swallowed unreflectingly the collective ideas of his time.

In the category of tools, weapons, and conveyances, what is *not* signified, from the Jungian point-of-view, is the fixed interpretation of the Freudian system which dogmatically assigns to all the thousand-and-one objects which are elongated, club-like, sharp, penetrating, protuberant or jutting, the meaning of penis, and for anything round, concave, or hollow—a cave, container, vessel, hole, *ad infinitum*—the meaning of the female genitalia. Nor, in any combination of these images, do Jungians feel compelled to see sexual excitation or wish-fulfillment of a sexually-toned nature. To be sure, these symbols *may* mean these things; but in every instance—and this cannot be stressed too strongly—the dreamer's personal associations to the images take precedence over any others, even those provided by the analyst if the dreamer is in analysis. (The exception, to be discussed later, is the case of archetypal dreams.)

6. TYPICAL MOTIFS. Common among motifs are: arrival and departure; journeying; flying; danger of falling from high places or in peril on a mountain top; difficulty in negotiating dangerous cross-overs; wandering along lonely roads, desolate and lost; exchanging, finding, or losing money. Money is another common symbol of libidinal energy, imaged also as gold, jewels, treasure, but just as often as excrement, urine, and other disgusting matter.

More typical motifs: being in the dark, or followed from behind; finding yourself stark naked or insufficiently clothed, or without shoes, thus inadequately equipped for some situation in real life; or wearing many hats, or a peculiar hat, or crowned, as a king or queen.

Altogether, typical dream motifs parallel the typical motifs of myths, folklore and fairy tales, and these, in turn, are closely related to the rituals, symbols and beliefs among primitive peoples. Fraser, Frobenius, Bayley and Müller, to name but four well-known scholars whose contributions to a new science of symbology are the product of years of research in the fields of anthropology, archeology, comparative religions and ethnology, show that the practices, rituals, symbols and beliefs prevailing amongst people widely separated by space, time and cultures are virtually identical.

Typical motifs in dreams will generally bear a relationship to the level of culture of the dreamer and such aspects need to be taken into account in interpreting the motifs. Where the motif represents a level of cultural history which reaches far into the past, long before the lifetime of the dreamer, that too is of significance in interpretation. The sword *Excalibur* appearing in a dream, for instance, is touching upon a bit of psychological truth consonant with the legend of the grail in King Arthur's time; a frogman's trident probing the water ahead of him belongs to an entirely different age in human consciousness, a much later development.

Other than the motifs typical of an archetypal situation there are, of course, motifs typical for the dreamer exclusively, as disclosed by the dreamer's records of his dreams which, over a long series, will gradually reveal the special life-problem of that individual. Such problems recur again and again on a spiraling scale as life is lived, and in the stages of progress depicted in dream imagery, the development of character and personality is unequivocally imaged.

7. MISCELLANEOUS INFLUENCES. In addition to typical motifs, motifs in the category of "miscellaneous" cover those conditions, situations, or problems that recur over and over again in the pat-

tern of dreams. These are chiefly idiosyncracies of dream image-formation and they include: contamination, condensation, multiplication, repetition, and metamorphosis.

A. *Contamination.* The contamination of one thing by another is an oddity about dreams probably resulting from stirring up complexes. Every mortal has his share, however "normal" the personality. Complexes are not the burden of neurotics only, and wisdom begins when acquaintance with your own odd quirks equals your estimate of the over-all queerness of everybody else.

As an illustration of "contamination," Dr. C. A. Meier, Zurich analyst, relates the story of the old woman in a mental clinic who constantly referred to herself thus: "I am the Lorelei." Dr. Meier unravelled the processes by which the patient had taken this title. It seems that the regular ward doctor in the clinic had the habit of shaking his head and saying, "I don't know what this means," when he paused briefly in making his rounds to listen to her incoherent statements. Now, "I don't know what this means" is the opening line of the famous *lied* of the Lorelei by Heine. This patient had elided all the intervening associations, but held onto this one remaining communication to identify herself as the Lorelei.

B. *Condensation.* Numerous qualities may be compressed into a single image but with one layer of meaning on top of the other like a piece of strudel pastry. A dreamer's spouse, lover, doctor, neighbor, relatives, pets or other familiars may be combined with animals, or with animal-, fish-, or bird-like images. The old woman who called herself the Lorelei also used to say, "I am the Socrates substitute," her meaning being that she had been put away unjustly, as had Socrates.

C. *Multiplication.* Two, three, several, a multitude of the same motif may appear in dreams, sometimes as an emphasis on the particular blind spot of the dreamer. In other words, the dream thus underlines its message by saying it over and over again.

Contesting trends within the personality can be imaged as two persons. A married pair in the dream can be the admixture of Shadow with either the Anima or the Animus, Jungian concepts to be described later in separate sections. Or, two of an image can mean two sides to the matter, good and bad, positive and negative, and the dream reminds the dreamer of this possibility in the situation imaged. In fact, the ambivalence of symbols may be taken for granted: every symbol, in the Jungian definition, expresses a *conjunction of opposites*.

D. *Repetitition.* Some dreams occur again and again, the underlying theme restated in a variety of ways. When a dream repeats itself, either the same night or on subsequent nights, the unconscious is restating the case because of its especial importance, as a teacher stresses through repetition some vital point essential for the pupil to grasp.

E. *Metamorphosis.* At critical stages in some dreams, as when danger threatens to overwhelm the dreamer, a metamorphosis may occur, rescuing the dreamer miraculously or magically. In one dream: "I was suddenly catapulted into a raging torrent. A bunch of wild leeks I had gathered on the banks metamorphosed into a life preserver and I floated to safety on the other side of the river." It will be plain even to a neophyte that the dreamer received a most positive message of encouragement from the unconscious at the time of a difficult and dangerous cross-over.

SUBJECTIVE LEVEL

1. "REMNANTS-OF-THE-DAY." In the bizarre arrangement of dream material, details plainly carrying over from the moods, impressions, and events of the preceding day or recent past are often woven haphazardly through the dream plot. Dreams are never simply photographic reproductions of waking-life events. Residual details will often filter into dream imagery, one thing "contaminating" the other, triggered off by emotions associated with the conscious situation of the moment.

On close scrutiny you invariably will discover little differences in what at first seemed to be an exact reproduction of a setting taken over intact from waking life. The image should be held in mind as you would examine a picture in real life; then you begin to detect a shift of features in the personifications, in the locale, in many trifles. In the end it is as though you were looking through a transparent curtain onto which your waking-life events had been painted, straight into another and deeper background merging the familiar with the strange inner scene, creating a new picture. James Joyce's *Ulysses* does something of that sort; its ever-shifting kaleidoscopic impressions are like a film-strip multiply exposed. Not only is the focus of instant, present attention caught but also the penumbral residue of past impressions as well, some clear, some blurred.

Another aspect to keep in mind: Some imagery will be presenting contents once in your consciousness but which are now forgotten, repressed or suppressed. Then there are the things you know but fail to realize that you know: *most of us know more than we know we know in some areas.* We are made aware of this fact occasionally, as when we read, or hear expressed, a conviction or a sentiment which immediately we recognize is exactly our belief, our conviction, our sentiment, too. Only, we have not *consciously* realized this was so, nor were we aware of having thought it out. But once verbalized, our instant assent has the effect of lifting such a matter to awareness and consciousness.

2. Somatic Stimuli. Physiological changes and conditions of the body are often portrayed through dream imagery. Hunger, thirst, heat, cold, sexual urges and other normal demands of the physical mechanism for its maintenance and repair are automatically pictured.

Abnormal conditions are imaged too. Various organs of the body threatened or affected by illness are imaged, as Scherner's investigations have demonstrated. From another and far older line of determination there are the correspondences established in Tantristic Yoga between particular bodily locations and corresponding psychological experiences, as designated in the system of *yoga chakras.*

As examples of dream imagery reflecting the bodily impairment of their dreamers: a patient suffering from pneumonia

82 THE MEANING IN DREAMS AND DREAMING

dreamed he was in a furnace filled with flames and blown upon by a powerful wind. As a matter of fact this is an accurate picturization of the inflammatory process menacing the respiratory system in a case of pneumonia. Another dream: a young girl patient of Jung's, early in his career, was suspected of muscular atrophy by other medical consultants on the case. Jung asked if she had had dreams, and learned of two. In one, the dead figure of her mother hung from a chandelier swaying to and fro in a cold wind coming from an open window. And in the other, a horse wild with fear plunged to its death from a high window. Both dreams pointed to organic destruction, a prognosis soon borne out by the actual death of the girl.

There is, of course, an immense literature beginning with Homer and Herodotus in the millennia before the Christian era, refined by Asclepius, Hippocrates, and Galen in the centuries between 480 and 130 B.C. dealing solely with the interpretation of dreams and diagnoses of bodily illness by dreams. Up to the time of Paracelsus in the 16th century, diagnosis by dream imagery was virtually a matter of looking up the solution to a problem in a textbook. Indeed, the Asclepiads in Greece numbered 320 abatons [4] at one period, all of them connected to the main temple at Epidaurus. Pausanias, an inveterate traveler and conscientious reporter, named the exact locations of the steles on which temple cures had been inscribed; these same steles were unearthed in archeological excavations in the 19th century and the report of what Pausanias had seen centuries before was corroborated. One specific requirement was understood to be the very essence of the cure: the petitioner was required to have a dream in the sanctuary. The dream was a boon reverently prepared for and awaited; so was the message of the dream. Sometimes that message foretold the doom of the dreamer; other times the longed-for healing dream, *somnia a deo missa*, the "dream sent by God," was granted.

Dream literature did not deal with health problems only; all the experiences which man has discovered to be critical turningpoints have been studied as they were reflected in dreams and recorded through the ages. One exemplary work is the five-volume *Oneirocritica* written by Daldianus Artemidorus, a Lydian who lived in Hadrian's reign in the second century of our era. His whole life was dedicated to the project of compiling everything known from the past and combining it with continuous and pains-taking research during his lifetime, documenting hundreds of dreams and researching the many facets of dream imagery. To this day his *Oneirocritica* stands unrivaled as the greatest dream book of all time, anticipating in many respects the discoveries of the depth psychologists by seventeen centuries.

For the enlightenment the comparison offers, here is a sample of Artemidorus' insight into the dream process:

"If someone with right understanding is affected with love for a woman, then she whom he loves does not appear in her own form but as a beautiful horse, or a mirror, as water, a boat, a fe-male animal, a garment or something of that sort which may be understood as a woman." What clearer parallel to Jung's state-ment that dreams speak a "pictorial and sensual language"? Nor can Artemidorus' insights in other respects be improved upon, either. He says that in order to make the correct interpretation of dreams it is essential to "know and take into account to what sort of person the dream occurs; what his trade is; what his class and name, what property and position he is endowed with; what his physique is; how life has dealt with him, the age he has reached. . . ." More, the dreamer's morals, customs, environ-ment, even moods, were considered to be indispensable informa-tion for the proper interpretation of his dreams. This view coin-cides with that of Jung, who insists that the "conscious situation" of the dreamer be known in every particular and considered to-gether with the imagery produced by the dream. The facts from *both* spheres, the conscious and the unconscious, provide the whole story. The Jungian principle of *compensation*, to be dis-cussed further on, is intrinsic to the interpretation of dreams.

3. PHYSICAL ENVIRONMENT. Sounds, or lights, may distort and color the dream imagery: an alarm clock going off, church bells ringing, a window shade suddenly rolling up with a snap, a back-

fire from a passing auto, and so on. Also, strange new quarters, a guest room, or a hotel, or other breaks in accustomed routine, may activate dreaming and trickle through the dream imagery which appears to take account of such changes in the outer experiencing.

4. PSYCHOLOGICAL FACTORS OF RELATIONSHIPS. Between closely related persons, as parents and child, husband and wife, lovers, intimates with a shared life pattern, the psychological problems of one can enter the other's dreams. This is especially true of children who are helplessly open to the psychic influences of their parents. If the parents are emotionally disturbed or unstable, the children invariably become infected. Unconsciously children "carry" their parents' psychic malaise and their unresolved psychic problems. Much of the psychological truth of the jealous God exacting tribute and justice "to the fourth generation" nests in this grave of familial conditioning.

Beyond the conditioning of family and clan, however, there is "participation mystique," a term coined by the noted anthropologist Levy-Bruhl to signify the state of *un*conscious identity which frequently exists between persons in an intimate relation, and even between persons and things, best observed among primitives, particularly in the cult of the totem. Among civilized people, however, participation mystique is the rule in the majority of close relationships founded upon unconscious assumptions about the other, and this is tantamount to saying participation mystique is the rule in human affairs. Sooner or later, in the course of most close relationships, there comes a stir for freedom by one of the partners. The bonds of intimacy and identity, once assumed to be blissful and desirable, become intolerable fetters to be cast off whatever the cost. (The ambivalence of close relationships founded on unconscious assumptions is discussed in the chapter on *Projections*.)

5. TIME FACTOR. Two aspects of time have distinctive meanings in the interpretation of dreams:

A. Imagery may depict something relative to past, present, or future experiences; space-time factors are demolished in the dream experience. Dreams in the categories of reductive, compensatory, or prospective, described in detail later, should be carefully examined for the time factor which could enable the dreamer to associate the dream experience with outer-life events.

B. The time of life of the dreamer is all-important. It makes a tremendous difference in the interpretation of a dream whether the dreamer is an adolescent, in early youth, in mid-life, or in old age; each of these stages of life has significance in terms of wholesome goals for libido.

The gradient of the first half of life is upward, toward the meridian. The instinctual drives and collective pressures upon the individual to get established in life, through launching his career, putting down roots in family and home, securing a place on the social scale commensurate with ambition and will, all belong to the first half of life. And Nature directs the full force of her mighty urges toward the attainment of these ends; if unimpeded, the gradient of libido is in the direction of *progression*.

But at high noon the sun already begins its setting. Somewhere between thirty-five and forty is the mid-point of life; what comes next follows as naturally and, at first, as imperceptibly as the changes of adolescence. Though it be one o'clock, five, seven, or eleven in the afternoon of life, the gradient of libido is downward, toward dusk, and dust. Libido is in the direction of *regression;* the climacteric of both men and women is as difficult and meaningful as the onset of puberty. Hypochondria, alcoholism, suicide, even murder can bowl over previously stable citizens in their late forties and fifties although their consciousness does not appear to have taken notice that time is running out. The general attitude accords with the observation of Harvard's Jerome Bruner, in *On Knowing:* "Today death has become somehow impersonal and unnecessary, perhaps like a fatal vitamin deficiency that might have been prevented or at least delayed. . . . One reads drug advertising with the sense that death must be an error on the part of the consumer . . . One dies nowadays in hospitals, hidden from view, victims of medical failure."

But whether the individual is conscious of the shortening span of his life or not, the psyche is fully aware. Dreams are not influenced by applications of estrogenous face creams or lotions for receding hairlines. When the meridian has been passed, dreams reflect the true situation without mincing imagery. There are problems belonging to the first half of life, and others belonging to the second half. The former reduce to whether or not the individual successfully adapts to the demands of external reality, for the most part. After the mid-point, however, the problem becomes just the opposite: *the requirement is to withdraw libido from external to internal realities.* "The afternoon of life is just as full of meaning as the morning, only its meaning and purpose are different," says Jung, pointing to the understanding the East long ago attained and incorporated into its culture, namely, that from noon on is ⁺he time for the development of cultural values, the opposite of the aims of nature in the first phase of life.

Western culture has no tradition for this turnabout; the transition period is largely fought; the cult of unfading youth is dinned into the collective consciousness by a thousand commercial voices. This visible, massive effort to hold onto the purposes and appearances of the first half of life goes on at every level of society.

The ability to interpret your dreams can be of the greatest value after middle age, the natural period for turning inwardly to a realm that was always there but which persistently, and even necessarily, was blurred by the incessant din of the preoccupations of the first half of life.

WHAT TO BE ON GUARD FOR

There are some, among them psychic, intuitive, creative personalities and markedly introverted types, who are closer to their unconscious than others. These may readily accept from the start the fact of the interior world.

The artist, for one, already knows the "inner eye" by which he reconnoiters the terrain of his inner artistic vision. The writer, too, is a veteran tourist in the realm of moving images and the interior enactment of the story he tells; he also knows about the images that move *him*. From first-hand experience he knows that the characters he creates soon take on a life and movement of their own; that his contribution is chiefly to maintain a Spartan discipline in controlling and shaping the material welling up in him into a particular form. If, in fact, the writer's work is not "taken over" by the inner power, once he is under way with it, he is better off to give it up for it simply fails to come out right when he is going solely on his own.

Now, such creative types are already acquainted with the image-producing faculties of the unconscious and they, far more than any other types, are readily able to experience the galvanic effect of a dream the meaning of which is clearly seen to dovetail with outer events in their lives. However, they are also prone to fall into the trap of interpreting every little twitch from their dream life as the equivalent of a cosmic explosion. Every picturization in dream and fantasy may burgeon the *subjectivity* of these dreamers. The qualities, functions, and possibilities about himself, as pictured in his dreams, can have the effect of inflating his ego. Suddenly he is more, much more, than ever he dreamed he was! His dreams prove it. And he is in trouble, or will be, unless he holds onto a realistic opinion of the rightful part he as an individual may claim in the great scheme of things.

Everyone who learns to make contact with his own unconscious through dreams is advised to keep in mind that sooner or later he will arrive at a stage where he imagines there really must be something a bit unusual about himself, something setting him apart from those who do not have this remarkable gift and the wisdom that comes with it. This well-known condition, termed "inflation," is almost always experienced by those who learn a great deal about Jungian psychology and dream interpretation. It may persist, to the dismay of your intimates, until at last the sobering realization strikes home: countless thousands of other persons the wide world over share your marvelous experience; it's as unique as feeling warm if you stand in the rays of the sun.

1. C. G. Jung, "General Aspects of the Psychology of Dreams," *Spring*, 1956.

2. Dr. Lawrence S. Kubie, an eminent U.S. Freudian psychoanalyst, writes in *Journal of the American Psychoanalytical Association*, Vol. I, 1953: "In recent years reconsideration of the classical picture concerning symbols has led several investigators to question the existence of fixity, universality, transition states between true symbolism and indirect representation, and to recognize the dangers of reification with respect to symbol-formation." Translated out of professional jargon, Kubie includes himself among those no longer holding Freud's view that dream symbols are fixed, that they are everywhere and always the same for whoever dreams them, and he warns of the danger of making mere words, or constructs, become actual things-that-exist: an ever-present danger in dealing with abstractions.

3. Jane Dunlap, *Exploring Inner Space* (New York: Harcourt, Brace & World, 1961).

4. The abaton was a combination of hospital and shrine, rather on the order of present-day Lourdes, to which the ill and troubled made pilgrimages.

CHAPTER FIVE

The Four Functions

The primary tools we have for adapting to external events are the Four Functions. These are of equal value in the economy of the psyche. Jung named them: Sensation, Intuition, Thinking and Feeling.

The Four Functions posited by Jung are irreducibly four in number, each distinctively different from the others and forming two pairs of opposites, thus: Sensation and Intuition, Thinking and Feeling; Hands-opposite-Hunch, Head-opposite-Heart.

They have directions as well (also four in number) namely: introversion and extraversion, progression and regression.

Early, very early in infancy, through the unique selectiveness exerted by heredity, personal choice and environmental conditioning, one function is chosen as the predominant function for adaptation to the external world. This function more or less becomes so fully differentiated by the individual who controls its use with his will that he can be as unaware he is using the function as he normally is of inhaling and exhaling.

Together with a characteristic bent for either introversion or extraversion, *the predominant function determines the psychological type of the conscious attitude.*

This superior function is ordinarily flanked by one or two *partially differentiated auxiliary functions,* never as responsive to the will or intention as is the predominant function, and the paired opposite to the latter sinks entirely into the unconscious. The inferior function is *always* the opposite of the paired functions, they literally represent a polarity for the experiencing of phenomena; it is not differentiated, that is, it comes and goes of its own volition beyond the rule of the will.

It does not disappear, however; its "absence" in the inventory of faculties at the command of the conscious personality does not mean that because it is unconscious it is disposed of; *energy cannot be dismissed, nor transferred to other functions!* From the unconscious the inferior function continually functions, but secretly, mischievously, often malevolently *against* the direction of the superior function which tries vainly to repress its opposite.

To put it plainly: *Your inferior function is your Achilles' heel!*

More: each function is as good as any of the others, that is, Thinking, for instance, is not a faculty superior to Sensation, nor is Intuition superior to Feeling, for each is a valid mode of adaptation to external life. But whichever function is chosen as the primary one, it automatically *excludes* the others. In fact the paired opposites *must* exclude the other. You cannot, for example, *think* about a problem and simultaneously have *feelings* about it. A thinker may take as his problem whether Kant or Sartre is the more profound philosopher. But if he injects his preference for one philospher over the other, then he is no longer *thinking,* he is *feeling.* His subjective prejudices color the facts by which *thinking* proceeds to its conclusions.

The upshot of the bias created by the superior function is: *you can ascertain only one-quarter of the truth of any phenomenon by it alone.* You need the other three to arrive at the whole truth. The situation is reminiscent of the fable of the blind men and the elephant. Each touched a different part of the beast and each swore a great oath that it must be (1) a long thick snake—his trunk; (2) a great, rough-barked tree—his leg; (3) a tremendous, wrinkled wall—his side; (4) a short, tough, skinny rope, his tail.

Sensation and Intuition form a polarity of irrational functions, Feeling and Thinking a polarity of rational.

SENSATION

Sensation is the function that tells you something *is*, and only that. It does not tell you *what* it is; Thinking does that.

As a type, the Sensation-dominant never doubt for a moment that all of "reality" that can ever come to anybody must come as it comes to them: through the five senses. The "proof of the pudding is the eating" in their view. At their best, they are great doers and can achieve practical, visible results; at their worst, they can be insensitive louts of the *genus Philistinus*.

An example: Two doctors enter a ward together and see a new patient in Bed 19. Dr. Hunch spots him from the doorway, says, "Well, well, looks like lobar pneumonia over there, eh?" Intensely annoyed, his companion, Dr. Hands, snaps back, "My dear fellow, jumping to conclusions like that is the bane of our profession! When I have the man's history, his temperature, pulse-rate, the physical signs in the chest, the blood count and the composition of the urine, I shall *know* what is the matter with the man!" The fact that it turns out to be lobar pneumonia in the end does nothing to endear Dr. Hunch to Dr. Hands, just as these opposite types in other fields fail to recognize that the other can be right, however much the methods contradict his own. In many areas not only the methods, but the conclusions as well, may differ and yet be valid. Apart from the claim of scientific proof of the validity of *this* phenomenon or *that* one, variant conclusions on an identical question have the authority of Gödel's theorem: either side may rebut the other; "certainty" is an illegitimate concept.[1]

INTUITION

Intuition tells you *what may be.* Out-of-the-blue possibilities can materialize into realities with this mysterious function which only recently, since quantum physicists acknowledge its importance in their work, has begun to achieve the luster of respectability. Knowledge comes straight from the unconscious, not from the senses, often like a revelation, an eruption, something "beheld," as the chapter on Images and Imagery related, or instantly discerned, a sort of omniscient "knowing."

You can almost always tell from his eyes whether a person is an Intuitive or not. An Intuitive radiates *at* things, taking in all with a diffused glance that scarcely sees the details but penetrates to the essence, the "atmosphere," the quality of the experience, just the opposite of Sensation who sees an astounding mass of detail.

An Intuitive, however, though he may uncannily sense the richest possibilities in some proposition or situation—"know" something favorable or adverse hangs in the atmosphere of a meeting, or in the nature of a new acquaintance—may not necessarily understand what to do about his impressions. He needs Thinking and/or Feeling to reinforce his Intuition for practical use. Of itself, Intuition is super-logical, not anti-logical nor merely logical. "An intuition which contradicts logic is not really an intuition but a prejudice," the scholarly Sinologist Richard Wilhelm says. "True intuition agrees completely with logic, only it surpasses it. It is not strung, so to speak, on the thin thread of logical procedure but has a broader base. . . ." [2]

The broader base is the Intuitive's proximity to the unconscious, as if there were no barrier between his mind and the psyche's resources, while other types have not the slightest inkling of such a free flow between the two spheres of the psyche.

At his best, the Intuitive is at home in realms of abstract thought and unlimited possibilities; at his worst he is lost on the mundane plane of practical matters. To an Intuitive, to be in a situation bounded by security and certainty of outcome, in which all the potentials have been realized, is a dreaded fate; he is imprisoned, and his sole concern is to be off to fresh new fields, just over the hill, vibrant with all sorts of possibilities. By contrast, his opposite type, Sensation-predominant, is frantic with anxiety and fright and subject to actual panic unless absolutely reassured about his solid footing in whatever he undertakes.

In the past two decades, the function of intuition has surpassed the respectability of the other three functions because physicists, acknowledging that intuition has a value equal to a thorough grounding in the symbolic logic of higher mathematics, have declared the function to be indispensable in quantum physics. The recognition has not come from one or two, but from a long distinguished line of the foremost authorities in the field: the late Nobel physicist Niels Bohr, the Nobel physicist Wolfgang Pauli, Robert Oppenheimer, Max Knoll, Walter Heisenberg, Philipp Frank and the late P. W. Bridgman, among them.

THINKING

In its simplest definition, *Thinking* tells you *what* a thing is. Thinking names things. Thinking differentiates, makes distinctions between just-this-and-precisely-that. Thinking formulates concepts to identify its cognition of things: it is apperception-with-judgment.

Where the Thinking function predominates, its opposite, Feeling, a rational function like Thinking, is inferior, undifferentiated. No one can do better than the Thinking type with a logical problem, but this type comes to think of every experience as a problem to which logic, applied, automatically and inevitably provides the only possible conclusion, overlooking the evidence thrust upon him time and again that, "The heart has reasons that reason never knows."

Emotionally, in the realm of Feeling, the Thinking type is very often soft and weak, and in private life falls under the heel of a

Feeling-type personality who, if equally unconscious and power-hungry, may ruthlessly dominate and exploit him.

Does this mean that Thinking types have no feelings? They have feelings, all right: strong, powerful emotions, which are necessarily and severely repressed; for these types have no control over their emotions, and they fear them, with sound instinct. Emotion, we should add, is not an activity of the person who feels it but something that happens to him, something that moves him out of "himself"; e-motion, from the Latin "to be moved."

While a highly differentiated Thinking function is truly one of the miracles of civilization, it is also one of the greatest hindrances to the individual's development toward wholeness. The collective scene is a witness to our meaning; we see the gigantic imbalance corroding our society because our emphasis on values is out of step with the technological advances which are the purest product of differentiated Thinking. Values are the function of Feeling, most conspicuously absent as criteria in the conduct of public affairs and business, both areas at present still under the old Roman principle of "*caveat emptor*."

FEELING

Feeling tells you what a thing is *worth* to you. Feeling is a *valuation* function. You can neither perceive nor apperceive without a feeling-reaction separate from and other than a cognitive and analytical determination about the object perceived. This function does *not* mean the capacity for warm and ardent emotion. In truth, *coolness not heat* is the distinguishing characteristic of Feeling types who can "turn it on" or "turn it off" at will. In other words, one with differentiated Feeling is perfectly capable of saying very nicely and icily, "I hate you!" and mean it. The Feeling type knows just how much expenditure of feeling a thing is *worth*, and gives it just that much and not a bit more. The type knows very well exactly what he wants and what others want too and is not above using this knowledge to get just what he wants regardless of others.

Feeling is a rational function when it is differentiated; that is, under the control of the will, or conscious intention. When it is not, then feelings just happen to happen to you chaotically, and that is uncontrolled emotion.

There is apt to be some confusion over the word "Feeling" in the context of the above definition and there is ample reason for confusion. "Feeling" is nearly as abused a term as the word "love" for describing states of emotions ranging from tenderness to wild passion. The distortion surrounding the whole complex of love-feelings is such that no attempt whatever can be made here to untangle the lines where Eros, the emotion of love and relatedness to another, begins, and Feeling, the differentiated valuation function, ends.

Just as the Thinking type has to pay dearly for his lack of Feeling development, so does the Feeling type come to grief with his Thinking problems. As a function, Thinking is beyond his ken but he will frequently find himself bedeviled by compulsive thoughts which he cannot dismiss by saying "I will not think," for the thoughts steal in anyhow and he is stuck with them. Each type is penalized for his short supply of the opposite functions and for scant measure in the auxiliary ones.

Cursory though the foregoing summary of the Four Functions is, you would be superhuman if you resisted attempting to pinpoint people in your own circle within the spectrum of these functions. It is certainly true that your comprehension of functional types can make an enormous difference in your understanding of people; in many instances in looking about your own milieu you will be round-eyed with sudden insight into the basis for some of the more incongruous pairs spicing the human comedy, or tragedy, as the case may be. You can fairly surmise which spouses, sweethearts, inseparable friends and intimates are living testaments to the irresistible attraction-of-opposite functions, *as though responding to a hidden command to find completion however vicariously through experiencing their opposite, inferior function*, expressed in another person. The opposite is easily spot-

ted as well: the insupportable tensions and frictions arising spontaneously between protagonists with differing primary functions;
neither side discerns that the other's position is as valid as his own
and both strain the civilized limits of polemics.

Practically speaking, determining accurately another's predominant function is, for a number of good reasons, extraordinarily
difficult, and not the least of these reasons is that people are by no
means even generally what they may seem to be. You will puzzle
over yourself, for that matter, for *not four* but *thirty-two* possible combinations of functions have to be evaluated before you
can properly form a conclusion. Why thirty-two? Because each
superior function will be either extraverted *or* introverted. Thus
to begin with there are *eight* modes of functioning: extraverted
Thinking, introverted Thinking; extraverted Intuition, introverted Intuition—and so on. Multiplying by four, the number of
irreducible functions, yields thirty-two primary possibilities. In
addition, the *auxiliary function* immediately supporting the superior one is invariably oppositely-motivated, that is, if extraverted
Thinking is the superior function and Intuition is the auxiliary,
Intuition will be *introverted*. Obviously, the complications become quite intricate as Jung's definitive study, *Psychological
Types*, relates.

The student will find Jung's classic of inestimable value in
learning how to distinguish his own type as well as others. Another excellent reference for laymen is P. W. Martin's *Experiment in Depth*, from which the following pertinent advice is
quoted:

"In attempting to arrive at what type a person is, the first thing
to note is what he does easily and well, the function into which
his energy (libido) naturally flows. In many cases this can be
checked up by seeing on which side he is inferior. There are here
one or two useful rules of thumb which, while far from infallible,
may be of help.

"Thinking and Feeling are alternative methods of weighing up
a situation. It is necessary, therefore, to distinguish what form

this weighing-up process takes. A Thinking type will normally rise to a problem—provided it is within his range of knowledge —and deal with it incisively. Seeing a situation in terms of problems is for him the natural line of approach. A Feeling type will not readily take to problems as such, but anything to do with people will at once claim his attention. The human angle is the one he understands.

"Sensation and intuition, being alternative methods of perception, may be distinguished by observing how a man perceives. The Sensation type, when sizing up an object, narrows his gaze, focuses his eyes upon it, really looks at it. The Intuitive, on the contrary, seems to envelop it with his gaze, looks around it and through it rather than at it.

"Whether the function is extraverted or introverted is more difficult to determine. It is true that the extraverted attitude can be readily distinguished from the introverted attitude by noting whether, in action or conversation, a person is going out freely to the object or audience, or whether he is staying within himself. What cannot so easily be decided is whether the superior function is being used or one of the others. The inferior function, compulsively running the man, may give a completely false impression. Generally speaking, the mark of the inferior function is that it escapes conscious control; comes and goes in its own fashion, at its own time; cannot be summoned at will; brings emotion in its train. The superior function a man will not even know he is using, it works for him so naturally." [3]

Jung's theory of psychological types covers the Four Functions and the direction of their expression, extraversion or introversion. Many other important characteristics of human personality are not a part of this study. For instance, capacity or incapacity for action; goodness of heart; artistic ability; intellectual integrity; sense of responsibility; sense of humor—none of these are measurable by the standards of the Four Functions yet they are important in the over-all structure of the individual personality, and of course, the individual's capacity for experiencing many facets of life. Despite these exclusions your command of the tenets relevant to the Four Functions is useful for something more than qualitative evaluation of yourself and others. As Jung points out, "To realise the order of our functions entails a severe psychological criticism," the truth of which comes home to you on the tender area of your inferior function. Because our resistance to becoming aware of personal limitations is matched only by our receptivity to approbation, everyone has to overcome a stubborn reluctance to admit the actuality of his inferior function. But this acknowledgment and acceptance is only a preliminary hint of what can be expected in confronting the Shadow, with which we deal in the next chapter.

As imagery, the Four Functions generally appear in dreams as *personifications*. Either the dreamer himself, or someone known to him who is representative of that particular function, is imaged—providing the function is *differentiated*. Where the function is not differentiated the imagery often expresses itself in animal forms. This is the general rule but there are always, of course, the exceptions that prove the rule as the following dream, taken from a series analyzed by Jung, will show.

The dreamer was a highly intelligent woman of thirty, a natural scientist, "suitably" married, the mother of two children. To her consternation, she found herself to be "in love" with another man—a situation which her mentality, her code of ethics, her upbringing, her whole philosophical orientation toward life, simply refused to accept. Literally, it was something that just couldn't happen to *her*. Beyond this brief synopsis of her "conscious situation" there is no need to illustrate the point further. She was distraught, but her intelligence was such as to recognize dimly that the "in-love" feeling was an *effect* from *causes much deeper than the attraction embodied by the man on whom her feelings of "love" had projected*. In consultation with Jung, she reported the following dream:

"I am with a mole and a canary. I have cut their nails and I am afraid I have cut them too short and caused them pain. Someone says to me, 'The mole has to go deep into the earth.' I took the canary out of its cage. It did not fly away. I had expected it would."

Here we have two animals: the mole, a creature living in the dark, digging underground, and the bird whose native medium is that of the light and air, like thought which seems to leave the head like a bird. They are completely opposite as instinctual forces, an above and a below.

This bird is decidedly domesticated: it is caged. The unconscious is the quintessence of arbitrariness in the choice of images and it does not choose an eagle, lofty on its aerie, swooping far and wide, nor for that matter an ostrich, with its penchant for putting its head in the sand not to see danger. No: this is a little sweet-singing canary, imprisoned. Canaries in a cage tend to grow their nails too long since their activities are so restricted; it is not a mistake to cut the nails of a canary in a cage. But a mole is a different thing. It is a wild animal that needs its nails to function properly in digging. To cut its nails is a serious mistake and a cause of suffering to the animal whose instinct to burrow is thereby hindered.

Symbolically, birds have long been associated with thought and inspiration, with the spirit, enthusiasm, and with communication, serving as messengers and bringing information. The dove of the Ark, for example, returned with the information of dry land where the remnant of mankind might put foot. The Paraclete is another bird-symbol of Wisdom which, in turn, consists of thoughts and ideas, the Divine *Logos*. In the dreamer's image, her Thinking function is pictured as a thoroughly domesticated canary-in-a-cage over which she has complete control; its wildness and freedom do not exist. But the opposite, emotional side of herself, Feeling, is most definitely not at her beck and call. She has no understanding of the nature of the mole or its needs. She does not recognize that to understand a wild creature one must study its habits in its own environment. Such understanding puts the burden of adaptation on the observer, not the wild creature.

Nonetheless, even in her dream the woman murkily realized something might be wrong about her action in cutting the nails too short; she is concerned about it even though she doesn't know just what is wrong. Then she is told what the nature of the mole is, as though she were being instructed; in other words, her attention is specifically called to the fact that the mole goes deep down into the ground, as if she might overlook this piece of news unless it were emphasized. Moreover, the idea being conveyed is that that is the *essential* thing about a mole's function, and that cutting its nails—the implication hangs in the air—impairs its natural functioning. Evidently something is required to go underground, because up above nothing is moving.

Of the canary, her Thinking function, nothing can be expected since it is so tame that even when she opens the cage door it does not fly around. Therefore no information useful for her predicament can come through her domesticated mind. But she can hope for something from her wild function, the primitive, inferior function that moves instinctually, as the mole moves, underground. The dream quite obviously stresses this function of the mole at the same time as it advises her not to expect solutions with her mind.

Because she was an intellectual this dreamer had assumed without question that the working out of any problem, even an analysis, was primarily a mental job: the analyst explained things and the analysand's part was accomplished by comprehending them intellectually. This was all very rational, very logical. And of course killed neatly every possibility of development. As Jung says, "We misuse our differentiated function in order to protect ourselves, very often in a wrong way; we use it to kill life when it threatens to become awkward. Up to a certain point this protection is quite valuable, but when you come to that place in your life where the development of your personality becomes an inevitable problem, then you are no longer allowed to kill life. Then you must accept life. . . ." [4]

This means, of course, that the development of other functions

is imperative for rounding out the personality; that the lopsided-
ness that results from the overemphasis of the predominant function must be painfully and painstakingly corrected.[5] However
well the facile superior function serves you—and serve well it
usually does at least in the first half of life—there comes the time
and the situation in which Thinking cannot resolve the dilemma
that cries for Feeling; the Intuitive cannot surmount the impasse
of the many unsolved problems his lack of reality creates until he
is finally nailed down by their mounting weight; the Feeling type
blunders from one confusion into another, prodigally dissipating
upon just and unjust alike energies better used in the development
of the discrimination and differentiation Thinking could provide;
the Sensation type finally reaches such a hole surrounded by
practical considerations weighty with reality that only intuition
could possibly lead him out of his self-imprisonment into the living realm where the play of chance and potential and possibilities
can kindle a feeling of the excitement and mystery of life and
that he is actually living it.

A single dream will not, in most cases, reveal the dreamer's situation, his progress in the development of personality or lack of
it. There are exceptions to the rule: the initial dream at the beginning of an analysis frequently describes the life-problem of
the dreamer as clearly as though a lighthouse beamed its powerful
light onto a dark sea. The dream quoted above was not an isolated
dream; it marked the beginning of a lengthy series for the
woman. We chose it as an excellent example of a dream imaging
the Functions, despite the fact that rarely will animals symbolize
differentiated functions.

Another point: the choice of mole and canary made by this
dreamer's unconscious to symbolize Feeling and Thinking, ap-
plies only in her case. Were you to dream of these creatures they
would undoubtedly mean something else, as amplification of the
imagery in relation to your conscious life, and the text of the
dream itself, would disclose. As a general rule, situations in which
the functions do appear as animals occur when opposing functions

are in conflict; then, in some instances, the conflict is imaged as a battle between two monsters or grotesque animals.

1. Gödel's Theorem: (1) Any consistent mathematical system which is sufficient for classical arithmetic must be incomplete. In other words, in a formal system which is expressible within the language taught to a student of a secondary school in any country, it is possible to formulate assertions which can be neither proved nor disproved; (2) Any such system remains consistent if one adds to it the axiom of choice and it also remains consistent if one adds the negation of the axiom of choice; (3) The so-called general continuum hypothesis is also consistent with ordinary mathematics and in fact ordinary mathematics remains consistent if the axiom of choice and the general continuum hypothesis are added simultaneously. (For lack of this proof, Bertrand Russell devoted years to the effort of proving or disproving *certainty*, an illegitimate concept by this Theorem.) *McGraw-Hill Encyclopedia of Science and Technology*, Vol. VIII, p. 177.

2. Richard Wilhelm, "The Circulation of Events," *Spring*, 1961.

3. P. W. Martin, *Experiment in Depth* (New York: Pantheon Books, 1955), p. 30. (Mr. Martin is Director of the International Study Center of Applied Psychology, Talbots, Sussex, England.)

4. C. G. Jung, "The Interpretation of Visions: Excerpts from the Notes of Mary Foote," *Spring*, 1960.

5. Many persons manage what is on the surface a well-adapted, agreeable life, without appearing to be in any way conscious of a lack in themselves of one or more functions. Many are, actually, cases of arrested development and often, as they grow older, their pattern of life and their attitudes express one of more and more conventionality, inflexibility, a sort of drying-up of life at the source.

CHAPTER SIX

The Persona and The Shadow

The web of our life is of a mingled yarn,
good and ill together; our virtues would be
proud, if our faults whipped them
not; and our crimes would despair,
if they were not cherished by
our virtues.
  WILLIAM SHAKESPEARE [1]

THE PERSONA

"I am in a railroad station about to take my departure from the place where I have lived since childhood," a dreamer related. "Old friends are there to wish me well; I am going to a new place I don't know anything about. Suddenly I am aware that while I am properly dressed in front, I have nothing on in back, and once I turn around I shall be exposed. I awaken in a terrible state of humiliation and embarrassment."

More dreams than there are stars in the heavens have imaged the dreamer in some humiliating situation like the one told above. To be naked in a public gathering, inadequately or inappropriately dressed, are commonplace motifs in dreams; they show the state of the Persona. Schopenhauer, whose general opinion of his fellow-man could only euphemistically be called sardonic, once described the outward cloak of manners with which people cover up their real selves as "that which somebody represents in contradistinction to what he actually is." Well he put his finger exactly on the Persona: it is our outer cloak of manners which Jung observed to be so intricately woven into our habitual pattern of behavior; dreams actually *personify* the Persona just as though it were a living creature itself.

The Persona as Jung describes this behavioral complex "is a complicated system of relations *between individual consciousness* and *society*, fittingly enough a kind of mask, designed on the one hand to make a definite impression upon others, and on the other, to conceal the true nature of the individual.

"That the latter function is superfluous could be maintained only by one who is so identified with his Persona that he no longer knows himself; and that the former is unnecessary could only occur to one who is quite unconscious of the true nature of his fellows. Society expects, and indeed must expect, every individual to play the part assigned to him as perfectly as possible, so that a man who is a parson must not carry out his official functions objectively, but must at all times and in all circumstances play the role of parson in a flawless manner. Society demands this as a kind of surety; each must stand at his post, here a cobbler, there a poet. No man is expected to be both. Nor is it advisable to be both, for that would be "queer." Such a man would be "different" from other people, not quite reliable. In the academic world he would be a dilettante, in politics an "unpredictable" quantity, in religion a free-thinker, in short, he would always be suspected of unreliability and incompetence, because society is persuaded that only the cobbler who is not a poet can supply workmanlike shoes. To present an unequivocal face to the world is a matter of practical importance: the average man—the only kind society knows anything about—must keep his nose to one thing in order to achieve anything worthwhile, two would be too much. Our society is undoubtedly set on such an ideal. It is therefore not surprising that everyone who wants to get on must take these expectations into account. Obviously no one could completely submerge his individuality in these expectations; hence the construction of an artificial personality becomes an unavoidable necessity. The demands of propriety and good manners are an added inducement to assume a becoming mask. What goes on behind the mask is then called "private life." This painfully familiar division of consciousness into two figures, often preposterously different, is an incisive psychological operation that is bound to have repercussions on the unconscious." [2]

"Angel abroad, devil at home," is just one homely folk-saying instinctively recognizing the existence of a "Persona," the term chosen by Jung from its original use in Greek plays to designate the mask worn by an actor to indicate the role in which he appeared on the scene. However, although the Persona is unquestionably a "mask" in the sense that a false face covers the true one, in dreams the Persona is only rarely represented by a mask. Usually reference to the Persona shows up by the state of your clothes, or your skin, an observation coinciding with the same view of two well-known Jungian analysts, Dr. Edward C. Whitmont of New York and Dr. C. A. Meier of Zurich.

Additionally, the former points out, "Clothes are indispensable realities, essential to our present life. They serve both for appearance and for needed protection. And our skin is an absolutely vital part of our individual organism; even a partial loss of skin function can result in loss of life. The *Persona* stands not only for a more glamorous uniform in which to present ourselves but also, in its role as clothing, skin, and the mask of the god or hero (as it did in ancient Greek plays), it represents a necessary form of extraverted adaptation to the archetypal demands of life around us. . . . We cannot evade the fact that *psychic life presents itself to us in a dualistic aspect, as both internal and external reality*, neither aspect can be dealt with as a mere epiphenomenon of the other. In life we have to accept them on equal terms even though the internal and external aspects are forever intermingled with, projected upon, and seemingly opposed to one another. . . ." [3]

Dr. Meier contributes further insight into the Persona and its derivation: "From . . . mask, we go to our clothes, therefore, the *costume* we wear. In French, costume, or *coutume*, is synonymous with *habit* which also means a relatively solid habitual complex of functions. . . . Considered as a function, the *Persona* is the *function of relatedness to the external world*—correlative to the function of Anima and Animus which represent the *function of relatedness to the inner world*. . . ." (Although the concepts of Anima and Animus have yet to be touched, your attention is called to this important distinction in the roles of these figures which show up in your dreams.) Continuing with the *Persona*, Meier adds,

"The stronger the *Persona* is, the more rigid it becomes and the more the bearer is jeopardized from influences from within. In such cases, a strong man, or confirmed rationalist, suddenly shows superstitious traits (or other such anomolies inconsistent with his outer mien of behaviour). . . . In dreams, the *Persona* is rarely personified since the *Persona* is something we wear, like clothes, rather than something we *are;* thus it becomes a dream *motif* rather than a dream figure. This becomes particularly clear when something goes wrong with our *Persona;* dreams where something is wrong with our clothes, we are exposed naked or partly naked. The *Persona*, when personified, *is always represented by somebody of the same sex.* . . . The father and mother images play a considerable part as examples in building up of our own *Personas*. . . ." [4]

As a rule, a man's *Persona* is both more elaborate and more rigid than that of a woman, who can change her hairdo, or for that matter the color of her hair, her hat, her frock, her whole appearance with much more facility than a man is able to change his to suit a whim or a mood. Hence, the Organization Man, the Specialist, the Banker, the Cleric, the Judge, the Professor, the Statesman and Politician, whose roles all too easily come to be taken *by themselves* as the real man, forgetting the human being and especially his uniqueness, his individual qualities, are often immured beneath the part they play to the observing world.

But, says Jung, "A man cannot get rid of himself in favour of an artificial personality without punishment. Even the attempt to do so brings on, in all ordinary cases, unconscious reactions in the form of bad moods, affects, phobias, compulsive ideas, backslidings, vices, etc. The socially 'strong man' is in his private life often a mere child where his own states of feeling are concerned; his public discipline, which he demands quite particularly of others, goes miserably to pieces in private. His 'happiness in his work' assumes a woeful countenance at home; his 'spotless' public morality looks strange indeed behind the mask—we will not mention deeds, but only fantasies, and the wives of such men would have a pretty tale to tell. As to his selfless altruism, his children have decided views about that." [5]

Improbably there could be in circulation some so naïve or primitive as not to recognize immediately from honestly appraising themselves and their circle that masks of all sorts abound. The *Persona* is a most necessary expedient, as even the minimally sophisticated recognize in meeting the multitudinous demands of daily life, as an adult among adults. But our *Personas* began to form in childhood, perhaps with Mummy who responded with a treat when we recited our little pieces to her visitors, perfectly aware that our virtuosity obliquely conveyed how clever Mummy was. Early our conditioning to please, placate, conform, tends to contort our natures, first for Mummy and Daddy, then teacher and classmates, friends, the boss, the powers-that-be, the world—*when it suits our needs and purposes!* We remain marvelously untouched, underneath it all, a fact we may be able to conceal from ourselves indefinitely if we avoid learning how to interpret dreams. The journey to self-knowledge through the terrain of the dream, however, is bound to take you *behind* the pleasant features of the Persona which is *always identical with a typical attitude dominated by the superior psychological func-*

tion! When that process is completed, *then* you are ready for—the *Shadow,* fully conscious that your Persona is a *convenient mask,* and not what *you* really are.

THE SHADOW

"The Shadow is a moral problem which challenges the whole ego personality; no one is able to realize the Shadow without a considerable expenditure of moral resolution. To confront it involves recognizing the dark aspects of the personality as *actually present and morally binding.* Such confrontation is the essential condition of any kind of self-recognition." [6]

There is a "strong sense of man's double being which must at times come in upon and overwhelm the mind of every thinking creature," Robert Louis Stevenson noted, later writing the story of man's inner torment and conflict, *Dr. Jekyll and Mr. Hyde,* which he dreamed in its entirety and wrote almost verbatim as he dreamed it.[7] Together with Wilde's *The Picture of Dorian Gray, Dr. Jekyll and Mr. Hyde* ranks high among classics in English literature, dramatizing the ever-recurrent constellation of the problem of good and evil and the duality of man's nature.

Granted, hardly a sentient being today is not braced to accept the view that there must be a dark side to humankind. A cursory reading of almost any daily newspaper—with its sordid accounts of crime, venery and corruption on all levels of society and among governments—or any evening of TV—the preponderance of television programs graphically showing mayhem, thievery and cunning acts of astounding viciousness—must force a consensus that improvement in man's bestial nature still has a long way to go before "civilized" can truly describe it. Additionally, we have had a "certain preparation through education," as Jung once trenchantly put it, to convince us that human beings are not 100% pure gold. Two millennia of theological indoctrination have indelibly drilled into Western Christendom that the sinfulness, degradation, and corruption of the human race is so total

that God Himself required the sacrifice of His Only Begotten
Son to redeem the worthless creatures He had formed in a
moment of impractical benevolence. *Why* man is to be found in
such a pitiable, deformed condition has been answered by a cartel
of deviously spun dogmas based on a preposterous incident of un-
authorized apple-eating about six thousand years ago. We are
heirs to this tradition and all its good that has been and still is incalculably enormous, and all its far-reaching evil, not the least of
which is the placement of the origin of all evil in that convenient
receptacle, the Devil. Naturally, no one can be found who will
undertake to reform the Devil!

There is a Shadow, the dark side of every man. Your portion
of your darkness will show up in the Shadow figure in your
dreams.

Actually, the Shadow is the reverse of the positive, gracious,
agreeable Persona. The Shadow is archetypal, but it feeds on all
the derogatory or nasty things thought but not said as we smil-
ingly shake hands, pretending a cordiality belied by our negative
feelings; it is our cold indifference, our procrastinations, our lazi-
ness, our self-indulgence. The Shadow is the way we over-do
some things and overstate others; our braggadocio and our cowardice, our ever-quick criticism of even our nearest and dearest;
our backbiting, our carping, our envy, our murkiness and smut.

The Shadow is the same sex as the dreamer, like, but inferior,
often incredibly so, and it comes in many guises. Be prepared for
the worst; dreams spare you not at all. The imagery the unconscious chooses packs a staggering wallop to sensitive self-esteem.
The Shadow may appear as a man's brother or a woman's sister;
as an alcoholic, drug-addict, pervert; a subordinate, foreigner,
servant, gypsy, tramp, prostitute; lame, hunch-backed, or blind;
as the person next door, or someone or something behind you, an
ominous adversary dogging your footsteps; as a burglar, a threatening, sinister and truly evil figure lurking in the dark; as a murderer, a Nazi, a prison warden, a torturer.

Any and all of these deplorable picturizations or others even

worse may show up your own share of blackness. But the archetypal Shadow is not all black. The Shadow is also strength and
power. You need only speculate on the paradox of the strength of
your weaknesses to grasp that the personal defects enumerated
are, on the psychological level, divorced from any moral connotation whatever, expressions of libido, psychic energy. "Energy
in itself is neither good nor bad, neither useful nor harmful, but
neutral since everything depends on the *form* into which energy
passes. Form gives energy its quality. On the other hand, mere
form without energy is equally neutral. For the creation of a real
value, therefore, both energy and valuable form are needed,"
Jung points out.[8]

Now then, we can speak of weaknesses and strengths only
from the moral point of view that puts positive value on the latter. Only a moral point of view can transform into strengths the
libidinal energies locked into misplaced expressions. Genuine
morality, where what is lived is in one piece with what is in the
secret heart, is possible only through the achievement of *conscious
free choice and will*. Neither choice nor will functions where the
individual is unconscious of the extent to which an authentic *mea
culpa* must come from him: he is subjectively bound by that to
which he is blind, and if he is bound he is unfree. In the Pauline
sense he may be absolved of guilt ("For until the law, sin was in
the world; but sin is not imputed when there is no law," Romans
5:13), but such innocence is on the infantile level of "Ignorance
is bliss. . . ."

The price of achieving conscious choice is high, as Jung implies in the passage with which this section opens, for the tension-
of-opposites that means the very spark of forward-moving life
requires that the inferior components of the personality bound
up in the Shadow be made conscious; the process is wholly secular, consonant with Kant's categorical imperative to the individual "that the principle of your action may become universal
law."

Identifying the Shadow is pioneer work for every dreamer

since every individual is unique although each shares in the collective gamut of human attributes. Generalizations can be more misleading than helpful, but the following rules-of-thumb should guide you *where to look in order to see.*

1. We can suspect our own Shadow by pinpointing *what makes us angry in other people.* There may be a truth about *us,* something we don't want to see because we hate that part of ourselves. Our *bêtes noires* are usually the carriers of the *projection* of that which we hate most about our own selves but our incredible self-duplicity manages to conceal the truth from our consciousness. Often we cannot forgive ourselves for having certain qualities and many punishments are meted out to ourselves by ourselves in secret unconscious rage over our repressed Shadows; we treat ourselves like illegitimate children in the Victorian age.

2. We can suspect our own Shadow by the amount of *satisfaction we feel at other people's weaknesses or failings.* Surprising? Well, lamentably perhaps, we are so constituted psychologically that we do not really resent the weakness of other people; it may even give us a pleasant feeling of superiority when not carried to the extreme of introjecting others' defects as our own shortcomings.

3. Our Shadows can often be detected by the *reaction of other people to us.* We have recognizable effects on those we meet which can tell us a great deal, if we want to read it the way it does read, and not like the washerwoman who always quarreled with everyone in her neighborhood. Rebuked once for this fault she replied, full of injured innocence: "How can I help it? I never saw anything like the tempers in the people I meet!"

4. We may experience *paralyzing inertia in the matter of living good qualities positively.* Curiously enough, there are people who live *below* their real level, actually repressing higher-than-average standards because secretly, though unconsciously, they do not want to take the responsibility involved in living some-

thing positive. *Good qualities carry an obligation.* And just the people with pure gold in their Shadow show the most resistance to digging it out! Among psychological curiosae, this perverse reluctance to live boldly to the utmost of what one could be has been well marked in such works as Fromm's *Escape from Freedom* and Menninger's *Man Against himself.*

In dreams the Shadow evokes strong emotion, for the inferiorities constituting the Shadow are of an emotional nature. At the beginning, its autonomous appearance is matched by the obsessiveness, or rather posessiveness, of the inferiorities in the dreamer's character and personality. With increasing insight and persistence the Shadow yields to the dreamer's awareness and if development warrants, the Shadow too "develops" through transformation.

The following series of dreams of a man's Shadow-image in the course of its development over a period of years is an exceptionally vivid portrait of the process. With a woman the Shadow qualities, not fundamentally different, would express similarly although with distinctively feminine features.

"I have, over the last fourteen years, experienced five different "shadow" figures in dreams. The first and most regular is my younger brother—sometimes more or less as he was some years ago, sometimes as he was as a child. It is never quite my brother, though, but someone like him. In the dream he is sometimes helping, sometimes opposing but for the most part passive. This, as I take it, is the shadow in its acceptable form: an autonomous complex, own brother to the ego, but almost devoid of energy. For years, although this figure appeared in scores of dreams, he never spoke a word.

"The second figure is the shadow in its unacceptable form: a dark, disreputable tramplike fellow, sometimes shabbily, sometimes flashily dressed. He is untrustworthy, thoroughly dislikeable; but virile enough in an unpleasant

way. In the dream where I first came upon him he had been
chasing little girls and, in concert with a number of neighbors, I helped round him up. When we captured him, he
and I stood by a deep still pool and I had to decide
whether or not I would throw him in and drown him [i.e.
thrust him back into the unconscious]. Fortunately, in the
dream I had the sense not to—or I should have had trouble.
Instead, I recognized that there might be that about me
which was like him.

"This had an interesting sequel. In a later dream the
younger brother and the tramp-like man coalesced to their
mutual advantage. I dreamed that I found myself sharing a
bed with some man I did not know. I got up at once; he
also. I looked at him and saw the most extraordinary combination of the better aspects of the 'younger brother'
shadow, and of the 'tramp' shadow: tall, decently dressed, a
little *louche*, but a man-like sort of person. I was on the
point of congratulating him on his transformation when, to
my intense astonishment, he anticipated me, speaking for
the first time. He said, 'You are twice the man you were.'
Which was precisely what I was going to say to him.

"The third figure is a soldier, the transmogrified tramp in
uniform, perhaps. Again, anything but a trustworthy character, a man who considers his own interests first, last, and
all the time; a rash and dangerous man, who could be very
vicious if cornered. His presence I recognize easily enough,
every time I put on any sort of uniform. For the time being
I am subtly different from myself—rougher, coarser, taking
a special pleasure in using bad language; and it is not hard to
recognize who it is speaking. On the other hand, unpleasant
though he is in many ways, he has a certain toughness of
fibre which I appreciate.

"The fourth figure is of a dark, stocky peasant, quiet,
steady, versed in the things of the earth, instinctively wise.
This aspect of the shadow goes beyond the purely personal,

down to the primitive origins. The fifth and most recent figure goes deeper still. In the night, in something between a dream and a vision, I saw a ruin. Up this pillar a shadowy figure was climbing, someone whom I know to be myself and yet not myself. He climbed expertly. The last part, over the great capital of the pillar, was especially difficult and I admired the way he got first a hand, then an elbow, then the chest, above the top. At that moment he gave a spring and was standing erect upon it. He had goats' feet. It was Pan—or a satyr?" [9]

To recapitulate:

1. The Shadow appears in dreams as a *person of the same sex as the dreamer*, like but inferior, often shockingly so.

2. The Shadow is the *reverse side of the Persona*, summed up by those contents repressed in the Personal Unconscious.

3. The Shadow is not all unrelieved blackness; moral strength also is bound up in this figuration, though lost to the conscious ego unless transformed by conscious choice and will.

4. Identifying the Shadow is not confined to paying heed to the clues listed, or to isolating those personalities in dreams which seem to fit the general descriptions given. Strangely, the Shadow cannot be realized until you are face to face with another person into whom you have projected it, and you suddenly *recognize your projection*. For example, you suddenly detect that it is not "their" unwarranted temper or "their" selfish thoughtlessness, but *your* unwarranted temper and *your* selfish thoughtlessness. Then the projection can be withdrawn, for the fault can be seen to lodge in your own personality. From that moment you may begin to walk toward the freedom that is based on having gained your own identity.

Freedom comes not from eliminating the Shadow—that can never be done with an archetype in any case—but in *recognizing him in yourself*. If you have read Conrad's story "The Secret Sharer" you may recall the young captain who runs terrible risks on his first command, with the gravest possible consequence to his future, by sheltering the outlaw mate who escaped from irons on another ship; he did so because instinctively he recognized what every law-abiding man has within him, his *own* lawlessness, his own Shadow. In the second dream of the series quoted above, the dreamer similarly faced the captain's choice when he might have thrown his Shadow-figure into the lake. Instead, like the young captain, the dreamer also took upon himself the task of coming to terms with his Nemesis not by eliminating him but by recognizing him and *accepting responsibility for him even at the risk of life itself*. The truth is, the least part of yourself, and the ugliest part of yourself, is still yourself, is still included in your *identity*.

The psychic process of *Projection* is responsible for seeing your Shadow *out there*, elsewhere than in yourself. We will need to understand how it works, how you can learn to see through and behind it, before taking up the august archetypes of *Anima* and *Animus*. These are first experienced *through* projections you make upon someone of the opposite sex; but they are generally inaccessible in dream imagery until the Shadow has first been encountered in projections and dream imagery.

1. *All's Well That Ends Well*, Act IV, Scene 3.

2. Jung, *Two Essays on Analytical Psychology*, pp. 190–91.

3. Edward C. Whitmont, "Individual and Group," *Spring*, 1961, p. 74.

4. C. A. Meier, The Cutter Lectures, Andover-Newton Theological School, Newton Center, Massachusetts.

5. Jung, *Two Essays on Analytical Psychology*, p. 192.

6. C. G. Jung, *Shadow, Animus and Anima* (New York: The Analytical Psychology Club, Inc., 1950).

7. Robert Louis Stevenson, *Across the Plains* (New York: Charles Scribner's Sons, 1888). See "A Chapter on Dreams."

8. Jung, *Two Essays on Analytical Psychology*, p. 46.

9. Martin, *op. cit.*, pp. 74–75.

CHAPTER SEVEN

Projection

*Depth psychology as well as biology have
shown that there exists a knowledge
connected neither with the cerebrospinal
nervous system, nor with any nervous
system whatever. It follows that we must
learn no longer to regard it self-evident
that every knowledge is "inner"—in
our consciousness, in our psyche, in us, in
some living thing. The more so when
we remember that inner and outer are
categories of our system of consciousness,
valid only for its own reality, but not, for
instance, for the reality of* participation
mystique, *nor hence of* projection.
*The understanding of biological, depth-
psychological, and parapsychological
phenomena is difficult for us just because
they cannot be grasped or even described
with our current conscious concepts.*
ERICH NEUMANN [1]

Jung repeatedly emphasizes, and I can do no less, that the
Shadow, Anima, and Animus are *not only concepts* and *not only
archetypal images* you observe in dreams, visions, and active
imaginations, but they are also encountered *externally*, in *projections* upon real people. Not only dramatic, but tragic and even
hopeless complications of destiny are wrought through activities
of the Shadow, which can be made conscious only through a rela-

tionship to a *vis-a-vis* of the same sex, and the Anima or Animus, through a relation to the opposite sex, as the case may be: man to Anima, woman to Animus.

A projection, however, is never made; it happens to you. You are *in* it before you know it. Experience shows that projections are an unconscious, automatic psychic process via which an unconscious content of a subject—say you yourself are the subject —transfers itself to an object—say a person you have just met—so that your unconscious content appears to belong to that object. All cases of "love at first sight" are notorious examples of this transference. Projections are never made consciously. Projections are always there first, and recognized afterwards, but not by the majority. Such transferences apply to the whole compass of our attachments to people, places, conditions and things. Put another way, our libido is commanded from us, drawn from us; we expend our libido in this way.

"Everyone creates an illusionary world which he takes for reality and which is then inevitably painful and a continual source of disillusion and disappointment through most of life," Jung points out. "This illusionary world begins by our assumption that the world is exactly as we see it and that people resemble our ideas of them. *All our human relationships swarm with projections.* . . . Every normal and not overly-thoughtful man (and woman) of our time is tied to his environment by a whole system of unconscious projections. As long as everything 'goes well' he is unaware of the compulsive, i.e. magical or mystical character of these relationships." Furthermore, Jung adds, "Projections are inherent in the natural state of the psyche." [2]

With projections inherent in the natural state of the psyche and, to boot, recognizable only *after* they are made, there's no doubt the phenomenon of projection must be added to the phantasmagoria of things which wring from us a cry of Why? Why flies? Polio? Death? But then—why Life?

We are entitled to probe and to ask: if projection consists chiefly in bestowing upon some person, object, condition or situation something out of yourself so that it is not what they have but what you yourself give that binds you to them or it, plainly, we *are* enshrouded by illusionary involvement. Then—what *is* real? And what is illusion?

We are right back where we were with Sir Arthur Eddington, contemplating our tracks on the time continuum. We are staring at the riddle eternal, *the nature of reality*, a topic of speculation which has provided at least three thousand years of contradictions as philosophers have attempted to race undisputed across the quicksands of interpretation.

You cannot hope to find here a definitive rendition of the nature of reality. If anything, depth psychology, flanked by cybernetics, computer technology, electrical studies of the brain and new knowledge in the field of neurophysiology, has succeeded in splintering to atoms the notion of Reality argued by the Scholastics as an Either-Or proposition. You sided with either the Nominalists *or* the Realists if you chose at all to be concerned with the ultimate nature of Reality, and their divisiveness has been fundamentally unchanged to the present time. Classical first-rate educations to this day copiously reflect intimacy with the speculative analyses of exquisite intellects such as William of Champeaux, Abelard, Berkeley, Bacon, Locke, Hume, Kant, and others right down to the present, for these men were masters of logical thought, in fact might be said to have either created or invigorated it over the course of centuries. Much of the sheer pleasure to be derived from their works consists in following the development of their arguments, arrayed logically upon a foundation asserting or inferring the nature and manner of how we perceive. Now, as in their day, our perceptions necessarily furnish us with the data leading us to our opinions about reality, and these continue to function in the polarities of an outer, physical, biological world which we recognizably experience through our peculiar, intermittent, ego-centered consciousness, and the inner, mental world that we call the sphere of the unconscious.

But our knowledge about the manner and nature of perception

has been vastly altered in the recent past. The Ames research indicates not only that the past history of the brain is involved in the complicated product a single act of perception really is, but also that a perception is valid only in *a context harmonious with that past experience.* In other words, *once the mental machinery is conditioned, we have little or no control over the ensuing perceptions.* The consequences of this insight into the way perception works will have their greatest impact in the next century or two as education and communication begin their task of integrating the new knowledge within our culture. The ramifications of the work to be undertaken has hardly begun to be understood beyond the very first step, which is the recognition that no one can ever get away from whatever mental conditioning has done to his mechanism of perception. Ideas about reality are contingent upon *how you perceive.*

But depth psychology has demonstrated another facet of perception: we are capable of perceptions which completely bypass the biological perceptive system connected with our ego and consciousness. Dreams, visions, creative imagination and substantial areas of creative work are *bona fide* phenomena of cognitive perception within the scope of our subject; beyond are the still-virgin realms of Psi, parapsychology, telepathy and manifold occult phenomena. In the Chafin will case mentioned in an earlier chapter, nothing in the neurophysiological and sympathetic nervous systems that trigger perceptual messages to the brain was implicated in the phenomenon of the Chafin brother who dreamed about his father's misplaced will; the perception of where to look for it came to him in a dream. The subsequent chapters on Prospective and Telepathic dreams cite many examples of this type of dream which, in effect, "perceives" what is unknown to the consciousness of the dreamer. Something other than our biological perceptual faculties function to inform or warn us, as these dreams demonstrate.

Further, in the psychic processes of *projections* and *participation mystique,* which is an even deeper unconscious identification

of subject-with-object, the polarities of the conscious and unconscious spheres are displaced; outer is experienced as inner and
inner as outer, so that the perceptual mechanism of our conscious
system simply ceases to orient us as normally it does by differen-
tiating what is subjective and what objective. That we learn later,
very often to our bitter grief, when we withdraw our projections
and illusion is replaced with "reality."

Reality, then, becomes a highly subjective experience for each
individual, for whatever reality comes to you comes entirely
through your relationships to people and things as a by-product,
not as immediate apprehension of their essential nature, as though
Reality itself were an extraneous object separated from yourself
like an exhibit in a glass case. The educated mind today knows
that any talk of "reality" to have any meaning whatever demands
that you *specify your field and define your approach,* since we
can speak of many kinds of reality as valid in the context of the
field of inquiry, but valid doesn't imply absolute certainty—
Gödel's theorem disposed of certainty as a legitimate concept.
This too is a piece of new knowledge that must certainly alter
future education, communications, and perhaps one other of the
past's powerful conditioners of the mental apparatus, religion.

Reality in the context with which we are concerned is that to
which you come when you see through and withdraw your projections, reintegrating them to your own consciousness. Plainly,
no one can tell you what *your* reality is and may be. That is the
paradox of reality and why it has as many planes as there are individuals enmeshed in the grand design constructed of our highly
subjective individual patterns, the sublime total adding up to the
preponderantly subjective outer reality we call "the world."

To become conscious of the *honest shape of your own experience of the reality behind your projections necessitates really intelligent and sobering labor,* a solitary task in which your
progress will match the Oxford don's observation of it as that
state you arrive at not by finding the answers but by progressively clarifying the questions.

Dreams are your number one ally for seeing behind your projections into relationships, situations, conflicts and problems and, besides, they are ruthless in puncturing your illusions. You have already learned how you use, misuse, abuse or not-use some of the Four Functions and how eloquent repercussions show up in dream imagery. No less forceful are the complications in human relations that result from projecting the Shadow, as you have also been informed, but when the Anima and Animus enter the scene, the complexities are enormously intensified, as the next chapter relates.

Projections are made thick and fast as bridges for libido expending itself in doing-and-becoming among contemporaries in the generations occupied with the first half of life. Intense attachments to ideas about desired careers, to moral, social and political commitments, to the beloved man or woman, are forged then. Without benefit of knowledge about projections, however, the sensitive person suspects the phenomenon early, uneasily aware of something false sifting as fine as mist through their closest relations and infiltrating the sub-basement of their seemingly solid convictions.

Time marches on, until finally there arrives an imperative need to backtrack to the source of blunders. At this stage reflective minds ponder the pattern of the past; a four-fold charting of causes shows:

1. From the beginning our need for love, self-affirmation, self-realization, feeds the psychic process of projections and contributes to the trajectory they take: our unfavorable ones fall at some remove from ourselves and our immediate circle while the favorable ones are close at hand, in effect becoming extensions of ourselves. They identify clearly to our milieu our status, and that with which our desires and aims are aligned.

2. Consistently, our projection-carriers actually *do* possess something of the property we project. However slight, there *is* a hook in them or it corresponding to that which is projected. It follows naturally, of course, that our intimates are presumed to radiate what we value too: consideration, sincerity, honesty, tact, wit, talent, warmth; the majority of us assume that this roster of

virtues fairly tallies with the facts about ourselves, and our immediate circle represents in a real sense the extension of ourselves
and that with which we are identified. Conversely, what is negative is never admitted to be nearby, let alone located *within* us;
therefore bad temper, trifling with the truth, an attitude of me-
first and something-for-nothing, bigotry and prejudice—in other
words the flaws little and great pitting the face of perfection—are
positively the evils *they*, some distance removed from us and ours,
are known to possess, just as our enemies in wartime are "known"
to be the source of all offense. As for four-star moral delinquency
or even criminality, such turpitude is incredible in "decent" people, ourselves included. Consequently, consternation and banner
headlines are touched off when an eminent president of a town's
leading bank absconds with the funds; a minister elopes with the
president of the PTA; the judge's wife abandons bed-and-board
for an Indian astrologist.

Behind our projections lurks the knowledge that requires
access to our full, clear consciousness: *we share all of everything,*
as much as we do the oxygen in the air! Nor could we begin to
be aware of the mote in the other's eye were it not to some degree the projection of our own beam. But the admission of such
dark aspects of the personality is a major moral challenge demanding rare moral resolution.

3. Some measure of our projections can be gauged by the
amount of emotion we register. Not only the Shadow can be detected in this way but our positive qualities as well, where the
inner assent freely yields itself as distinct from mere lip-service.

4. The projections made have later come home to roost. Illusions have been withdrawn in favor of—"reality." But what has
been found? How unnerving to discover that what you find is
just what you have put into anything! But here it is important
not to be deceived again, by labels, and to be able and willing and
honest enough to *see* what you look at. If, for example, a love has
come to an end and now you see it was, after all, only a projection and not love, the question remains: *what* was projected?

Loneliness? Expediency? Ambition? Lust? The treacherous wish for a-lot-for-a-little? *Real* love is not a projection, so cannot be withdrawn.

Now what a dilemma to find, in withdrawing your projections, that this is the one signal achievement guaranteed to treble the difficulties of human relations, at first at any rate; later on you do come into your own but not before you learn there is justification for the saying, "Knowledge increaseth suffering." For one thing, you learn there are no longer easy bridges over which libido can pour unconsciously, binding you to persons, places, and things, or lulling you with the notion that "happiness" is a place arrived at, like alighting from a bus when your destination is reached. A sad feeling of isolation intensifies. *Now* what?

Only this: the libido that unconsciously streamed out into projections is yours, available for your use either through conscious choice or, it may again be expended in other projections of which you are unconscious. All-in-all, seeing through projections is not the easiest thing in the world to do. You are actually in an entirely new field of psychological experience in venturing behind your projections. As Jung says, "It requires an unusual degree of self-awareness to remain above, rather than below, one's projections, for these projections are inherent in the natural state of the psyche." It is the uncommon personality who feels called to undertake such a task, attuned to his need "to be aware of the situation in which he finds himself," as Hellmut Wilhelm expresses it,[3] aware too of the consequences that may grow out of it which "must be the aim of every person who wants to guide his life rather than merely drift with the current."

1. "The Psyche and the Transformation of the Reality Planes," *Spring*, 1956, 87.

2. C. G. Jung, "General Aspects of the Psychology of the Dream," *Spring*, 1956.

3. Hellmut Wilhelm, *Change* (New York: Pantheon Books, Bollingen Series, 1960), p. 8.

CHAPTER EIGHT

The Syzygy: Anima and Animus

*According to my experience a certain
number of human beings can grasp what is
meant by Anima and Animus without
special intellectual or moral difficulties;
however, one encounters a larger number
who have great trouble in understanding
these concepts or recognizing that* they
represent observable phenomena. *This
indicates that with these concepts we
have moved outside the usual range
of experience. . . .*
    C. G. JUNG [1]

When the Anima and Animus emerge in dream imagery you
can be sure the deepest levels of the unconscious have been penetrated. The initial experience of these powerful archetypes for
whom the majority have had no advance preparation whatever is
positively uncanny. A feeling of incredulity at the phenomenon
is the most marked response, and even after having repeated experience of their presence in your dreams and insight into their
projection in outer life, a bewildered sense of unreality clings to
the recognition of their potency and reality. It is far easier to
come to terms with the Shadow than with the Anima and
Animus; it is, in fact, a major step forward in your exploration of
your own psychic processes when you finally consciously recognize empirical experience of them both inwardly and outwardly.
    Reiterating once again what has been declared about the Shadow

and other images: these archetypes are not inventions but observable, spontaneous productions of the unconscious. Their unsuspected activities in the lives of men and women are often responsible for grotesque entanglements, compulsive bondages, deep suffering and real tragedies in outer life. You cannot know too much about them although, since they are archetypal, therefore psychoid images of the collective unconscious, they can never be raised into full consciousness.

The Anima is the *feminine image* in man, and the Animus is the *masculine image* in woman, to put the matter in the simplest terms. Both the Anima and the Animus may appear as (1) personifications of the opposite sex in an incredible number of shapes and complicated entanglements from newborn infants to ageless sybils and wise ancients; (2) as animals of every variety and combinations in hybrid forms (3) as strange mythological creatures, half-serpent-half-bird, or mermaids, or satyrs, and so on.

In substance, a man's Anima is his unconscious feminine side; the Animus is the masculine imprint on the woman's unconscious. In a nutshell it could be described this way: the Anima produces *moods* in a man; the Animus produces *opinions* in a woman. Effeminate, inadequate males, masculinized, immature females, are overrun by their syzygy who actually lives in their stead.

There may be some who will be outraged at the connotation of bisexuality in thus identifying the psychological counterpart of the feminine in man, and the masculine in woman. But the facts cannot be dismissed in order to protect illusions. Not only the *psychological* image of the opposite sex is present in each individual, but the *physiological* aspects are clearly present, as biology demonstrates. The reproduction process, which can be either asexual or bisexual, depending upon the organism, shows that in the former the cells split into two and keep on splitting with rare conjunctions of the cells. Only with two opposite cells, as is the case with the sperm and egg, is there a conjunction in which the resulting cells do not separate again but remain together to build a new individual.

Moreover, the physiological factors of gender extend right into the genes controlling sex, in which a special pair of sex chromosomes are to be found. There, according to Dr. Edward F. Griffith, it is found that:

". . . female sex cells have two similar chromosomes termed XX. Men have an unlike pair, XY. One, the X chromosome, is derived from the mother; the other, Y chromosome, from the father. All the eggs receive an X chromosome but, in the case of the sperms, only half of these contain an X chromosome, the other contains the important Y chromosome which is male-determining. So, if an X-bearing sperm joins an egg the result is a female-XX, but if a Y-bearing sperm joins the egg the result is a male -XY.

"That, presumably, is one of the reasons why there are so many sperms and so few eggs; the chances of fertilization need to be greater and the chances of the egg being fertilized by a Y-bearing or X-bearing sperm made more equal.

"It seems, however, that the X-bearing properties are really in the majority. The egg is feminine anyway, and the sperm tends that way. It takes a special Y cell to bring about the change. Left to themselves 'female' cells produce females—if they develop at all, which in certain instances can happen. . . . One cannot help feeling that these facts have a psychological bearing as well as a physiological one. . . . .

"The concept of bisexuality and hermaphroditic unity— meaning that each of us has the potentialities of the other sex within us—was not only misunderstood by our forefathers but frequently rejected as being not nice, abnormal or pornographic. That the hidden biological factor had a psychological counterpart in the unconscious and that the one was closely related to and influenced by the other was not fully understood either. . . ." [2]

The physiological background just explained is likely to please those accustomed to acquiring all knowledge along intellectual and rational lines. The genetic analysis of the duality of the sexes can then be checked off as still another penetration of nature's secrets in this century of such splendid ground-breaking. They are the very ones who are likely to experience considerable resistance at the thought of taking the Anima and Animus personally, *as real personalities*—"the more personally taken the better," Jung tells us. Literally, Jung recommends the valuable technique of holding a conversation with these archetypes, the art of which consists in: "Allowing our invisible opponent to make [itself] heard, in putting the mechanism of expression momentarily at [its] disposal, without being overcome by the distaste one naturally feels at playing such an apparently ludicrous game with oneself, or by doubts as to the genuineness of the voice of one's interlocutor. This latter point is technically very important: we are so in the habit of identifying ourselves with the thoughts that come to us that we invariably assume we have made them. If we were more conscious of the inflexible universal laws that govern even the wildest and most wanton fantasy, we might perhaps be in a better position *to see these thoughts above all others as objective occurrences, just as we see dreams*, which nobody supposes to be deliberate or arbitrary inventions. . . ." [3]

Before taking up the Anima and Animus separately, the following generalities about them can be stated:

(1) The first experience of these archetypes takes place between the infant and the parent of the opposite sex.

(2) Subsequently, the image is *projected* onto a suitable candidate who does actually provide an appropriate hook for capturing the projection and reflecting it back, an event ordinarily occurring at adolescence in the first earthshaking experience of "falling-in-love."

(3) Although personally we believe it would not hurt any young adult to be at least aware of these potent archetypes, especially in view of the many catastrophic blunders with life-long consequences that can be attributed to blind ignorance, in Jung's

view it is of secondary importance to become acquainted with the Anima or Animus before mid-life. The important thing in the first half of life is, without doubt, that Nature be paid her tribute; the man has to be a man, the woman a woman, in all the essentials necessary to fulfill the biological role as well as adapt to the social and economic demands of the environment. Many hurdles have to be surmounted, not the least of them the enormous requirement of separation from the dominant parental influence; the realization of sexual maturity in a natural orientation of the sexes to their opposites; putting down roots in family and career with the concomitants of a favorable adaptation of the ego-self to these multifarious requirements.

THE ANIMA

The Anima is the factor of utmost importance in the psychology of a man wherever his emotions and emotional reactions are involved. Unlike the Persona and the Shadow which accumulate, as it were, from infancy on into maturity, the Anima image is *innate* in each male child and begins to develop from the mother's effect on her son. The mother is the first feminine being with whom the man-to-be comes in contact, and she cannot help playing, overtly or covertly, consciously or unconsciously, upon the son's masculinity, just as the son, in his turn, grows increasingly aware of his mother's femininity. A mother-complex, either positive or negative, develops, but by no means necessarily a pathologically or psychologically disturbing one. This is in the *normal* course of development, and since a man, insofar as he is not constitutionally homosexual, can only be a masculine personality, the normal male will effect in the first half of life the projection of his Anima onto real women who in some way catch and reflect the image he has within.

As Jung explains it, "In the first half of life, the projection of his Anima onto a real woman draws him (the man) into living life, fulfilling the masculine role, establishing himself as a man and head of a family. But in the second half of life the Anima can no longer be projected; she is a function of his inner being and he must come to terms with her as a function relating him to his own unconscious.

"No man is so entirely masculine that he has nothing feminine about him.[4] The fact is, rather, that masculine men have—carefully guarded and hidden—a very soft emotional life, often incorrectly described as "feminine." A man counts it a virtue to repress his feminine traits as much as possible, but the repression naturally causes these contrasexual demands to accumulate in the unconscious."

Strongly constellated in a man, the Anima softens his character, makes him touchy, moody, jealous, vain, unadjusted. On the inner side, from about thirty-five onward, when it becomes vastly important to forge a working relationship with inner realities the Anima becomes the key figure for this functioning just as the Persona is outwardly. Her ambivalence manifests in dream imagery when one moment she appears in a positive aspect, and next negative; now young, then old; now a good fairy, then a witch; now a saint, then a whore; now his wife or sweetheart, then an unknown; now a maiden, then a mother or goddess.

Her versatility is spectacular, as Jung describes in the following: "To the young boy a clearly discernible Anima-form appears in his mother, and this lends her the radiance of power and superiority or else a daemonic aura of even greater fascination. But because of the Anima's ambivalence, the projection can be entirely negative. *Much of the fear which the female sex arouses in men is due to the Anima-image.*

"Naturally, the image of woman, his Anima, becomes his love-choice and often the man strives to win the woman who best corresponds to his own unconscious femininity—a woman who can unhesitatingly receive the projection of his soul. Although such a choice is often regarded and felt as altogether ideal, it may turn out the man has married his own worst weakness, explaining some highly remarkable conjunctions."[5]

Examples of the *Anima* [6] in literature are prolific, far more than the *Animus,* actually, because men outnumber women as writers and have from Antiquity. Writers literally draw pen-portraits of their Animas or Animi, as the case may be, and some men have provided such excellent descriptions that Freud, for example, wrote about his vexation with the creative writer's ability to look into the motivations of his characters with ease. He, a psychiatrist, had to laboriously prod, analyze and deduce to come to their same insights.

In *On Love,* for example, Ortega y Gassett writes:

"There are individuals who in the course of their lives love several women; but with clear persistency, each one is a repetition of a single feminine type. Sometimes the coincidence is so great that these women even share the same physical features. This kind of masked fidelity, in which actually a single generic woman is loved under the guise of many women, is exceedingly frequent."

Another Anima image is described here by Charles Morgan's young hero in *Portrait in a Mirror:*

"Is this she whom I have loved? It is she whom *love* has loved and I am as nothing before her; I have no existence in her eyes. I am neither boy nor man, but an idea to which she offers her being, a projection of her longing, by it created. Therefore in my heart I fall down before her as before my Creator, yet stand before her a giant, the image by which her imagination is enslaved."

Celia Coplestone, addressing her lover, Edward Chamberlayne, in T. S. Eliot's *The Cocktail Party* describes vividly the moment of recognition of the projection of the Animus:

[You are] only what was left
Of what I had thought you were. I see another person
I see you as a person whom I never saw before.
The man I saw before, he was only a projection—
I see that now—of something I aspired to—
Something that I desperately wanted to exist.
It must happen somewhere—but what, and where is it?

The somber reflections of Don Fabrizio, Prince of Salina, in *The Leopard*, by Giuseppe di Lampedusa of Sicily, are well-known to the mature who have come to the end of their projections. He describes his discernments thus:

> "Tancredi and Angelica were passing in front of them at that moment, his gloved right hand on her waist, their outspread arms interlaced, their eyes gazing into each others. They were the most moving sight there, two young people in love dancing together, blind to each other's defects, deaf to the warnings of fate, deluding themselves that the whole course of their lives would be as smooth as the ballroom floor, unknowing actors made to play the parts of Juliet and Romeo by a director who had concealed the fact that tomb and poison were already in the script. Neither of them was good, each full of self-interest, swollen with secret aims; yet there was something sweet and touching about them both; those murky but ingenuous ambitions of theirs were obliterated by the words of jesting tenderness he was murmuring in her ear, by the scent of her hair, by the mutual clasp of those bodies of theirs destined to die. . . . The two young people moved away, other couples passed, less handsome, just as moving, each submerged in their transitory blindness."

Verification of these examples of projection taken from literature can be seen millions of times over in real life; it is the universal human experience of "first love" and, too often, the mechanism behind a lifetime of many "loves."

Usually, an infantile or immature man has a maternal Anima; an adult man, the figure of a younger woman; the much older man, or senile, has an Anima of a very young girl, or even a child.

Jung's delineation of the Anima, in his published works, creates a full-scale portrait of the image of woman in man which simply cannot be adequately condensed. The metamorphoses of the Anima can be estimated from this short series of dreams Jung interpreted, tracing the transformation of the Anima throughout:

Dream 1: A white bird perches on a table. Suddenly it changes into a fair-haired seven-year-old girl and just as suddenly back into a bird, which now speaks with a human voice.

This dream shows the Anima as elflike, that is, only partially human. She can just as well be a bird, which means that she may belong wholly to nature and can vanish, i.e., become unconscious, from the human sphere, i.e., consciousness.

Dream 2: In an underground house, which is really the underworld (of the unconscious) there lives an old magician and prophet with his "daughter." She is, however, not really his daughter; she is a dancer, a very loose person, but is blind and seeks healing.

This dream shows the unknown woman as a mythological figure from the beyond (the unconscious). She is the *soror*, or mystical child, of a "philosopher" a parallel to those mystic syzygies to be met with in the figures of Simon Magus and Helen, Comarius and Cleopatra. This dream figure fits in best with Helen. A really admirable description of Anima psychology in a woman is to be found in Erskine's *Helen of Troy*.

Dream 3: The unknown woman sits like the dreamer on the tip of a church-spire and stares at him uncannily across the abyss.

The dreamer is confronted with his Anima, a place high above the ground, i.e., above human reality. Obviously the Anima exerts a dangerous fascination.

Dream 4: The unknown woman suddenly appears as an old female attendant in an underground public lavatory with a temperature of 40 degrees below zero.

The Anima has taken a deep plunge into an extremely "subordinate" position where the last trace of fascination has gone and only human sympathy is left.

From this series and others like it we get an average picture of the strange factor which has such an important part to play in the masculine psyche.

THE ANIMUS

The masculine figure in a woman's unconscious, the Animus, corresponding to the Anima in man, is essentially different from man's, just as the woman's whole psychology and nature is not inferior but simply different. As Jung says, "A woman is often clearly conscious of things which a man is still groping for in the dark, so are there naturally fields of experience in a man which, for woman, are still wrapped in utter darkness. Personal relations are as a rule more important and interesting to women than objective facts and their inter-connections. The man's world of commerce, politics, technology and science, the whole realm of the applied masculine mind, woman generally relegates to the penumbra of consciousness while, on the other hand, she develops a minute consciousness of personal relationships, the infinite nuances of which usually escape the man entirely."

While the Anima is notorious for producing moods in a man, the Animus produces opinions in a woman. They are spurious, for they do not rest on the solid ground of real knowledge or thought, but on assumptions or inferences. Animus opinions often have the character of unshakable conviction, and the principles on which they appear to be based will be lofty and unassailable. On analysis, however, or pricked with the needle of incontrovertible evidence to the contrary, they will collapse like a deflated dirigible.

Jung says, "Unlike the Anima, which is invariably a single figure that a man seeks over and over again, the Animus is usually a plurality of males, and it goes without saying that the Animus is just as often projected as the Anima. In intellectual women the Animus may, in its negative aspect, encourage criticism, disputatiousness and would-be highbrowism which, however, keeps harping on some irrelevant weak point and ridiculously making it the main one. The arguments of a negative Animus are just off the mark; they *seem* right but are wrong; an irrelevant assumption lies at the base of the argument. Positive relationship with the Animus develops creativity in the woman . . ."

Not, we add, in a masculine way. The creative woman in good relationship with her Animus is a thoroughly feminine woman but may have an invincible character and speak with power, as of inspired wisdom. She can well be "more terrible than an army with banners" in a cause she believes to be just and right; the history of notable women in the past few centuries, with their emergence into a world previously the exclusive province of men, offers many examples of such women. Florence Nightingale, for one; to the fallen in Crimea she was a veritable angel of mercy, but to the stuffy old-guard established in the British War Ministry she was a tough, sabre-tongued harridan, and they would sooner face cannon than keep appointments with this single-minded heroine whose dedication transformed nursing into a profession.

Creatively gifted women in the arts and in literature abound: the Brontës, George Sand, Emily Dickinson and others have been acutely aware of the man-like spirit inspiring their work and have bequeathed to posterity their written testaments to their awareness. *Animus* means spirit, breath, pneuma, and also has the meaning of *Logos*, the word, or the power of the idea, which is essentially the *masculine principle*, as *Eros* is the feminine principle of love and relatedness.

Like the Anima, the Animus is ambivalent and autonomous. His activities can have favorable or unfavorable results. Naturally, the unfavorable are more easily pinpointed than the favorable for the same reason that a screeching wheel draws more attention than the others. Already mentioned is the strongly opinionated female who would rather win an argument than keep harmonious relations, and there are other stereotypes of Animus-possession. For example, the strong-weak woman, wily actresses uncannily able to size up the image the man expects to have mirrored back to him, such as baby-doll, cool, remote princess, or understanding

sybil, and, perennially, the mother-type, comfortable, undemand-
ing, forgiving and ever-loving. Also painfully evident are "they-
quoters." These women will quote some authority, often un-
specified, but if specified will generally be that of husband, father,
brother, priest or parson, as indisputable proof of the validity of their assertions. They are overrun by masculine authoritar-
ianism and have but a rudimentary thinking mind of their own.
All the foregoing are instances of *Animus possession* instead of
what ought to be, *relation to the Animus*.

The true function of the Anima and Animus is to connect the
individual with his unconscious in the same way that the Persona
connects him with the external world. While the Anima and Animus remain personified, as imaged in dreams, visions or active imagination, they are not being purposefully used as functions. Jung
states, "They cannot be integrated into consciousness while their
contents remain unknown. The purpose of the dialectical process [7] is to bring these contents into the light, and only when this
task has been completed and the conscious mind has become
sufficiently familiar with the unconscious processes reflected in
the Anima and Animus will they be felt simply as a function."

The Animus often appears in dreams as a person known to the
dreamer. He may be imaged as father, lover, brother, teacher,
judge, wise friend, parson. When unknown, his appearances are
astonishingly varied: he may be a phantom lover, often enough
the occupant of her daydreams as well; or magician, artist, philosopher, priest, monk, minister, aviator, a young boy, stranger at
the gate, companion on a journey, conductor or tour guide. In his
negative aspect he may be imaged as a ruthless and brutal jailer or
torturer, a murderer, sadist, rapist. For many a woman the Animus appears in plural form, as a council passing judgment on everything that happens to her and may even lay down the law, tell-
ing her what and what not to do.

What there is to say about the Animus cannot be condensed
adequately any more than the whole story of the Anima. A thor-

ough study of these two archetypal figures as Jung discusses them in his works will be well worthwhile: especially recommended are *Two Essays on Analytical Psychology*.

One final and pertinent sidelight touching on these two figures whose activities in the unconscious can wreak devastation in human life solely because they are ignored, is this. Feminine psychology, totally different from masculine, is distinctive in the woman's innate response to being needed personally. Actually, woman cannot come into being at all *as a woman* until this personal response is awakened in her. As the fairy tale puts it, Prince Charming kisses Sleeping Beauty *first* and *then* she awakens. Her awakening means the fulfillment of her feminine role as mate to man.

Difficult though it may be to believe, the switched-on charm of the girl frugging away in white Courreges boots is simply the current cover-up for her instinctive gambit to please, to captivate, to stay "empty" in order to better reflect the Anima projection of the male. For the average male is not only unconscious but strongly bent on remaining so. That requires the woman to be as unconscious as he is, submerged in the role traditionally assigned to her: wife, mother and homemaker. Many women manage it—more correctly *have* managed it in the past, but the present time shows the cracking-up of many outmoded attitudes, social mores and expectations about the female. Whether, underneath the façade of a "happy" marriage, the pair involved are genuinely satisfied, is increasingly recognized to be a valid condition to be insisted upon by two sentient, complex human beings who individually possess immeasurable potential for development. The best-selling success of such books as Betty Friedan's pungent *The Feminine Mystique*, documenting the "problem that has no name" suffered by women in "the housewife trap" is no mere straw in the breeze. It is rather more a significant indication of the new Animus infecting this and the rising generation of women who are conscious of their compelling need for an identity as a person, beyond that of a Sleeping Beauty awakened by a kiss to fulfill her biological role. The "problem that has no name" *is* the throbbing one of awakening consciousness. And, as Mrs. Friedan so perceptively reports, the time is *now* when the inner voice driving women on to become complete can no longer be smothered. It is coming on strong, although, granted, plenty of women will continue to live mentally and emotionally as women lived in the Middle Ages, as there are men today who might just as well have been born Neanderthals.

In every generation not the mass but the restless, striving, searching, creative few are the leaven for their time. These, in our day, despite the seeming odds against them, have a great deal going for them as they attempt to ease, if they cannot solve, some of the problems the on-coming generations will inherit along with the Strontium 90 in their formulas.

Our main asset in constructing a Great Society is our new, clearer understanding of how we perceive. Already mentioned are the Ames research centers, which have demonstrated conclusively that once our mental machinery has been conditioned, we have no choice over the perceptions which result, and our world is shaped by how we perceive it. Coincidental with this new consciousness is psychological knowledge of the dynamic processes of the psyche, among which the mechanism of projection is seen to be a lever that opens Pandora's box when operating blindly. Of course, we shall never change the ways of Nature, and it appears that Nature's way is to involve humans in life's tangles through projection. But, we may reflect thoughtfully on Jung's observation on the psyche: "The psyche is the world's pivot: not only is it the one great condition for a world at all, it is also an intervention in the existing natural order, and no one can say with certainty where this intervention will finally end." New knowledge, new awareness, new consciousness, changes the old order and constitutes an "intervention in the existing natural order," as was Galileo's, Newton's, Einstein's, Freud's and Jung's. We don't have the faintest idea where their interventions will finally end, but we do know this: enlarging our own consciousness, as in seeing through our projections is one change in Nature's ways we can individually effect.

The poet Tagore, in the decade before World War II, voiced the problem that *does* have a name and speaks directly to our time thus:

"Civilization is almost exclusively masculine, a civilization of power in which woman has been thrust aside in the shade. Therefore it has lost its balance and is moving by hopping from war to war. Its motive forces are the forces of destruction and its ceremonials are carried through by an appalling number of human sacrifices. This one-sided civilization is crashing along a series of catastrophes at a tremendous speed because of its one-sidedness. And at last the time has arrived when woman must step in and impart her life rhythm to the reckless movement of power."

Women must step in with their own unique gifts—their perceptions, their acute sensibilities and feeling-values, instinctive discernment of relationships, which in effect balance the weight of masculine Logos which is predominant in the affairs of the world. It is a tragic misconception of what they can contribute when educated, intelligent women are sidetracked into tasks demanding that they function as pseudo-males, circumscribed by conditions set up by masculine psychology for men in economic competition.

Women almost inevitably fall victim to their own Animus thrusting for power, however much that end may be muffled in a velvet glove, as the economic terms are now laid down for "achievement." Their gain individually, and the gain of society collectively, will come when a living relationship with their Animus has been accomplished by a substantial number of women. It is *their* influence which shall constitute a genuine "intervention" in the existing natural order for only in this way can the feminine principle of Eros be made to balance our Logos-based civilization.

The outline of Anima and Animus presented here will doubtless be as serviceable as a catalogue of an art exhibit you have not personally attended. Nothing can really take the place of seeing the exhibit yourself; likewise, only your personal experience of these potent archetypes can bring home to you their reality, immediacy, importance and power.

1. "Schatten, Animus und Anima," *Wiener Zeitschrift für Nervenheilkunde und deren Grenzgebiete*, Band I, Heft 4, 1948.

2. Edward F. Griffith, M.R.S.C., L.R.C.P., "Psycho-Somatic Medicine," Guild Lecture #108, Guild of Pastoral Psychology, London, England.

3. Jung, *Two Essays on Analytical Psychology*, pp. 199–200.

4. Not touched upon here is the question of the creative man and woman; the feminine or masculine in their natures brings about special circumstances that are not generally applicable. But it may be noted that the creativity of the creative man *is feminine* while that of the creative woman *is masculine*, in part accounting for the many personality disorders such as homosexuality and bisexuality conspicuous among creative persons of both sexes which are widely misunderstood, both as to content and significance, just as much by those involved as by the general public.

5. Jung, *Two Essays on Analytical Psychology*, p. 187.

6. Not dealt with in this section is the homosexual relationship, a pathological deviation beyond the scope of our concern with the Anima. However, it may be noted that always one of the partners in a homosexual alliance assumes the "feminine" role, and it is his Anima that captivates the "male" consort. Conversely, the female homosexual aggressively assumes the male role of an extremely dominant Animus. Interestingly, the Sioux Indians formally recognized homosexuals in their society. They were called "Berdache." They lived as women, wearing women's clothes, from that time in puberty when they underwent initiation rites which included the necessity to ritually dream of themselves as men. The Berdache failed to dream the image of themselves as warriors, or see the image in a vision. That decided their fate and thereafter they chose a companion with whom to live and were treated with courtesy. Many were talented and able to do artistic work; their beadwork, for example, was highly valued for its aesthetic quality. Their consorts, however, were looked on with contempt for having chosen "the easy way."

7. The dialectical process means confronting the Anima or Animus by the conversation technique; that is, literally talking with them, asking questions and *listening for their replies* which, uncannily, come. Or, by tracing the development of the Anima or Animus through dreams and assimilating the meaning of their activities.

CHAPTER NINE

Procedure

You have just awakened, let us assume, and still hover in the hazy border-world between sleep and full wakefulness. Vaguely a thought stirs that *something* has been happening; barely a split-second ago you were participating in something. Then you have it; it was in a dream you just left.

1. WRITE IT DOWN RIGHT AWAY. As fast as pencil can fly over the pad forehandedly placed by the bedside for just this purpose, put down your recollections of the dream in explicit detail. If you recall only one trifling incident, put *that* down. More often than you can imagine, the context of which that small incident was a part will begin to enlarge as you write; that incident will link to another and then another, until the whole inner story eventually emerges into recall.

Or you may awaken convinced you haven't dreamed at all. Focus on what it was you were thinking when you first awakened; perhaps it was not a thought, exactly, but an image, or an impression about yourself in some action in the past, or speculation about the future. Recollecting that initial thought many

times triggers off a train of associative thinking connected to it
and the contiguous recollections reconstruct the dream for you
in a fantastic way. When you are genuinely concerned with re-
calling your dreams, the unconscious will return the compliment
of your paying attention to it; your attitude of receptivity and
willingness helps. As sleep research proves, we do dream every
night, and people who begin analysis firmly convinced they never
have dreams invariably find a wealth of dreams pressing forward
into consciousness once the analysis is under way.

The instruction to write it down right away is meant *literally*.
No matter if it is the dead of night and will power of the kind
that makes heroes is necessary for you to resist the engulfing
drowsiness. Time and again experience proves there is nothing so
evanescent as a dream. You can go over and over it in your superlative memory, branding it there thinking it could not leave you
any more than the memory of your birthday, graduation, marriage, first child; slip back to slumber smugly secure; awaken to
remember only that you had a dream, but of which you remember nothing.

Or you may awaken remembering quite well the vivid dream
you have had; proceed about the business of getting showered
and dressed first, before you commit the dream to paper, all the
while mulling over this-and-that aspect of the dream, only to find
that when the convenient time for you has arrived the dream has
departed, like smoke in a stiff breeze.

These and a surprising number of derivative experiences will
finally impress upon you the importance of writing the dream at
once.

Occasionally you will be astonished to read, in the morning, a
dream that awakened you in the middle of the night, arousing
you just enough to scribble it down blindly before forgetting it
completely. It will seem to you an utterly strange document,
hard for you to associate with yourself at all; only the witness of
your own handwriting on the paper could convince you of the
nocturnal adventure.

2. CREATE FAVORABLE CONDITIONS FOR DREAMS. Exhaustion; absorption in a great many activities; even the routine of a full schedule, can inhibit the free rise of dreams to the surface of your recollection, although they occur anyway but on a deeper, inaccessible level. An increase in emotional tension, not much but enough to break the monotony of the rhythm of your days, will provide the stimulus on the outer side to constellate dreams on the inner. A trip; something unexpected, outside your usual routine, a sudden piece of news not necessarily of monumental importance—occurrences like these can build up the necessary interior tension to start you dreaming.

3. DON'T INTERPRET AS YOU WRITE. Forget any attempt to "understand" or "interpret" the meaning of your dreams as you are writing them out. Dreams often have to "go cold," sometimes for weeks and even months, before you can see plainly what they mean. And a common hazard to guard against while you are writing the dream is the invidious attack of your intellect trying to depreciate the *worth* of what you are committing to paper. This assault is apt to be particularly withering the more rational and intellectual the dreamer is by type. "What nonsense! I must be out of my mind trying to make anything out of this!" Prepare yourself for that kind of thinking in the early learning period. The assaults might easily undermine your perseverance; you need to be on guard about the possibility—nor will they vanish until you have had, not once but a number of times, *the living experience of the dream.*

It is not easy to grasp the reality of Jung's comment that, "To experience a dream *and its interpretation* is very different from having a tepid rehash set before you on paper. Everything about this is in the deepest sense experience. . . ." The italics stress the significance of the *two* events coalescing into a single experience: dream *and* interpretation, or rather, your comprehension of the dream's meaning. When this occurs your understanding is no longer intellectual only, it is felt emotionally also. The first approach to taking the unconscious seriously, as a sphere of experience as genuine in its own right as anything in conscious life, is extraordinarily tenuous. Even though the intellect "understands" all the technical terms, the concepts, the processes formulated by the theory of a particular psychological school, and readily concedes the significant part dreams play in expressing activities of the unconscious, nevertheless the unconscious continues to *seem* to be an unreal appendage of the conscious self, until the meaning of your dreams strikes home again and again with unmistakable pointedness.

The right formula has to be found to resolve the conflict between the conscious mind and the unconscious products brought before that mind through the dream. This can be done only by *living it through.* "Every stage of the process must be lived through," Jung declares uncompromisingly. "There is no interpretation or other sleight of hand capable of getting the individual around this difficulty by deception. The coalescence of conscious and unconscious can succeed only a step at a time." [1]

"Living it through" brings, eventually, understanding, for one thing, of what the unconscious is communicating. Out of understanding comes a gradual change in outlook, then in attitude, for something is added to your knowledge by what you integrate out of the unconscious. An enormously important dimension is added to your experience of living: *you are able to enter a sphere of irrational experience,* through the dream. This alone alters the commonplace and the habitual; you can no longer look on the ordinary things of your life as you used to, and since everything depends on how we look at things rather than on how they are in themselves, the meaning of what is transpiring in the unconscious is a personal guideline of unimaginable worth.

4. RECORD THE DREAM WITH GREAT CARE. Note carefully how the details are introduced in the dream sequence. For example, if a person known to you shows up in your dream, bustling into a room, or backing into it, it is important to note just which and not merely record: "Jack came into the room."

Stick as closely as possible to the dream's images, Jung advises.

"When somebody dreams of a 'deal table' it is not enough for him to associate it with his writing-desk, which does not happen to be made of deal. Supposing that nothing more occurs to the dreamer; this blocking has an objective meaning for it indicates that a particular darkness reigns in the immediate neighborhood of the dream image, and that is suspicious. We would expect him to have dozens of associations to a deal table, and the fact that there is apparently nothing is itself significant. In such cases I keep on returning to the image and I say, 'Suppose I had no idea what the words "deal table" mean. Describe the object and give me its history in such a way that I cannot fail to understand what sort of thing it is.' " [2]

Jung's advice is, of course, indisputable. But do not take it to mean that every single dream you ever have will, with sufficient diligence, decode itself to your understanding. There are dreams, as Jung himself points out, that are simply impenetrable. Dreams which do not yield their meaning after honest and intensive effort to penetrate them will usually repeat their message in another dream and in other analogies.

In actual practice, all the more relevant to you who approach dream interpretation as a cultural development rather than a therapeutic measure—although both goals merge and become synonymous in the process—it will be impossible to understand every little thing in your dream. Nor would it be sensible to try, although every effort should be extended to amplify the images of the dream (see next chapter) particularly when you have an archetypal dream.

5. KEEP SERIES OF DREAMS. In general it is the series of dreams, really amounting to a running conversation with the unconscious, that provides the undercover information about your hidden inner life.

The series, however, is not sequential, as Dr. Meier explains: "A series of dreams is usually not a sequence where one dream is the result or a product of the preceding one, in such a way that A of necessity produces B and B of necessity produces C, and so on. . . . The arrangement in a series is a *concentric* one; the various single dreams of a series deal with one and the same central problem and thus group themselves around this problem. Moreover, a series of dreams gives a number of different aspects of one and the same situation in such a way that one dream gives one aspect and another dream another, so that through the series the situation becomes clear. Thus Dream B may well add whatever has been overlooked in the interpretation of Dream A, for example; and Dream C may add more information or correct a misinterpretation.[3]

Martin's experiences corroborate the above. He points out, "Many dreams say practically nothing to us, appear meaningless, and yet these same dreams looked at afterwards as part of a series, make astonishingly good sense. To use a somewhat fanciful analogy, it is as if the unconscious were showing several films at once, films taken at different levels. Each dream is a brief 'shot.' A particular shot at a particular time may be meaningful or it may leave us completely nonplussed. It is only when we piece together the 'shots' and have a wider knowledge of the living background that we get some idea of what the total performance represents." [4]

The diagram which follows fully illustrates the interconnections between the images in a dream. Drawn by Dr. Jolande Jacobi,[5] this example assumes that the dream under investigation has four clearly defined elements in it, represented by, say, four images: son, horse, river, mother, to choose at random for the sake of illustration. The nodal points, interconnected by the lines with each other, trace imagery in all possible directions and correspondences, the purpose being, of course, to supplement, broaden and enhance the key images: son, horse, river, mother. Dr. Jacobi's instructions regarding the amplification of all the imagery is included in the subsequent chapter on Amplification.

There are exceptions to the rule that the series of dreams, not the single dream, will tell the dreamer's life-problem clearly. Initial dreams at the beginning of an analysis are often extraordinarily informative, disclosing to the analyst the etiology of the dreamer's difficulties from remote past cause to future probability. Such dreams act like flares casting a beam of light over the dark scene of a possible shipwreck.

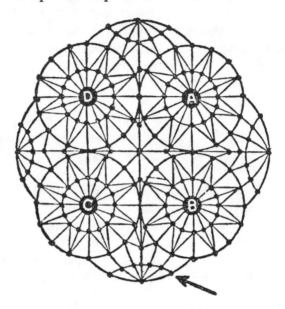

DIAGRAM OF DREAM ELEMENTS
A, B, C, D are the dream elements. The nodal points of the net of connections shown by the little arrow represent the various correspondences, the amplifications. (Reprinted with permission from *The Psychology of Jung* by Dr. Jolande Jacobi, Yale University Press, 1951.)

Occasionally there are other solo dreams of remarkable lucidity, one of which Jung tells in the following account, which is also unusual because he interpreted it without prior knowledge of the dreamer.

"Sometimes . . . one comes across fairly intelligible dreams, particularly with people who know nothing about psychology, where personal knowledge of the dreamer is not necessary for interpretation. Once on a train journey I found myself with two strangers in the dining car. The one was a fine-looking old gentleman, the other a middle-aged man with an intelligent face. I gathered from their conversation that they were military men, presumably an old general and his adjutant. After a long silence, the old man suddenly said to his companion, 'Isn't it odd what you dream sometimes? I had a remarkable dream last night. I dreamed:

" 'I was on parade with a number of young officers, and our commander-in-chief was inspecting us. Eventually he came to me, but instead of asking a technical question he demanded a definition of the beautiful. I tried in vain to find a satisfactory answer and felt most dreadfully ashamed when he passed on to the next man, a very young major, and asked him the same question. This fellow came out with a damned good answer, just the one I would have given if only I could have found it. This gave me such a shock that I woke up.'

"Then suddenly and unexpectedly addressing me, a total stranger, he asked, 'D'you think dreams can have a meaning?' 'Well,' I said, 'Some dreams certainly have a meaning.' 'But what could be the meaning of a dream like that?' he asked sharply, with a nervous twitch of the face. I said, 'Did you notice anything peculiar about this young major? What did he look like?' 'He looked like me, when I was a young major.' 'Well, then,' I said, 'It looks as if you had forgotten or lost something which you were still able to do when you were a young major. Evidently the dream was calling your attention to it.'

"He thought for a while, and then he burst out, 'That's it! You've got it! When I was a young major I was interested in art. But later this interest got swamped by routine.' Thereupon he relapsed into silence, and not a word more was spoken. After dinner I had an opportunity of speaking with the man whom I took to be his adjutant. He confirmed my surmise about the old gentleman's rank, and told me that I had obviously touched on a sore spot, because the general was known and feared as a crusty old disciplinarian who meddled with the most trifling matters that were no concern of his.

"It would certainly have been better if the general had kept and cultivated a few outside interests instead of letting himself be drowned in mere routine, which was neither in his own interest nor in that of his work; he might have been able to realize his one-sidedness, and correct it. In other words, if he had *looked through* his own actions to search for the reasons that prompted him to go poking about in his soldiers' knapsacks—an occupation better left to his subordinates—he might have discovered the reason for his irritability and bad moods, i.e., his genuine need to give expression to an artistic talent which he was repressing." [6]

6. YOUR ATTITUDE MUST BE RIGHT. Developing techniques that in effect link together conscious and unconscious is a real art and art is a hard mistress exacting, prior to anything else, two indispensables: (1) serious attention, and (2) a basic steadfastness of spirit.

We have said that the unconscious returns the compliment when you pay attention to it by attempting to recall dreams; that is a first step in according the unconscious "serious attention." Recording them systematically in a special book kept for that purpose only, is another step. Doing your best to amplify the images and interpret the dream goes beyond the mere recording of them; now the unconscious has been given your libido, your energies, with deference equal to that which you might consciously give to a proposition in real life.

As for the second indispensable, steadfastness of spirit, Martin's comments are particularly apt: "When we deal with the deep unconscious, we are dealing with the depths from which only yesterday as it were consciousness emerged. In doing so, inevitably we place consciousness in peril. To take it upon oneself to apply the constructive technique (i.e. the interpretation of dreams) a man needs not only resolution but psychological stamina. *Without it the risk is too great.* If you do not have it—and we are all made as we are made—keep away. To recognize that there are some things one is not fitted to do is not cowardice but wisdom."

Jung's own warning is not to be dismissed lightly, either. "One never knows what one may be releasing when one begins to analyze dreams," he says, and although referring specifically to those in analysis, the application to others is pertinent. "Something deeply buried and invisible may thereby be set in motion, very probably something that would have come to light sooner or later anyway, but again, it might not. It is as if one were digging an artesian well and ran the risk of stumbling on a volcano. *When neurotic symptoms are present one must proceed very carefully.* But the neurotic cases are not by a long way the most dangerous. There are cases of people, apparently quite normal, showing no especial neurotic symptoms—they may themselves be doctors and educators—priding themselves on their normality, models of good upbringing, with exceptionally normal views and habits of life, yet whose normality is an artificial compensation for a latent psychosis. Those concerned suspect nothing of their condition. Their suspicions may perhaps find only an indirect expression in the fact that they are particularly interested in psychology and psychiatry and are attracted to these things as a moth to the light." [7] Jung's emphatic warning should not be ignored; the psychological stamina to hold your ground with a foot in both realities is of prime importance.

Mental breakdown is not the only dire consequence of a hostile unconscious; psychosomatic illnesses and the instigating of accidents are other manifestations of inimical unconscious activity. "A very large number of accidents of every description, more than people would ever guess, are of psychic causation, ranging from trivial mishaps, like stumbling, banging oneself, burning one's fingers, etc., to car smashes and catastrophes in the mountains; all these may be psychically caused and may sometimes have been preparing for weeks and even months. I have examined many cases of this kind and often I could point to dreams which showed signs of a tendency to self-injury weeks beforehand. All those accidents that happen from so-called carelessness should be examined for such determinants. We know, of course, that when for one reason or another we feel out of sorts, we are liable to commit not only the minor follies, bur something really dangerous which, given the right psychological moment, may well put an end to our lives. . . . In the same way, bodily ills can be brought into being or protracted. A wrong functioning of the psyche can do much to injure the body, just as conversely, a bodily illness can affect the psyche; for psyche and body are not separate entities but one and the same life. Thus there is seldom a bodily ailment that does not show psychic complications, even if it is not psychically caused." [8]

Pointing to dangers is not intended to dash cold water but to make clear that the unconscious is not to be trifled with. However, the individual in basically sound psychological health will not experience difficulties; the unconscious responds with a friendly face to those at one with it; its hostility is reserved for those at variance with it.

7. ANALYZE THE DREAM'S STRUCTURE. As you already know, many dreams are strikingly similar to stage plays. The *dramatis personae*, time, and place are stated; the lines of the plot are drawn as the story unfolds; the conflict comes to a head and something good or ill has to happen to resolve the deadlock; finally comes the "*lysis*" or solution.

The dramatic structure of the following simple dream will illustrate how the plot may be broken down into its parts. A woman dreams:

"I am riding a small motor scooter, very pleased with myself for maintaining my balance since I have never ridden one before. I am riding 'side-saddle' and my feet and legs are bare. My feet are pretty, I think, admiring their long, white, clean, straight-toed lines.

"Bravely I ride down a steep ramp and into a bank, despite misgivings about managing the sharp turn at the foot of the ramp. With skill that surprises me I avoid the walls and desks as I drive on through the interior of the bank toward the exit at the far end of the building. Business is going on as usual, I observe as I ride along. I notice a young mother with three tots at one teller's window. She has a tiny, diaperless infant in arms, a small three-year-old boy and a younger girl child; the latter two are scrambling playfully together. Just as I arrive abreast of them they roll directly into the path of my scooter; an accident is inevitable. But somehow, with a dexterity I would never have imagined I could command, I swung the scooter away, missing them by a hair."

The *dramatis personae* are the dreamer who is herself riding the scooter, the mother at the teller's window, and the three very young children. Time and place are the interior of a bank, a place where money and valuables are stored.

The exposition of the plot tells us the dreamer has a new accomplishment; now she rides a motor scooter for the first time. A motor scooter is quite particularly a vehicle for an individual operator; the woman steers it herself and she can even negotiate difficult turns and maneuver the vehicle in circumscribed surroundings. Moreover she is riding side-saddle, the traditionally feminine mount on a steed. Inferentially, the dreamer has learned a new way to travel on a self-steering, highly-individual form of transport which she manages very well despite the side-saddle mounting of a decidedly womanly woman. But there are incongruities, to which we will return later.

Then there is the crisis, the near-accident to the two small children and herself. The disaster is averted by her quick-thinking action in the instant of danger as she swerves the vehicle away from them. Obviously her instinctive sense of balance is also very keen for she meets the unexpected with the aplomb of an expert although it is her first venture on a scooter. In fact the *lysis* of the dream shows that within herself, from the instinctual realm, even more than from *thinking* how to save the children, was the power to contravene the accident that seemed inevitable.

In addition to analyzing the structure, various personations may be recognized which illustrate the concepts you have read about in the technical section of this book. The dreamer herself appears, identified as her ego or conscious self. The young mother is another aspect of herself, rather than the Shadow, for she has borne three small children, one still an infant in arms. These are new potentials in the dreamer's developing personality, in actual life she was in the process of growing in depth, having begun almost four years earlier as the three-year-old boy, her first-born in terms of new potential, new life, indicates. She had come to terms with her unconscious positively as the dream clearly reflects. A bank is a place where treasure, money and valuables, are stored; these are symbols of libido, psychic energy, and in this domain of the unconscious, the storehouse of psychic energy, she is relatively at ease, operating her motor scooter by herself, indicating the same mastery and flexibility in relation to the unconscious.

However, the children are in need of constant maternal watchfulness in order to thrive and grow up; the slightest ineptitude on the driver's part—her ego-self—might have killed them when they rolled into the path of the scooter. And there remains one peculiarity about the driver: her feet and legs are bare. Thus if for any reason she were forced to dismount she is inadequately equipped for walking. You could say that a basic *standpoint*, i.e. feet that are shod, ready to stand on the ground and walk about, in touch with the earth and earthly things, is apparently still lacking at the present time. An extraverted-Intuitive type, Sensation—"reality" —was her weakest function.

Occasionally the meaning of a dream may come in a flash while you are looking over the story it tells which, coupled with your own personal knowledge of the conscious situation at the time, fits both parts together like pieces in a jigsaw puzzle. On the other hand, the dream can be positively impenetrable, in which case considerable amplifying of the dream imagery has to be undertaken before you can even hazard a guess as to the dream's meaning. And this is likelier to be true as you progress deeper into dream interpretation, strangely enough.

8. WHY THIS DREAM NOW? Your answer to this question put literally to the dream is most important because essentially, dream action is a finely-attuned compensation process on the unconscious side correcting something lacking in the conscious attitude of the dreamer at the time of the dream.

You will recall that in the chapter on the Psyche the principle of *compensation*, or *complementation*, was posited as axiomatic. Jung says: "The psyche is a self-regulating system that maintains its equilibrium just as the body does. Every process that goes too far immediately and inevitably calls forth *compensation* and without these there would be neither a normal metabolism nor a normal psyche. *In this sense we can take the theory of compensation as a basic law of psychic behaviour.* The relation between conscious and unconscious is compensatory. *This is one of the best-proven rules of dream interpretation.* When we set out to interpret a dream it is always helpful to ask: what conscious situation does it compensate?" [9]

Compensation and its partner *Complementation* are two differing, purposeful reactions of the unconscious to an unnatural and dangerously one-sided conscious state of the dreamer, the unconscious reacting exactly as the body reacts in a purposeful way to injuries, infections, or abnormal ways of living.

Compensation means rounding-out, and smoothing-out, in the sense of *Compenso*, the Latin root, which means to weigh one thing against the other and to smooth out. Implicit is the idea of some more complete standpoint superior to or different from the one the dreamer has in conscious life.

Complementation, from the Latin root *compleo*, signifies filling-up completely, as a dream may do by adding details left out of the dreamer's consciousness for one reason or another as, for example, repression, resistances, wrong moral judgment, etc. (Compensatory dreams illustrating the principle involved are to be found in Chapter Twelve.)

In a series in which many facets of the dreamer's problems are imaged, each dream reacts to the momentary conscious situation, reflecting a single compensatory aspect in each dream; the whole series together reveals the total compensatory effect of the dreams. How essential dreaming is to the physical well-being of the dreamer has been shown by the Dement-Kleitman researches,[10] mentioned in the first chapter.

In addition to dreams, *compensation* as an expression of psychic activity seeking equilibrium can take these forms: (1) Compensation lived-out; (2) Conscious suffering; (3) Uncharacteristic behavior; (4) Opposition to the cultural canon.

The brief accounts of each which follows will be useful:

1. *Compensation lived-out* sometimes consumes years of an individual's lifetime in psychosomatic illness or in one of the myriad forms of neurotic maladaptations which are commonplace in modern life. It is one penalty exacted by the unconscious for the extremely one-sided, thus unbalanced, development of the personality characteristic of our culture. Evidence abounds on this point, but here is just one index of the extent of the impairment of the adult population constituting the contemporary generation in power which has been provided by the recent sensational A. C. Rennie research studies in mental health among residents of midtown Manhattan, conducted by survey methods outstandingly excellent in a consensus of social scientists.[11] Heretofore estimates of the incidence of mental illness centered around a figure of one-in-ten. According to the Rennie studies made among a research pool of 175,000 adult residents, 23% of the population are seriously enough impaired to need immediate help. Another 58% show mild or moderate symptoms suggesting they are often bedeviled but not entirely crippled by their symptoms. Only 18 to 19% are described as "well." The conclusions of this

study, which deviated widely from common expectation of its results, project one startling fact: an immerse load of personal anguish is borne by great numbers of people, never suspected before; in fact three out of four of those troubled have neither sought help nor have they any idea where to go or what to do to be helped.

Another trouble area exists among the older population, among the retired, the so-called "golden age" or "senior citizens" group. What government and social service agencies call "Problems of the Aging" includes one striking problem: the increase of mental illness with advancing age. An astonishing revelation about the great majority arriving at retirement is the widespread prevalence of the notion that *now* they will start "living" since at last they have the leisure to "live"—but great numbers are totally uninformed as to what could effactually give them a sense of zestful living, and are unprepared for fruitful leisure. Other acute problems, such as failing health and lack of sufficient means, plague a substantial proportion of the group, but the aimlessness and the confused fancies about what constitutes "living" pose the most serious threat to their chances for a serene old-age.

2. *Conscious suffering.* Nothing to do with sickly religiosity or self-conscious piety is intended by *conscious suffering.* Jung observed that repressing disagreeable thoughts creates something like a psychic vacuum which usually becomes filled with anxiety. Consciously understanding and recognizing your thoughts and what it is that occupies the subliminal strata of your thinking and wishing makes you aware, "brings to consciousness" in other words, something you lack. You substitute knowledge and awareness which might very well and indeed often does bring with it *conscious suffering,* for now you know what it is you lack, and desire, and the lack of it is a cause of suffering. But you no longer suffer unconsciously, in chronic anxiety states which are the substitute for conscious suffering and awareness.

Of itself suffering has no psychological value but the anomaly of *un*conscious suffering in the form of chronic anxieties because of repression or refusal to accept consciously the challenges in the pattern of each individual's life gives a symbolic value to conscious suffering consciously assumed.

3. *Uncharacteristic behavior*. The human's enormous potential resides in his being the repository of many tendencies, a great many of which must be curtailed or suppressed in favor of others. As Joseph Campbell writes: "In his life-form the individual is necessarily only a fraction and distortion of the total image of man. He is limited either as male or as female; at any given period of his life he is again limited as child, youth, mature adult, or ancient; furthermore, in his life-role he is necessarily specialized as craftsman, tradesman, servant, or thief, priest, leader, wife, nun, or harlot; he cannot be all. . . ." [12]

But no one can ignore any element that is a part of himself and many tendencies simply refuse to be passed over. Strong tendencies strongly repressed have a way of sooner or later erupting into that life seriously interfering with the course *willed* by the individual. Thus, the serious-minded professor of mature years suddenly elopes with a burlesque queen; a distinguished senator dies of suicide or heart attack following a yellow journal's thinly-disguised exposé of the private life of a highly-placed public official which includes his habitual recourse to a brothel specializing in boys for men; the older woman, most frequently among well-to-do widows whose adult children have left home, develops a benevolent interest in aspiring young and comely men of more-or-less talent but discernibly suave charm; and their covert sisters-under-the-skin, the ladies who flock to doing good works, or become avid disciples of variously-qualified group leaders, including *bona fide* religionists, but also the cultists of the quasi-religions and esoteric philosophies of many shades.

A *modus operandi* has to be worked out by the individual, taking note of all that he is in order to direct his life decently and in accord with what he might be as a whole individual. By the time most adults come to this awareness they also realize how many gaps the educative processes in the first 25 years of their lives have left in their equipment to experience life meaningfully and fully. Although economically they may "have it made," the deeper questions that have been shunted aside in the competitive struggle have simply bided their time. When they emerge again, as they do, neither panaceas nor computers will quell them.

4. *Opposition to the cultural canon.* The opposition of the creative minority to the collective majority is most graphically portrayed in modern art, the butt of many vulgar jokes among the uncomprehending; in literature and its subsidiary arts, the cinema and theatre, including modern dance; and modern music as well.

Modern art, particularly imageless abstract art, reached the nadir of representation of the phenomenal world with Mondrian, Kandinsky, Picasso, Klee, Ensor, Chagall, Munch and de Chirico, among the great painters of the 20th century, their genre bringing to culmination about a century of gradual disintegration and eventual disappearance of a strictly pictorial imaging of outer appearance, at its peak with Courbet in the mid-19th century.

At odds with the dominant currents of our rationalistic and scientifically-oriented civilization, modern abstract artists such as Klee, finding no vocabulary "for the ultimate mystery that lies behind the ambiguity which the light of the intellect fails miserably to penetrate," as he articulated the artist's position, trended backward to the role of the primitive artist in tribal life. Then the artist's necessary and privileged function was to make magic symbols venting the *inner feelings* of the tribe. In similar capacity the shaman or chief was specially privileged to have the "ota," the Big Dream, of importance for all the tribe, as distinct from the little insignificant dreams happening to ordinary members of the group. The modern artists, having dropped through one false bottom after another on the way down to the ultimate bottom level of primitivity, finally began to express what Neumann calls "opposition to the epoch's consciousness and sense of values." [13] This is what modern art shows, what the artist feels and paints from the inside-out: grotesque distortion; distress; the sinister fear of world catastrophes—a Picasso's tortured, fragmented "Guernica" and Marini's sculptures of famine-bloated horsemen staring vacantly toward the sky from which bombs may rain: merely two examples of human anguish from a somber register of art about the disorganization of a whole society.

The *avant-garde* in art are flanked by the writers, spearheaded by great talents such as Mann, Joyce, Huxley, Orwell, Camus, Aiken and others in an outpouring of literature resembling the mill of the sorcerer's apprentice. Floods of words are venting writers' awareness of shattered forms and bleak meaningless- ness and the horror of purposeless vacuity in a mysterious world incalculably rich in possibilities and in deadly danger of strangu- lation from inability to choose to live.

As for music, Schoenberg, Bartok and Copland hardly make melody, only harsh sounds in atonal discord, and a dirge for the race sounds through the lament of Menotti's *The Consul*.

Volumes could be devoted to explicating themes barely hinted in the foregoing, well beyond our concern with dreams and their interpretation, yet germane to the phenomenon of compensation. For the artist uniquely expresses the unconscious through the pipeline of his work as the need of his times works inside him without his necessarily wanting, seeing, or understanding the true significance of his function. The more divergent the *authentic* expression of his inner vision of a deeper level of reality than that reflected in the phenomenal world, the more he demonstrates compensation for the existing cultural canon and fulfills his indi- vidual role in helping transform and overturn it. Collaterally, the individual who is not an artist and who lives by and within the canons of his culture also demonstrates compensation but individ- ually, in dreams and through external commitments which are also the workings of the psychic processes as, for example, through projections, or lived-out compensation, mentioned above.

The declaration that the psyche automatically *compensates* raises the question: Compensates *why?*

The logical supposition must be that there exists some more complete standpoint for the individual, superior to or different from the one he consciously has. Taking into account the corrective, healing, directive expressions the unconscious provides through dreams, as many thousands of persons released from savagely crippling neuroses can testify, the supposition appears to be on firm ground.

Plainly then, *compensation appears purposive.* But, as the Zurich analyst C. A. Meier comments, "Only retrospectively can it be seen that this goal, this *telos*, was a *causa finalis;* nor could this *causa finalis* be found had not the theorem of compensation been applied consecutively . . ." [14]

This *causa finalis* Jung calls "wholeness." Wholeness can be sought by successful adaptation in two directions: outwardly, in profession, family, society, and inwardly, by the viable relationship maintained with the unconscious, as delineated in the chapters on the archetypal figures we encounter in dreams.

When an individual deliberately takes upon himself these dual goals, most particularly the inner relationships (for presumably outer commitments will have long since been undertaken before the inner world makes itself felt), he sets upon a process of development which Jung has termed "individuation." As individuation is a special field beyond the scope of our present subject, we will not comment further on it, with this exception. The interpretation of dreams and their integration into the dreamer's consciousness constitute a partial step in the direction of "individuation." But as to the end-goal, Jung says: "While I am quite ready to believe that an intelligent layman with some psychological knowledge and experience of life could, with practice, diagnose dream-compensation correctly, I consider it impossible for anyone without knowledge of mythology and folklore and without some understanding of the psychology of primitives and of comparative religion, to grasp the individuation process which, according to all we know, lies at the base of psychological compensation." [5]

1. C. G. Jung, *The Integration of the Personality* (New York: Farrar and Rinehart, 1939), p. 105.

2. C. G. Jung, *The Practice of Psychotherapy* (New York: Pantheon Books, 1954), p. 149.

3. C. A. Meier, "Jung and Analytical Psychology," The Cutter Lectures, Andover-Newton Theological School, Newton Center, Mass.

4. P. W. Martin, *op. cit.*, p. 44.

5. Dr. Jolande Jacobi, *The Psychology of Jung* (New Haven: Yale University Press, 1943), p. 82.

6. C. G. Jung, *The Development of Personality* (New York: Pantheon Books, 1954), p. 101-2.

7. Jung, *Two Essays on Analytical Psychology*, pp. 112–113.

8. *Ibid.*

9. Jung, *The Practice of Psychotherapy*, p. 153.

10. Dement, *op. cit.*, p. 1707.

11. A. C. Thomas, Rennie Series in Social Psychiatry, Vol. I, *Mental Health in the Metropolis: The Midtown Manhattan Study*, (New York: McGraw-Hill, 1962).

12. Joseph Campbell, *The Hero with a Thousand Faces* (New York: Meridian Books, 1956), pp. 382–3.

13. Erich Neumann, "Art and Time," *Man and Time* (New York: Pantheon Books, 1957), p. 11.

14. Meier, *op. cit.*, p. 53.

15. Jung, *The Structure and Dynamics of the Psyche*, p. 290.

CHAPTER TEN

Amplification

Amplification and its corollary *Integration* are the final steps in the interpretation of dreams, the former taking precedence in the sometimes lengthy and painstaking task out of which the latter ideally matures.

Amplification is the process of elaboration, of making fuller and more explicit, all parts of the imagery of dreams in order to create a comprehensive background against which the motifs, movements, and signal information of specific dreams stand out clearly, illuminating the problems of the dreamer in somewhat the same way a design stands out on a great tapestry.

Two steps are involved. The first is *Personal amplification;* that is, questioning what each dream element signifies to the dreamer subjectively. The dreamer makes associations to each of the images in the dream, interconnecting them in all possible directions and all possible correspondences and analogies. Extraordinarily penetrating insights are won by the dreamer in this way. Sometimes they are painful, extremely so, but also they have a liberating effect as progressively he becomes better acquainted with the contents of the Personal Unconscious.

Beyond the personal is the *objective amplification* by which associations made to the dream imagery are not at all personal or subjective but *collective* in the broadest meaning of the term. At this level dream imagery corresponds to the symbolic material of mythology and the dreamer in effect touches, or rather enters into, the pre-logical realm of the Collective Unconscious. Dr. Jolande Jacobi, to whom reference was made in the previous chapter, specifically instructs as follows: "When a snake, for instance, appears in a dream, then its significance lies precisely in the fact that it is a snake and not a bull, the snake having been chosen by the unconscious to express what it means. What the snake means to the dreamer is *not* determined through a chain of associations but through amplification, i.e., by supplementing the snake symbol with all the references, as, for example, myths, significant for its nature as snake and corresponding to the meaning that the 'snake' as such has for the dreamer. For just because the snake is not regarded as a 'substitute figure' but in its actual and real meaning for the dreamer, the still obscure meaning of the dream is not cleared up by the investigation of what that figure possibly conceals. On the contrary, all the surroundings, the context in which it is placed, are taken into consideration and investigated. As the representative value of a colour only results from its being placed in a pictorial context—for whether a spot of grey represents a bit of shadow or a reflection of light, a fleck of dirt or a strand of hair, is decided only by its surroundings, by the colours and forms of the total composition—so the role and meaning of a dream symbol only reveal themselves when it has been evaluated according to its position and meaning in the context. When one further takes into consideration the total situation and the specific psychic structure of the dreamer as well as his conscious psychological attitude, to which the dream content, as experience proves, is complementary, then the real meaning of the figure in its subjective reference appears of itself. . . ." [1]

Amplification of dream imagery in such careful and exacting detail will, in a long series of dreams extending over a period of time, sometimes years, unmistakably show that the activities of the unconscious, as Jung says, "no longer appear as a senseless string of incoherent and isolated happenings but resemble the successive steps in a planned and orderly process of development." [2]

Obviously, *research* is called for in all the studies which may shed light on the dream images: symbology, religion, myths, fairy-tales, and so forth. Identical motifs to those in your dreams are to be found in the latter two. The situation in which you yourself are caught in real life, as imaged in your dreams, can be an age-old human situation, reflected in the myths of the race, the constellation of which in another individual human life, yours, may well evoke an archetypal symbol. Once Jung wrote this writer pointedly with regard to the question of research, in response to material we sent him which we *intuitively* understood. He wrote, "Symbolism and its interpretation are not an intuitive task but rather a scientific one and they ask an unusual amount of knowledge. People usually think that when they succeed in having some imagination on a symbol they have also interpreted it, but an interpretation has to be substantiated through objective material."

Now, this sort of research thrusts the dream-interpreter straight into the techniques of *Hermeneutics*, an ancient and honorable art widely practiced in former times, defined as, "The science or art of the interpretation of literary productions, especially the sacred scriptures; the study or teaching of the principles of interpretation." Hermeneuts flourished as teachers among the early Christians who were known as "saints," for so the communities of the faithful were described, and the term is still verbally alive to this day in the Confiteors of eastern and western Catholicism, and with Anglicans and Episcopalians. But long before the Christians took over "hermeneutics" the pagans had it, as indeed they had a great deal more that Christianity absorbed intact into its bloodstream of practice and principle, quite the opposite of the common misconception that Christianity outwardly maintains unbroken continuity with Judaism.

As might be expected, at the pagan level "hermeneutics" exposes the Greek roots invariably struck on turning over the first spadeful to examine the underpinnings of our civilization. Hermeneutics is directly connected with the god Hermes, known also as Mercury in the Roman pantheon, where he is pictured with the *petasus*, a low-crowned, broad-brimmed hat commonly worn by messengers in ancient times, and with small wings at his ankles, or on his sandals (*telarius*). Hermes' family connections are impeccable: his father was the supreme deity Zeus, his mother Maia, eldest of the Pleiades, the seven daughters of Atlas and the Oceanid, Pleioni. This background has a bearing on Hermes as a *symbol*, the elucidation of which affords an excellent opportunity to demonstrate the amplification of an image, which is the essential character of hermeneutics.[3]

Hermes' genealogy is enlightening. On his father's side he touches the topmost power in the heavens and on his mother's, the bottom depths of the watery realm: thus he combines the elemental opposites of air and water, sometimes expressed by his representation as hermaphroditic, which is the conjunction of extreme opposites, the masculine-and-feminine. Hermes was official messenger of the gods when they meant peace; his symbol was the caduceus, a long winged wand around which two serpents entwine. The caduceus signifies, among many other meanings too numerous to go into here,[4] the integration of the four elements; the Romans interpreted it as a symbol of moral equilibrium and good conduct. The caduceus is a very ancient symbol; it has been traced back to 2600 B.C. in a design on a sacrificial cup but the symbologist Heinrich Zimmer states that it probably dates back beyond the Mesopotamian culture. Now this is borne out by penetrating into prehistoric times when "*the mythic process*" first began to enclose *perception*, and language was nothing more than grunts and growls of sound, emitted by the earliest humans.

The Lost Language of Symbolism[5] traces the primal meanings of the earliest onomatopoeic sounds, from which we extract the following:

M-E-R-C-U-R-Y breaks down to "Fire of MERAK." Merak is the

Great Mare; Mare is also Mother, sometimes Mind. What we understand, then, is: MERAK derives out of MA=*Mother*; UR=Fire; AK=Great or Almighty; the meaning is: the power of communication. Mercury is *carrier* of the *messages* of the gods, i.e. *communication*; he is the offspring of the Great Almighty Fire, the supreme god of light, and the Great Mare, or Mother, the ceaseless regenerating power of the womb.

TABLE OF THE PRIMITIVE LINGUAL ROOTS OF SYMBOLOGY [6]

P or B
OP = *hoop* or *eye*; as in hoop, optics
PA = *Father*, as in pa, pater, parent

T or D
OT = *hot*, as in hot
DI = *brilliant* as in Diana, diamond, etc., and Sanscrit Dyu, Dyaus

CH or J
AJ = *aged*, as in age
JA, IA, or YA = *ever-existent*, as in Jah, Jehovah, Yahweh

K or G
AK = *great* or *mighty*, as in Karnak, Carnac, Zodiac

L
EL = *God* or *Power*, as Semitic El
LA = "That which has existed for ever"

M
OM = *Sun*, as in Hindoo Om or Aum
MA = *Mother*, as in ma, mama, mater

N
ON = *one*, as in one
NE = *born of*, or *born*, as in French né

R
UR = *Fire* and *Light*, as in Semitic ur
RA = *The Sun-God Ra* or *Re*, fundamentally *ur A*, the *Fiery A*

S or Z and SH and ZH
ES = *essence* or *light*, as in esse, to be
ZE = *Fire* and *Life*, as in Zeus, Zoology, Zodiac

F or V
EF = *Life*, as in Eve, alive, and ivy
FI = *Life* and *Fire*, as in feu and vie

But *communication* is not the only attribute of Mercury; something *prior to communication* is implicit within his powers and that is, *apperception as a phenomenon; communication* is in the relation of a twin to the phenomena of *apperception* impressing itself upon the earliest human consciousness responsible for creating the *differentiations* expressed in the lingual sounds referred to above. As Cassirer states: "Language never denotes simply objects, things as such, but always conceptions arising from the autonomous activity of the mind." We have to journey back mentally to that very long ago time in human history when early man's disposable attention (the bulk of it was consumed by instinctual needs for survival as individual and species) had accumulated enough to focus on this *or* that thing and clearly distinguish differences between them. Some individuals were better able to do this than others, reaching a degree of objectivity permitting them to *see* what they *looked at* somewhat differently from their tribal brothers. Thus, the leafy *branch* of the tall oak tree which stirred when the leopard sprang; the *rock* by the bush with the red berries where the woman gave birth on her way to fetch water; the *instant* when the sun broke the rim of the expectant horizon, these specific differentiations registering in the apperceptions of primordial man were in effect a break-through for expanding human consciousness. As phenomena they were accorded a place of significance along with the leopard, the birth, and the appearance of the sun heralding another dawn; in fact they became deified as "gods-of-the-moment," [7] for early man projected onto gods he created all of the powers greater than himself.

In summary: Hermes-Mercury, the messenger of the gods, deifies primordial man's *apperception as a phenomenon* and the *power of communication*, both attributes differentiated from earliest times and imbedded in the lingual fundamentals of primitive language. The sharpest tool of the hermeneut for penetrating to fundamental conceptions will be found to be etymology, the study of the origin of words. Language ranks with the opposable thumb as the singularly distinctive feature mutating man from primate, permitting the generations to transmit to posterity the knowledge accumulated in the past. Language proliferates vertically *and* horizontally, however. Horizontally, an ever-expanding number of things can be named and described by the human facility of thinking-in-words; vertically, meaning-upon-meaning becomes superimposed upon the buried primal roots of words which remain still alive within us, still functioning on our prelogical level, still operative as emotionally with us as with the primitive.

The difference between yesterday's virgin mind and today's sophisticated intellect is like that of night and day but in this respect the former has the advantage: yesterday's *knew* that powers greater than it, forces that moved-by-themselves, abounded in the world and had their effect on all living things. These were powers that had to be worshipped, propitiated, and taken into account in all human affairs; they were "gods." But today's superior intellect "knows" the gods are so much poppycock. The more sophisticated understand quite well that "psychic processes" explains such a lot that was never before understood in the history of humankind. But "knowing better" has not supplied a better answer than the primitive had; in fact the answer is still missing. For those powers that used to be divinized keep right on acting as if they were still divine in the ancient understanding of that term, namely: they are autonomous, powerful, great-and-almighty in-and-of themselves. The primitive deified the phenomena confronting his pristine mentality, but you cannot because you know better. But what are you going to put in place of divinity? Possibly a concept? Borrowing from Henry Adams because he hits the mark: "The flimsiest bridge of all is the human concept unless somewhere, within or beyond it, an energy not individual is hidden; and in that case, the old question instantly reappears: *what is that energy?*"

Moot and irksome though the question may be, unanswerable for many, answered by many through the certainty of this-or-

THE MEANING IN DREAMS AND DREAMING

that creed, the remainder must retire with Adams' conclusion: "Where we know so little we had better hold our tongues," but with one extraordinary advantage afforded in our day. We look to the dream, the direct, pertinent, meaningful and uncorrupted expression of the unconscious; in due course we may be privileged to fashion an answer uniquely our own.

1. Jacobi, *op. cit.*, pp. 85–86.

2. Jung, *The Structure and Dynamics of the Psyche*, p. 289.

3. "The essential character of hermeneutics, a science which was widely practised in former times, consists in making successive additions of other analogies to the analogy given in the symbol; in the first place of subjective analogies produced at random . . . , and then of objective analogies found (by the analyst) in the course of erudite research. This procedure widens and enriches the initial symbol, and the final outcome is an infinitely complex and varied picture, in which certain 'lines' of psychological development stand out as possibilities that are at once individual and collective." (Jung, *Two Essays on Analytical Psychology*, p. 287.)

4. J. E. Cirlot, *A Dictionary of Symbols* (London: Routledge & Kegan Paul, 1962), p. 35.

5. Harold Bayley, *The Lost Language of Symbolism* (New York: Barnes & Noble, Vol. II, 1952), pp. 365–66.

6. *Ibid.*

7. Herman Usener, *Götternamen* (Frankfurt: Schulte-Bulmke, 1948). Usener points out that the very oldest phase of mythic thinking deified everything, even fleeting mental contents (i.e., perceived on the instant), thus objectifying the content externally (pp. 87–280).

CHAPTER ELEVEN

Integration

Integration is probably concurrent with amplification in many instances; obviously, once you *see* the meaning of the imagery you have worked out in amplification you can hardly avoid *understanding* it, which is tantamount to "integrating" it. That is: what-was-unconscious is now assimilated-by-consciousness.

Understanding a dream is not always the main thing, however, although unquestionably, insofar as intellectual understanding belongs to the totality of experience, it is valuable for the dreamer. But sometimes understanding may not come for a considerable period of time or for that matter ever, about certain dreams, in the sense of intellectually comprehending their meaning. The emotional impact of dreams is an effect transcending intellection, however, since there is an immediately salutary effect precisely like that exerted upon an audience by a powerful drama. The verisimilitude of a stage play to real life is such that audiences experience emotional catharsis through vicarious participation in the action. Dreams serve the identical function; they are nightly dramas released by the unconscious for psychic equilibrium. We

remind you again of the effects upon those deprived of dreaming, indicated by the Dement researches, mentioned in the first
chapter, disclosing that dreaming appears to be a healthful necessity, and lack of dream-time can result in serious psychic disturbances.

The methods of a professional analyst and his comments about
amplification of dream imagery can be helpful in understanding
the typical difficulties which can stand in the way of integration.
The following two cases from the files of Dr. I. Jay Dunn, of Los
Angeles, are especially relevant.[1]

A man in his early forties consulted Dr. Dunn, arriving with
two large, well-filled notebooks, one crammed full of paintings
and the other containing his record of dreams, visions, and Anima
dialogues (i.e., "conversations" held with the Anima, a technique
described earlier). The man was well-acquainted with Jungian
techniques and had been in consultation with another analyst
who had been called away for an extended period and who referred him to Dr. Dunn.

The man's complaint was that "nothing happened"; in spite of
all his careful and devoted work on himself, he felt untouched.

The following dream was presented at the first meeting:

"I am on a high land near the ocean. It is a rocky coast, and the
slope between me and the water is strewn with huge boulders
jutting high. The way to the water is not easy, but possible.

"There are a few others scattered about, like parties having a
picnic. They are along the top of the crest and on a few flat areas
down the slope. Some are beginning to leave. There are also two
or three young fellows. I am not a part of any group and am not
on good terms with these fellows.

"Now most of the others have gone, possibly because of the
approaching rain. I want to go down to the sea in spite of the
rain. That is what I came for. The young fellows have already
been down there, and they know the terrain well. Therefore they
are not too concerned with going now. They prepare to leave,
too, but they seem to hang around in the distance for a while. I

feel they think my wanting to go down there is foolhardy.

"I start wending my way down. Not straight down, but at times parallel to the shore, heading north. Soon I come to an empty shelter. S. is there. I continue on. Now I feel that the venture will take a long time. When I get to the water, I will keep on going into the ocean. I come to another landing on the hillside. It is not much further to the ocean now. It is raining. I think about struggling through the water to my destination. It will be a very long trip—cold, wet and with hazards. I realize that I have no equipment for such a long venture. The main thing would be matches to light a fire. I have none with me. I know that I will be lost without them. I look about the campsite and find a penny-box full of wooden matches. This is helpful, but I worry about there being enough for the whole trip. I figure the length of time I will be gone against the amount of matches, and see that I can just about make it if (a big if) I can keep the matches dry and use them sparingly. I know that if I make them stretch, I'll be out too far to get more and will perish or at any rate will never get back. It is frightening but I feel that perhaps luck will be with me. I decide to go on. I reach the ocean and keep going. It is raining and the ocean swirls about me."

The dreamer's associations are:

"Boulders"
These make travelling hard, but they are not boring. . . . They break the monotony of a small hillside. . . . I always wonder what surprise is waiting for me around the next corner.

"High land"
Where regular, everyday things go on. . . . I like panoramic views.

"Three young fellows"
Like teen-age youths in other dreams. . . . Self-sufficient, practical, efficient, shrewd. . . . Not as rowdy and ruthless as in other dreams, but they have this potential.

"Rain"

> I like rain. . . . The feel on the face and the sound on the roof. . . . It is refreshing and intimate, especially if one has a warm cottage. Stresses how exposed I am to the weather and how awful to be wet.

"S"

> Daughter, now with first wife. . . . Here she is eighteen. . . . Good mind and matter-of-fact. . . . But she is not stable and could not study anything. . . . More stable now.

"Ocean"

> On top: huge, awesome, mysterious. . . . I like the tang of salt air. . . . Underwater: deep, fearful, endless. . . . Contains scary, slimy undersea life, crawling, snapping shellfish. . . . Like the unconscious.

"Box of wooden matches"

> More substantial than paper matches. . . . Used to light stoves, campfires, etc. . . . Toothpicks, wedges, as poker chips, make a house plan. . . . Received a box covered with a veneer of matches from my mother last year. I was impressed because it seemed unlike her to devote time to such a long, detailed job. . . . "Children shouldn't play with matches" an old saying.

Commenting on the dreamer's associations, Dr. Dunn analyzes why "nothing happened" as far as this man was concerned:

"They are passive reflections that reveal only a small amount of work. A type of 'anima-thinking' lacking focus and discrimination. The dream symbols are merely described. Rain makes him think of the feel on the face and the sound on the roof, with no attempt to understand it as an inner content. The associations are not made objectively. They are personalized. 'I like the tang of salt air.' He does not like to give up possibilities, nor to be one-sided, and he takes all aspects into consideration. Boulders make traveling hard, but they are not boring. Most important, there is no attempt to relate the dream contents to his immediate life. They are discussed as though they had little connection with the dreamer."

The conscious situation of this dreamer is described by Dr. Dunn in this way: The course of this man's life reflected the same passivity and lack of involvement he showed toward the unconscious. Well-known in his field of commercial art and respected for his special talents, he was unable to stay in any one place for long. As he expressed it, he had to leave because other men disliked him so. This was due to his nasty temper and to his meanness. He was forced to do freelance work with sporadic success. Married twice, he showed very little responsibility toward his first wife and child. He also had reservations about his present wife who tried hard to understand him but from time to time burst out in annoyance with him. He began to think: Is she the one for me?

Although Dunn attempted to persuade the dreamer to put more work into amplification of his dream material, he would not, justifying himself with the retort that one does not question a dream. It just *was*. Shortly thereafter he withdrew from consultations entirely. Of course, his statement is nonsense. Taking the unconscious seriously does not mean taking it all that literally. To turn over the direction of your life entirely to the unconscious as it expresses in dreams is the equivalent of a psychosis and an abdication of conscious direction that can lead to serious trouble. And that dreamer certainly appears to be headed for trouble although his dream offered a number of encouraging images that, had he taken the trouble to amplify, might have had a most positive effect on his future.

I have no personal knowledge of the dreamer other than the foregoing, but tentatively, the images that stand out in his dream state the unconscious situation quite clearly. The *landscape* is desolate, cold, and rocky and he heads North: this is a motif signifying return to the mother-world, or Earth Mother; he is approaching the *shore of the ocean:* the border between the Unconscious and Consciousness. *Ocean* is a multi-faceted symbol from time immemorial, of the deep unconscious; of libido, the life-giving element; it is the medium in which life on this planet originated—indeed, you cannot live without it; the ritual of re-birth or birth-of-the-spirit, baptism, involves sprinkling or im-mersion in water. There is water everywhere in this dream, even descending from the heavens in the form of *rain*. *Rain* is a ferti-lizing, generative flow of water from above, releasing tensions, liberating the life-force in germinating seeds. Rain is conceived as urination of a divine being, as creative fertilizing, in ancient reli-gions, as the Rudra songs of the Rig-veda set forth. The dreamer *journeys* over a strange *way* that is difficult: the way of life is individual fate following its course, and to be on the road recur-rently in dreams points to the inner movement, the mysterious way leading inward, although the desolation of this dreamer's way, which seems rather a wilderness, would indicate an isolated ego-consciousness. Casting about the campsite (looking about the resources he has at hand) he finds a small box of *matches:* man-made *light*, which he anticipates will be sufficient for his needs. The matches are an ambivalent symbol: they can bring fire for man's use, but also to be noted are his personal associations. One is a warning, "children shouldn't play with matches," sternly ut-tered by countless mothers to their offspring; the other a refer-ence to his own mother, and her gift to him of a box she deco-rated by veneering matches to the surface. Here the dream touched lightly and significantly in multiple ways upon his fun-damental problem: he was a mother's-boy. His "fear of life," of "exposure" to the demands of relationship to a wife, child, and colleagues, and his refusal to face up to his own Shadow and its hostile masculinity (as might be recalled from comparison with the dreams related in the chapter on the Shadow) suggest the un-derlying psychological problem often to be found in the arche-typal mother-son constellation with its crippling train of mal-adaptations.

The next dreamer related to Dunn another seaside drama. "There hadn't been any traffic along the beach in a long while. At one time the railroad tracks had followed the coast line, now they were hanging limp, broken and dusty off the edge of the wind-swept dunes. Toys of children living along the beach were packed in light-blue cartons, dusty and worn, and it is easy to tell they have not served for fun for a long time. Also, that no new toys had reached the isolated community in ages."

The dreamer's associations were as follows: "My life near the sea has been interrupted, especially the one that shuttled parallel with the unconscious (ocean) for a long time without ever getting wet. The safe roadway has been destroyed. No more can I watch the sea from a safe arrangement. The young life along the beach still hugs the old means of gratification. No new ones are being put at their disposal. The new life is going to survive, but without new toys, it's going to be serious."

The conscious situation of this dreamer was this: A man of forty-five or more, intelligent, highly cultured, he had lingered in an analysis for many years. In writing out dreams he demonstrated a great deal of passivity, half-heartedly and superficially digging into the amplification. Dunn's insistence that he pay considerable more attention to the associations he made to dreams had, after three months, finally produced the dream just quoted, and his associations are self-explanatory. "Like leaving a scene of childhood, times have changed," Dunn remarks of his client's situation depicted in the dream. "Life has moved on. His play with fantasies is now over. Like the outlived preoccupations of youth they are now shabby and boring. The road that ran parallel to the unconscious has fallen into disuse. The dream impresses him with the fact that where he once lived has become a 'ghost-town.' Not only will he have to work to realize some of his ambitions, but the process will wet the skin. It will really touch him."

Eight weeks later the dreamer voluntarily if reluctantly left the analyst, stating that he knew he had to leave, that he had leaned too long and it was time he went on his own, to which Dunn agreed. Some weeks later he wrote Dunn a note about his progress, reflecting the lessening of dependency as well as a new sense of responsibility toward himself.

"What I miss since I decided to go it alone is multi-faceted. But one facet became clear, and I am glad about the enlightenment. I became aware of lacking a convenient 'pater confessor' as of now. The confession I seemed to crave consisted mostly of complaints about my own little aches and pains. I suddenly remembered that I prepared myself for the interviews by collecting observations on how different I was from the norm. The norm—in my estimation—being a smooth, satisfying, happy existence. I used to busy myself during the week by collecting material that permitted me to ask, 'Oh, why was my fate so different and thereby so harsh?' Like a writer sketching down ideas to be woven into a valid literary statement, I stitched together a Jeremiad of incompetence and failing, so as to create compassion and illuminate my individuation from a multitude of deplorable sides. I would be surprised if this attitude would not change after this realization.

"Throughout, I am eagerly watching my dreams, and since I now live minus analytical help, I devote much time toward understanding what they say.[2]

Once the techniques of Hermeneutics have been mastered and you experience the indescribable emotion that accompanies your interpretation of dreams, *knowing* in some inexplicable way that *that* is what it means, you will know that you have also mastered the art of interpretation. You can then expect to see revealed in the imagery of your dreams more and more of the infinite complexity of your own hidden nature. In Jung's words, "Certain 'lines' of psychological development stand out as possibilities that are at once individual and collective. There is no science on earth by which these lines could be proved 'right'; on the contrary, rationalism could very easily prove that they are not right. Their validity is proved by their intense value for life. And that is what matters . . . the important thing is that men should have life, not that the principles by which they live should be demonstrable rationally as 'right.' " [3]

To take a cue from professional practice, in an analysis the progress of a patient is contingent upon the activity of the unconscious, a good deal of which is determined by the analyst from the dream material brought to him. The latter often reveals not only the current aspect of the basic conflict or problem but also implies the "line" to be taken. So marked are these "lines" that Jung specifically declares of them: "The elaboration of the 'life-line' reveals to consciousness the true direction of the currents of the libido. . . . The life-line constructed by the hermeneutic method is . . . temporary, for life does not follow lines that are straight, nor lines whose course can be foreseen far in advance. . . . These life-lines, therefore, are never represented by widely recognized principles or ideals but by points of view and attitudes that have a provisional value. A decline in vital intensity, a noticeable loss of libido, or a feeling of constraint, indicate the moment when one has quitted one line and entered upon another, or rather ought to have entered upon it. Sometimes it is enough to leave the unconscious to discover the new line but . . . it is not good to acquire the habit of letting oneself go; and the least that one can safely do is attentively to observe the dreams, those reactions of the unconscious which indicate barometrically the imperfect state of our adjustment.

"Unlike other psychologists, I therefore think it necessary for the patient, even after analysis, to remain in contact with his unconscious, if he wishes to avoid a relapse. That is why I am persuaded that the true end of analysis is attained when the patient has arrived at an adequate knowledge of the methods by which he can maintain contact with his unconscious and at a psychological understanding broad enough for him to discern, as far as possible, and whenever necessary, the direction of his life-line, for without this his conscious mind will not be able to follow the flow of libido and consciously sustain the individuality he has achieved. . . ." [4]

1. I. Jay Dunn, "Analysis of Patients Who Meet the Problems of the First Half of Life in the Second," *The Journal of Analytical Psychology*, VI, 1 (London: 1961).

2. *Ibid.*

3. Jung, *Two Essays on Analytical Psychology*, p. 287.

4. *Ibid.*, pp. 288–89.

CHAPTER TWELVE

Compensatory, or Complementary, Dreams

Compensation as a principle of self-regulation of the psyche is a fundamental postulate of the Jungian frame of reference. In Jung's thought the compensatory, or complementary, factor is always present in dreams, as described earlier.

Dreams analyzed in this chapter have been taken from the files of Jungian analysts and the writings of Jung. Some are self-evident instances of compensation-at-work, and in others, a brief explanation accompanies the dream text supplying the necessary information, generally about the "conscious situation" of the dreamer in question.

DREAM ONE [1]

"I was on a highway at the foot of a high hill, and upon the hill was a castle, and in that castle was a high tower, the donjon. On top of that high tower was a loggia, a beautiful open contrivance with pillars and a beautiful marble balustrade and upon that balustrade sat an elegant figure of a woman. I looked up—and I had to look up so that I felt a pain in my neck even afterwards—the figure I saw was my patient!

"Then I woke up and instantly I thought, 'Heavens! Why does my unconscious put that girl so high up?'

"And immediately the thought struck me, 'Because I have looked down upon her.'"

The conscious situation was this: Jung's patient was a young woman in her early twenties who had been born in India of wealthy Europeans and raised by an Indian amah. When the family returned to Europe the girl had "gone wrong," as the saying goes. In short order her reputation had sunk to the level that earned her the nickname "the great whore of Babylon." Her make-up and flamboyant dress were such that Jung reported he felt ashamed in front of his own maids when she was in his office for an hour. As a physician called in by the embarrassed family of the girl, Jung naturally attempted to contain his personal feelings about her and to all intents was able to do so—but the fact remained, their consultations got nowhere. After a time Jung felt obliged to tell her there was really nothing he could do for her. Then he had the above dream. He related subsequently, "I really had thought she was bad. My dream showed me that this was a mistake and I knew that I had been a bad doctor. So I told her the dream at once and it worked miracles."

DREAM TWO [2]

The compensatory factor is not always such an open-and-shut case, as the following, brought to Jung by a well-adjusted, happy and successful young man, illustrates.

"My father is driving away from the house in his new car. He drives very clumsily and I get very annoyed over his apparent stupidity. He goes this way and that, forwards and backwards, and maneuvers the car into a dangerous position. Finally he runs into a wall and damages the car badly. I shout at him in a perfect fury that he ought to behave himself. My father only laughs, and then I see that he is dead drunk."

The conscious situation of the dreamer was this: The young

man's relation to his father was excellent; he admired his father enormously because his father was successful and a good father to him. Nor is there a shred of fact in the dream story; his father would never behave like that even if drunk. And the young man himself was a most careful motorist; bad driving and even slight damage to the car would have irritated him greatly to be sure— but nothing like this had happened in real life. Now, obviously, the dream presents a most unattractive picture of the father and on the basis of a naïve application of the idea of compensation, you could not fail to conclude that underneath the seemingly good relations, the son must be harboring an intense animosity for the father which shows in the dream. But, Jung says, he could detect nothing of the sort; the son was not neurotic; his relationship with his father was genuinely one of affection and respect. What, then, was the dream trying to convey? Jung reasoned; "But, if his relation to his father is in fact good, why must the dream manufacture such an improbable story in order to discredit the father? In the dreamer's unconscious there must be some tendency to produce such a dream. Is that because he has resistances after all, perhaps fed by envy or some other inferior motive? But—before we burden his conscience . . . with young people a dangerous proceeding . . . we would do better to inquire not *why* he had this dream, but *what its purpose is*. The answer in this case would be that his unconscious is obviously trying to take the father down a peg. If we regard this as a compensation, we are forced to the conclusion that his relation to his father is not only good, but actually *too good*. In fact, he deserves the French soubriquet of *fils à papa*. His father is still too much the guarantor of his existence, and the dreamer is still living what I would call a provisional life. His particular danger is that he cannot see his own reality on account of his father; therefore the unconscious resorts to a kind of artificial blasphemy so as to lower the father and elevate the son. . . . An unintelligent father would probably take umbrage, but the compensation is entirely to the point, since it forces the son to contrast himself with his father, which is the only way he could become conscious of himself.

"The interpretation . . . struck home. It won the spontaneous assent of the dreamer. . . . But this interpretation was only possible when the whole conscious phenomenology of the father-son relationship had been carefully studied; *without a knowledge of the conscious situation the real meaning of the dream would have remained in doubt.*" (Italics mine.)

You will note that Jung was careful not to jump to conclusions and say anything which could have altered the young man's positive relationship with his father. "It is of overriding importance that no real values of the conscious personality should be damaged," says Jung,[3] "much less destroyed. . . . The recognition of the unconscious is not a Bolshevik experiment which puts the lowest on top and thus re-establishes in the reverse the very situation it intended to correct. . . . We must see to it that the values of the conscious personality remain intact, for unconscious compensation is only effective when it cooperates with an integral consciousness. . . . Assimilation (of the unconscious information) is never a question of 'this-*or* that' but always of 'this-*and* that.' " In other words, the unconscious *adds* to what you are in your conscious life, enlarging your awareness and increasing your insight into yourself and others.

DREAM THREE [4]

This dream and the next are brutally frank "comments" by the unconscious, quite clearly compensatory in character.

A highly gifted but indolent young woman dreamed that while she idled away her time in daydreams all of her belongings were removed from her room on her sister's orders. Here the dream is declaring that unless she can rouse herself to a personal effort she will become completely "destitute" and "homeless." In conscious life the dreamer passively drifted, without direction, relying on her family for support and waiting for a rich man to marry her, instead of making use of her talents. This dream penetrated sufficiently to effect a slight change in her attitude and she had another dream in which she saw herself beginning to make a half-hearted effort to repair her ramshackle rundown house. To her surprise as soon as she began to exert any effort at all, neighbors and workmen, more competent than herself, began to congregate in order to help her; now the work proceeded efficiently.

The sister was her Shadow, in this case the energetic and positive aspect buried in the dreamer's unconscious. She was one of those about whom, as the section on the Shadow related, it could be said that their Shadows contain gold, but these personalities prefer to funk the responsibilities of developing their native gifts.

DREAM FOUR [5]

Another woman dreamed that she was taking a pleasure trip with a very superficial and frivolous chatterbox of a friend. Although they were having a wonderful time she noticed that their car was being pursued by a truck driven by a madman who seemed intent on running them down and destroying them.

They tried to escape, but to her terror, she realized that the driver of her own car seemed to have a secret understanding with the murderous pursuer. She realized that destruction must be her inescapable fate unless she herself took the wheel.

Here too the dreamer is warned about the murderous effect of passively permitting another to "take the wheel," or "drive her car." The driver of her car is her Shadow; the mad pursuer, her Animus, with whom she is not in good relation. Often the Shadow and Animus contaminate each other in dreams as in real life. Sometimes they are represented as a married pair, a particularly tough constellation posing an extremely difficult challenge to that dreamer's consciousness.

DREAM FIVE [6]

Another record from Jung's own personal dream-experiences: "I once had a personal conflict with a Mr. A. I gradually came to the conclusion that the wrong lay more on his side than on mine. At this time I had a dream in which I had consulted a lawyer regarding a certain matter. He demanded for the consultation to my complete astonishment, no less than five thousand francs, to which I strenuously objected.

"The lawyer is an irrelevant figure remembered from my student days. The period is important because at that time I had many disputes and arguments. I associate this brusque type of lawyer with my emotion toward Mr. A.'s personality, as well as with the continuing conflict. I could now proceed along the objective level and say, Mr. A. is concealed behind the lawyer; therefore, Mr. A. demands too much from me. He is in the wrong. Shortly before this dream a poor student had tried to get me to lend him five thousand francs. Mr. A. is therefore a poor student, incompetent and needing help because he is at the beginning of his studies. Such a person has no business making claims nor holding opinions. The wish fulfillment would be as follows: My opponent is to be gently depreciated and pushed to one side and my peace of mind protected. In reality, however, I woke up at this place in the dream with the liveliest emotion about the presumption of the lawyer. I was by no means quieted by the "wish-fulfillment."

"Certainly the unpleasant A. affair is hiding behind the lawyer, yet it is worth noting that the dream has dragged up that unimportant attorney from my student days. The word lawyer brings to mind lawsuit, having rights, being right, and, with that, the remembrance of my student days when, right or wrong, I often stubbornly, obstinately, and opinionatedly defended my thesis in order to gain at least the appearance of superiority for myself. I feel that this trait has played its part in my encounter with Mr. A. Whereupon I know that it is really myself, a part of myself unadapted to the present, demanding too much, just as I used to. In other words, this part of me, still convinced right is on its side, wants to extort too much libido from myself. I know, then, that the moot question with Mr. A. cannot die because the obstinate contender in me still continues to care about a 'just' outcome."

As is obvious from Jung's comments, his "conscious situation" included the conclusion that he was right and his opponent wrong, to which the dream responded with images evocative of opinionated obstinacy—not at all the sort of thing he could wish for to substantiate his conclusion. Such compensatory functioning is always very individual in nature.

"It is therefore not easy to set forth any sort of special rules for the type of dream compensation," says Jung. "Its character depends at times upon the innermost character of the individual's whole being. The possibilities of compensation are countless and inexhaustible, although, with increasing experience, certain fundamental traits will gradually be crystallized out." [7]

DREAM SIX [8]

"My car had broken down; the steering wheel was broken off. I tried to repair it with an umbrella. Then somebody said: 'That has to be done differently. This way will never work.' I find that I live in a house which is dangerous in the evening and at night because it is ghost-ridden. I live on the top floor and have all the lights on. I hear steps and am terror-stricken. Then a voice says to me: 'It is better not to be alone here.' "

In conscious life, this dreamer's problem was not "aloneness" or loneliness, as might be expected from the remark he heard in his dream. As Dr. Whitmont analyzes the dream, the interpretation unfolds thus: Where, then, is one to look for the "aloneness"? The dream states it quite clearly: Here, on the *top floor*, living on the level of the head, with an overemphasis on intellectual consciousness (*all the lights on*). The dream also points out that his way of moving through life (the *automobile*) had failed. To the *umbrella* the dreamer associates the attitude of a distracted professor, one who is too absorbed in speculations. Objectively, an *umbrella* is one's means of protecting oneself against the weather, against the vicissitudes of nature. Thus the situation cannot be remedied by reliance on his intellectual capacities and self-protective efforts. In the *evening* and *night*, that is to say to-

ward the dusk of life (he was in his early sixties), there is danger
from ghosts, from energies which, owing to the limitedness of his
intellectual orientation, have been reduced to specters, to free-
floating anxieties and fears. In such a situation "it is better not to
be alone."

1. Jung, *Two Essays on Analytical Psychology*, p. 177. Jung himself had this dream.
2. Jung, *The Practice of Psychotherapy*, pp. 155–156.
3. *Ibid.*, pp. 155–156.
4. Edward C. Whitmont, "The Religious Aspects of Life Problems in Analysis," *Spring*, 1958.
5. *Ibid.*
6. C. G. Jung, "General Aspects of the Psychology of the Dream,"
Spring, 1956, 15–16.
7. *Ibid.*, p. 5.
8. Whitmont, *op. cit.*, pp. 51–2.

CHAPTER THIRTEEN

Reductive Dreams

DREAM ONE [1]

"I dreamed that I was reshingling our roof. Suddenly I heard my father's voice on the ground below, calling to me. I turned suddenly to hear him better, and, as I did so, the hammer slipped out of my hands, and slid down the sloping roof, and disappeared over the edge. I heard a heavy thud, as of a body falling.

"Terribly frightened, I climbed down the ladder to the ground. There was my father lying dead on the ground, with blood all over his head. I was brokenhearted, and began calling my mother, in the midst of my sobs. She came out of the house, and put her arms around me. 'Never mind, son, it was all an accident,' she said. 'I know you will take care of me, even if he is gone.' As she was kissing me, I woke up."

The conscious situation of the dreamer was this: An eldest child, 23 years old, he had been separated from his wife for a year; "somehow we could not get along together. I love both my parents dearly," he says, "and have never had any trouble with my father except that he insisted that I go back and live with my wife, and I couldn't be happy with her. And I never will."

The young husband who wants to stay home with mother appears, on the basis of his own "innocent" statements about himself, to be in the grip of a first-class Oedipal configuration, one of the reasons why we chose this dream as an example of the "Reductive" type. "Reductive" signifies *"reductio ad primam figuram"*; that is, "reduce-to-the-first-figure." The Freudian method concentrates primarily on getting to the root of complexes through techniques of *reductio ad primam figuram*. With significant frequency the analysis trails retrospectively back to childhood and a marked attachment to one of the parents, a complex which successfully disturbs normal adult development of sexual expression with a partner of the opposite sex. Dreams image complexes, as you have already been informed; thus, "reductive" dreams are those leading to the disturbing complex, eventually leading to the "first figure."

The Oedipus complex, positing incest and parricide as primary human motivations in the Freudian formula, is flatly refuted by Jung as "prime cause" and the qualitative divergence between the two approaches crystallizes at this bottom level of differing viewpoints on the Oedipal configuration. For these reasons, the presentation of the opposing Freudian and Jungian views on a widely misapplied "understanding" of the Oedipus complex is especially apropos.

In a nutshell, the orthodox Freudian position posits the Oedipus complex as inherent—those successful in adapting to the demands of adulthood, i.e., the attainment of normal genitality in both aim and object, do so by *sublimation* of this powerful impulse. The incest wish is understood literally as the wish for actual coitus with the real mother in the case of the male, and with the father in the case of the female. Civilization was possible because the psychical mechanics of sublimation made it possible, therefore sublimation "constitutes the primary constellating pattern of all impulse, thought and feeling, imaginative art, philosophy, mythology and religion, scientific research, sanity and madness." [2]

Jung rejects this hypothesis: "From this angle the whole edifice of civilization becomes a mere substitute for the impossibility of incest." To be sure the "first figure" to which the Freudian method leads points to the mother, in the damaged male, or the father with the impaired female, but Jung shows that however important the parental figures, they are so only in a certain context. Much more significant than the parent *per se* is the evidence that *incest as a motif is the primary figure*, recurring over and over again in primitive cultures, religious rites, myths, legends and folk tales. The basis of the incest is not "cohabitation but, as every sun myth shows, the strange idea of becoming a child again, of returning to the parental shelter and of entering into the mother in order to be reborn through her. But the way to this goal lies through incest, i.e., the necessity of finding some way into the mother's body. . . . The incest prohibition intervenes; consequently the sun myths and rebirth myths devise every conceivable kind of mother-analogy for the purpose of canalizing the libido into new forms and effectively preventing it from regressing to actual incest. For instance, the mother is transformed into an animal, or is made young again, and then disappears after giving birth, i.e., is changed back into her old shape. It is not incestuous cohabitation that is desired, but rebirth." [3]

But Jung does not dismiss the Freudian identification of the existence of a regression of libido to the complex called Oedipal, and his remarks are worth including for their bearing on this very important point.[4] "As you know, I am critical of Freud in this particular respect, but my criticism would not go so far as to deny the extraordinary power of the retrospective tendency (of the libido in regression). On the contrary, I consider it to be of the greatest importance, so important that I would not call any treatment thorough that did not take it into account. Freud in his analysis follows this regressive tendency to the end and thus arrives at the findings you all know. . . . I have suggested that it is not just a relapse into infantilism, but a genuine attempt to get at something necessary. There is, to be sure, no lack of infantile perversion. . . . When we try, conscientiously and without theoretical bias, to find out what the patient is really seeking in his father or mother, we certainly do not, as a rule, find incest, but rather a genuine horror of it. We find that he is seeking something entirely different, something that Freud only appreciates negatively: the universal feeling of childhood innocence, the sense of security, of protection, of reciprocated love, of trust, of faith, a thing that has many names. . . . I believe that incest and the other perverted sexual aspects are, in most cases, no more than by-products, and that the essential contents of the regressive tendency are really those which I have just mentioned."

The Jungian viewpoint casts quite a different light on the phenomenon oɪ the ubiquitous mother-complex charged to the Oedipus configuration, the term itself a misnomer if the compilation by Robert Graves [5] may serve as a criterion. *Graves traces at least twelve versions reaching back to the 13th century* B.C. Satirically commenting on the Freudian theory that the "Oedipus complex" is an instinct common to all men, he observes: "While Plutarch records (on Isis and Osiris 32) that the hippopotamus 'murdered his sire and forced his dam' he would never have suggested that every man has a hippopotamus complex."

"The Oedipus complex is a symptom," Jung declares uncompromisingly. "Just as any strong attachment to a person or a thing may be described as a 'marriage' and just as the primitive mind can express almost anything by using a sexual metaphor, so the regressive tendency . . . may be described in sexual terms as an 'incestuous longing for the mother.' But it is no more than a figurative way of speaking. The word 'incest' has a definite meaning and designates a definite thing, and as a general rule can only be applied to an adult who is psychologically incapable of linking his sexuality to its proper object." [6]

The young husband who wants to stay home with mother appears from the Jungian point of view to be failing to achieve the first plateau of adulthood, the successful transfer of his Anima-image to a woman other than his mother. Still, the full "conscious situation" is not known, and a Jungian requires it in order to deal with the current problem. His mother's participation in emasculating the dreamer, and his father's too—for all too often the dominance of the mother merely cloaks the abdication of the father from the masculine role in the family—are not known. What, for instance, is the psychological orientation of this family? Presumably each wants "happiness" for himself individually and for each other as well but what is their notion of this state? Is it assumed to be a condition arrived at as though it were the destination of a Sunday outing? Can it be inferred that the family understands that the realities of daily life shared with living people must necessarily reflect quite a number of educated awarenesses about individual give-and-take that in the long run insure their mutual happiness? On this basis Freudian and Jungian would agree: the young man lacks education in manhood and the recognition that the conditions of life include conflict, struggle, effort and will-ing.

DREAM TWO [7]

Another instance of a Reductive-type dream, very different from the first, was related to Jung by a friend of his.

"I saw horses being hoisted by thick cables to a great height. One of them, a powerful brown horse which was tied up with straps and was hoisted aloft like a package, struck me particularly. Suddenly the cable broke and the horse crashed to the street. I thought it must be dead. But it immediately leapt up again and galloped away. I noticed that the horse was dragging a heavy log along with it, and I wondered how it could advance so quickly. It was obviously frightened and could easily cause an accident. Then a rider came up on a little horse and rode along slowly in front of the frightened horse, which moderated its pace somewhat. I still feared that the horse might run over the rider, when a cab came along and drove in front of the rider at the same pace, thus bringing the frightened horse to a still slower gait. I then thought, now all is well, the danger is over."

The conscious situation of the dreamer was as follows: He was an ambitious and capable businessman, headed for success because of his capabilities and capacity for hard work. He had been disappointed in beginning a business venture of his own in the past, but had not given up hopes for the future in that direction. His pastimes were mountain-climbing and travel; just about the time of the dream he had had a great desire to do both. His wife, however, was pregnant and could not accompany him; she would not permit him to go alone, so he had abandoned his plans. Her pregnancy had obliged them to give up a trip they had intended to make to America. They both loved traveling and had traveled a good deal. They realized, however, that as soon as there are children in the family it becomes much more difficult to move about and that one cannot go everywhere. The disappointment to him in having had to give up the trip was especially disagreeable as he had hoped to establish some new and important business connections.

Jung took up the individual points of the dream thus: He asked his friend to amplify the dream imagery at each point, the hoisting of the horses, for example. To the dreamer it seemed as if the horses were being hoisted onto a skyscraper but tied up just like horses that are lowered into mines to work. Other imagery: the dreamer had recently seen a magazine illustration of a skyscraper being built and had been struck by the dizzying height at which men had to work. *Skyscraper*—America; *height*—his ambitions for his business. *Mines*, means, literally, "moutain-work" (*Bergwerk*). *Mountain* is also height; to-climb-a-mountain is to get to the top; work-labor. The underlying idea might be: "By labor one gets to the top." Height is expressed very vividly in the dream by the "dizzy height" of the skyscraper which stands for America, the goal of the dreamer. The image of the horse is obviously associated with the idea of labor, heavy work: as heavy as the work the horses have to do in the mines. Moreover, in colloquial speech there are expressions such as "to work like a horse," "to be in harness" and so forth, which substantiate this interpretation.

The powerful brown horse which impressed the dreamer particularly, seemed to Jung to image the dreamer himself. But there was some contradiction in the interpretation that "By labor one gets to the top" in view of the dream imagery whereby the horses were being hoisted by thick cables and not actually functioning under their own power. Here the dreamer remembered how much he scorned tourists who had themselves hoisted up the moutain peaks like "sacks of flour." He himself had never needed anybody's help. The various horses in the dream are therefore "other people" who have got to the top but not by their own efforts. The powerful brown animal who crashed into the street, who at first seemed dead to the dreamer but eventually galloped away, yielded this association: The street was the same in which his business was, where he once hoped to make his fortune. Nothing had come of those plans. His disappointment was intense—but the horse did get up and gallop away; so had he not allowed himself to be "got down."

The log that the horse dragged along with it made him recall that once he had been nicknamed "the log" on account of his powerful, stocky figure—Jung's conjecture was correct. As for the horse galloping away in fright, Jung's interpretation is crystal-clear:

"A new section of the dream obviously begins at this point, probably corresponding to a new period of his life, if the interpretation of the preceding part is correct. I therefore asked (the dreamer) to fix his attention on the horse galloping away. He stated that for a moment in the dream he saw another but very indistinct horse appear beside the brown one; it too was dragging a log and started galloping off with the roan. But it was very indistinct and disappeared immediately. This fact (together with its late reproduction) indicates that the second horse was under a special repressive influence and was therefore very important. (The dreamer) was dragging the log with someone else, and this person must be his wife, with whom he is harnessed 'in the yoke of matrimony.' Together they pull the log. In spite of the encumbrance which might easily hinder his progress he was able to gallop, which again expresses the thought that he can't be got down. (The dreamer) associated the galloping horse with a painting . . .'A Moonlight Night,' where galloping horses are shown on the cornice of a building. One of them is a lusty stallion, rearing up. The image of the galloping horse, therefore (which at first galloped in a pair) leads to the very suggestive painting . . . Here we get a quite unexpected glimpse into the sexual nuance of the dream, where till now we thought we could see only the complex of ambition and careerism. The symbol of the horse, which so far has shown only the side of the hard-working domestic animal, now takes on a sexual significance, clearly confirmed by the horse scene on the cornice. There the horse is the symbol of passionate impulsive desire, which is obviously identified with the sexual drive. As the associations show, the dreamer feared that the horse would fall or that the impetus of the moving log might "pitch it into something." This . . . can easily be interpreted as (his) own impetuous temperament, which he feared might involve him in thoughtless acts.

"The dream continues: 'Then a rider came up on a little horse and rode along slowly in front of the frightened horse, which moderated its pace somewhat.' His sexual impetuosity is bridled. (He) described the rider as resembling his superior in dress and general appearance. This fits in with the first part of the interpretation: his superior moderates the rash pace of the horse, in other words, he hinders the dreamer from advancing too rapidly by keeping ahead of him. But we still have to find out whether the sexual thought we have just discovered is developed further. Perhaps it is hiding behind the expression 'a little horse,' which seemed to me significant. (He) stated that the horse was small and dainty like a rocking horse, and this reminded him of an incident from his youth. While still a boy he saw a woman far advanced in pregnancy wearing hoops, which were then in fashion. This comical sight seemed to need an explanation, so he asked his mother whether the woman was wearing a little horse under her clothes. (He meant one of those little horses that used to be worn at carnivals or circuses and were buckled to the body.) Since then, whenever he saw women in this condition, it reminded him of his childish hypothesis. His wife, as we have said, was pregnant, and her pregnancy was mentioned as an obstacle to traveling. Here it bridles an impetuosity which we must regard as sexual. This part of the dream is obviously saying: 'The wife's pregnancy imposes restraints on her husband.' Here we have a very clear thought which is evidently strongly repressed and extraordinarily well hidden in the meshes of a dream that seems to be composed entirely of upward-striving symbols. But evidently the pregnancy is still not a sufficient reason for restraint, for the dreamer feared the horse might nevertheless run over the rider. Then comes the slowly advancing cab which slows down the pace of the horse still more. When I asked (him) who was in the cab, he recalled that there were children. The children, therefore, were obviously under a repression, with the result that the dreamer only remembered them on being questioned. It was a 'whole cartload of children'. . . . The cartload of children checks his impetuosity.

"The meaning of the dream is now perfectly clear and runs as follows: the wife's pregnancy and the problem of too many children imposes restraints on the husband. This dream fulfills a wish, since it represents the restraint as already accomplished. Outwardly the dream . . . looks meaningless, but even in its top layer it shows clearly enough the hopes and disappointments of an upward-striving career. Inwardly it hides an extremely personal matter which may well have been accompanied by painful feelings."

Reductive Dreams may be understood as fulfilling their purpose when their dreamers, particularly younger people, can come to an understanding of their repressions and projections in terms of a purely personal psychology. For others, notably those who have successfully adapted to the demands of the first half of life, interpretation of dreams on the Reductive level simply does not resolve their problems and the unconscious sends forth quite different types of dreams demanding from the dreamer another adaptation to another reality.

1. Quoted in *The Hero With a Thousand Faces* by Joseph C. Campbell (New York, Meridian Books, 1955).

2. Joseph Campbell, *The Masks of God* (New York: Viking Press, 1959), p. 76.

3. C. G. Jung, *Symbols of Transformation* (New York: Pantheon Books, 1956), pp. 223–224.

4. C. G. Jung, *The Practice of Psychotherapy* (New York: Pantheon Books, 1954), p. 32.

5. *Op. cit.* (Oedipus Rex, according to the 1950 *Columbia Encyclopedia*, was the hero of Greek mythology who killed his father and married his mother. Laius, King of Thebes, and his queen, Jocasta, had a son, Oedipus, of whom it was foretold that he would murder his father. The baby was exposed on Mt. Cithaeron, but he was brought by a shepherd to the King of Corinth. When Oedipus was grown he learned from an oracle that he would kill his father and marry his mother, so he fled Corinth, thinking his foster parents were his real parents. At a crosssroad he met Laius, quarreled with him, killed him, and then proceeded to Thebes. There he gained the widowed queen's hand by answering the riddle of the Sphinx, and thus the prophecy was fulfilled. After many years Oedipus learned the truth from the seer Tiresias and the shepherd. In an agony of horror he blinded himself, and Jocasta killed herself.)

6. Jung, *The Development of Personality*, p. 75.

7. C. G. Jung, *The Psychogenesis of Mental Disease* (New York· Pantheon Books, 1960), pp. 57–62.

CHAPTER FOURTEEN

Reactive Dreams

DREAM ONE

Here is a dream that could hardly have spoken more plainly to the dreamer if it had called on the telephone to warn her.

This woman, a writer and long-time friend of the author, had been driving herself unsparingly to meet a deadline which was drawing near. Although she felt harassed almost beyond endurance, the thought of how much still remained to be completed before the date she had agreed to turn in her manuscript prodded her to keep going night and day. Then she had a dream in which appeared a man known to her in real life, who ranked very low in her opinion. She thought him a coarse and obstinate man, totally insensitive to the needs of anyone but himself, as she had observed in his relations to his wife and family. In her dream that man entered the room where the writer was working, went to a closet, opened the door and looked inside, said something harsh to somebody there, then slammed the door, turned and left the room.

As soon as he had left the dreamer looked into the closet.

Chained to the floor was a young man, pitifully emaciated, his head hanging low on his breast. The dreamer was aghast at this evidence of the man's cruelty, it was really torture, to the unknown, esthetic-looking prisoner.

Awakening with lively emotions of burning indignation and pity mingled, the writer thought it over. She was well-versed in the ways of dreams and understood a great deal about depth psychology. Very quickly she recognized the brutality of one aspect of her own Animus, in the figure of the jailer; he was powerful, and unbridled, he tortured the other aspect of the Animus, the creative, esthetic side, who was no match for him—without the aid of her conscious will! Very quickly she made different arrangements with the publisher about the deadline and pulled herself up short from the role of torturer to her own creative side.

DREAM TWO [1]

Here is another dream expressing Reaction, of one of Jung's normal patients—that is, one who was neither neurotic nor pathologically disturbed.

The young man dreamed of the illness of his sister's two-year-old daughter.

Some time before this his sister had, in fact, lost a son through illness, but at the time of the dream, none of his sister's children was ill. At first the dreamer was baffled by the dream because it failed to fit the facts. Also, there was no particularly close tie between the dreamer and his sister and he could not feel that this sick child was personally significant to him. However, Jung pressed him for the ever-important subjective associations he might have and suddenly the dreamer recalled that two years earlier (the sick child's age was two) he had taken up the study of occultism. In the course of pursuing this interest he had discovered psychology. The child-image evidently represented his interest in the psyche and it struck the dreamer forcibly that the study of occultism had something sickly about it. Through the implied criticism certain changes of attitude were brought about, of a kind one could never think up rationally, and a dead point in his life was overcome.

DREAM THREE [2]

A man in modest circumstances decided to leave his wife and children in order to marry a wealthy girl, many years his junior, with whom he had "fallen in love." He had not, of course, arrived at his decision without agitation of mind, but finally his mind was made up. Then he had a dream.

He was about to set out on a trip to a rather out-of-the-way destination. Rushing off hurriedly he passed a group of respectable-looking elderly men who disapprovingly shook their heads. Disregarding them he pushed on, when suddenly, from out of the clouds, a huge hand appeared, took hold of him, and shoved him right back to his starting-point.

The dreamer knew something of depth psychology; the dream had frightened him very much and he sought counsel. Dr. Whitmont's remarks follow in their entirety.

"The dream shows that what he (the dreamer) sets out to do is 'out of the way' and contrary to generally accepted moral standards (the disapproving elders: Freud's superego). It shows he may disregard these considerations with relative impunity and still manage to get by. Something else, however, will not be disregarded. A power that reaches from heaven to earth does not allow him to proceed. Whether we call this power the inner judge or conscience, the moral integrity of the personality, the will of life or, like the symbolic image of this dream, the hand of God, we merely substitute various words and varying symbolic representations which all express the same thing: that is, an entity both unknown and unknowable, yet objectively real, transpersonal, and supreme, which, in many symbols and under many names, has been instinctively acknowledged by mankind throughout the ages. The warning of the dream is that the 'hand of God' will not permit him to proceed.

"Of course one is justified in asking: May not dreams of this sort express the patient's own unadmitted and unconscious wishes, rather than 'objective demands'? Perhaps the dreams show that these people were in fact scared, anxious to get out of the fight, and rationalising their escapist attitudes under the cloak of traditional religious symbolism. Perhaps the dreams 'invented' all this impressive symbolism merely for the purpose of furnishing the dreamer with plausible alibis. And indeed there is no question but that quite often analysis of the personal unconscious will uncover just such tendencies.

"Quite as frequently, however, the dreamer is startled, even shocked, by material like the above, which far from fulfilling his wishes or repressing any attitude he can even remotely recognize as his own, seemingly actually makes a demand upon him, confronting him with a point of view apparently entirely unacceptable and opposed to his own desires and convictions. Moreover, if we observe (when we are able to) how such dreams relate to the dreamer's further development and what happens if their warnings or demands are disregarded, we may seem further justified in accepting, at least as a practical working hypothesis, the 'objectiveness' of the nonpersonal source of the 'absolute' meaning. The man who dreamed of the hand from heaven came, subsequently, to face his responsibility and decided himself to remain with his family."

DREAM FOUR [3]

Jung tells the following short dream and interpretation (condensed here).

A young man dreams: "I was standing in a strange garden and picked an apple from a tree. I looked about cautiously, to make sure that no one saw me."

The young man's conscious situation was this: He remembered as a boy having plucked a couple of pears surreptitiously from a neighbor's garden. He had a bad conscience about it, which reminded him of the fact that yesterday he had also had a bad conscience or rather a feeling of embarrassment as if he were doing

something wrong when he met a young lady—a casual acquaintance—in the street. He also associated the apple-picking with the
Garden of Eden and with the fact that he had never really understood why the eating of the forbidden fruit should have had such
dire consequences, for it seemed to him an unjust act of God, because God had made men as they were, with all their curiosity
and greed. Another association: sometimes his father had pun-
ished him for certain things in a way that seemed to him incomprehensible. The worst punishment had been bestowed on him
after he was secretly watching girls bathing. This reminiscence
led to the confession that he had recently begun a love affair with
a housemaid but had not yet carried it through to its natural conclusion. On the evening before the dream he had had a rendez-
vous with her.

The total effect of the dreamer's associations point to his feeling of guilt—and a strong reference to the affair he is involved in
with the housemaid which has not yet culminated. In this
dream his erotic experiences have a tinge of guilt—which he
feels, but his association with the Fall is that he had never really
grasped why the punishment should have been so drastic. This association throws light on the reasons why he did not think simply, "What I am doing is not right." He didn't think that, for the
simple reason that he didn't know that he might *himself* condemn
his conduct as morally wrong. So far as his conscious ideas on this
matter were concerned, he believed that his conduct didn't matter
in the least, morally, as all his friends were acting in the same way.

Jung's remarks are thought-provoking, to say the least, with
respect to this demonstrable insistence on a moral standard, as
dreams will image. "Now whether this dream should be considered meaningful or meaningless depends on a very important
question, namely, whether the standpoint of morality handed
down through the ages, is itself meaningful or meaningless. . . .
Mankind must obviously have had very strong reasons for devis-
ing this morality, for otherwise it would be truly incomprehensible why such restraints should be imposed on one of man's

strongest desires. If we give this fact its due, we are bound to pronounce the dream to be meaningful, because it shows the young man the necessity of looking at his erotic conduct for once from the standpoint of morality. . . . We should have to say that the young man, hypnotized by his friends' example, has somewhat thoughtlessly given way to his erotic desires, unmindful of the fact that man is a morally responsible being who, voluntarily or involuntarily, submits to the morality that he himself has created."

Morality, in the light of depth psychology, is a *secular matter*, not an ecclesiastical impost.

The outstanding characteristic of the dreams related in this section you will recognize to be a morality factor. The "Hand of God" dream is particularly striking. Nothing whatever is asserted about a "God," you will notice. What is evident is rather more an implied but existent standard of ethical action, the violation of which causes psychological repercussions.

Jung says of this factor: "It should never be forgotten that morality was not brought down on tables of stone from Sinai and imposed on the people, but is a function of the human soul, as old as humanity itself. Morality is not imposed from outside; we have it in ourselves from the start—not the law, but our moral nature without which the collective life of human society would be impossible. That is why morality is found at all levels of society. It is the instinctive regulator of action which governs the collective life of the herd . . ."

We have particularly brought forward this characteristic emphasis by Jung on the morality factor as innate in the psyche as the sexual factor. From this instinct for morality the religious function is considered by Jung to be the flower in the hierarchy of the instincts. We shall not digress to a discussion of the religious function, but we may note that the individual psyche is not stamped with any creed or form; it is these which are imposed from the outside, most influentially by parents and through education. The religious function Jung speaks of stems from the

Latin root *"religio"* or *"religiare,"* which meant "careful observation." Such was the attitude essential for those who sought healing in the ancient abatons through the "dream that came from God." After their vision they were called "religious," that is, they were "bound-to" the healing God. The same attitude of "careful observation" precisely describes how to attend to the activities of the unconscious.

1. Jung, *The Practice of Psychotherapy*, pp. 44–45.
2. Edward C. Whitmont, *Spring*, 1958, p. 53.
3. Jung, *The Structure and Dynamics of the Psyche*, pp. 243–44.

CHAPTER FIFTEEN

Prospective Dreams

A New York analyst, Dr. Eugene Henley, contributes the following two dreams from his files. Both are of the Prospective type, but the elements of Compensation and Reaction are plainly discernible.

"I want to give you two dreams, one of an extravert, the other an introvert, each around fifty years of age. First, the dream of the extravert at a place in life where he feels himself blocked. He can't manage his libido. In his office, though up to now he has always been a shining model of efficiency and resourcefulness, he finds himself quavering and asking advice of his subordinates. His memory fails him, he can't make decisions. The office staff is alternately worried about and amused over him and urges him to take a vacation. 'We'll get along without you for a couple of months, you'll see,' they tell him. But the thought of being so little needed makes him feel useless. He's always been the 'big shot' in the office; they certainly couldn't let him go for a couple of months. He wouldn't let them down. Not he.

But the doctor is finally consulted after some rather serious lapses in his business life and at home, and his wife begins to plan a vacation. But our friend doesn't want to go. He doesn't want to be any place where he has to 'see people,' he insists. 'Don't know what to say to anybody these days.' And at home he's so 'nervous,' how could he stand any time there? The house would smother him if he were 'tied' down to it. No, he'd have to keep on at the office, where he was 'interested.' But was he interested? Sometimes everything would go blank there, he remembered. What a hell of a mess! All these years he'd slaved at his desk, and now where was he? Gee, wouldn't it be great to be a kid again? Then he dreamed the following:

"He is on the ground floor of his office building in New York, in the marble lined lobby of its solid structure built high into the air. Suddenly the building begins to tremble and sway. Perhaps it is going to collapse. Everybody is rushing out. He darts about, even tries to enter the elevator. But somebody shouts to him to 'Beat it!' and he runs to the street—just before the building falls. Now all the buildings are swaying, they totter and crash. The whole city topples into ruins.

"Then the city is gone and in its place is a vast plain, or *desert*. Nothing is seen except a restless black *horse* roving over the desert-plain apparently seeking something. The dreamer watches intently and notes that the black horse stops once or twice and paws the earth as if in search of an object. After a time he seems to have found this thing and the dreamer goes over to where the animal stands. There, almost submerged in the ground, lies the inert figure of a man. The dreamer observes his swarthy skin and heavy black beard. Strange, this fellow seems to be an *Arab*. He thinks he must 'get the Arab somewhere for help,' so he tries to lift him up to set him on the horse. But he can't lift this fellow, partly pinioned in the earth. He tugs and strains to no avail. He is terribly scared. The scene shifts, apparently to another part of the plain where a reddish stone tower stands before him. Now he is mounted on the black horse and riding into the arched door-

way of the tower. He expects to be carried into the inner court-
yard, but the horse suddenly careens helter-skelter onto the stone
stairway of the building. The rider can't stop him nor regulate
him in any way, and as they dash madly upwards the tower
changes into a modern house, like his own, actually, and the powerful brute is smashing into its walls. The animal's great strength
crashes the dreamer into the brick and mortar. The house topples, just as the office building had. The man wakes himself up
with a fearful outcry.

"Here we have a fairly obvious dream of a man so one-sided
that he has built up nothing against the time when mere ego interests fail him. He is a decent, kindly sort of man with an I.Q.
well above average and with his emotional development at a
childish level. A 'family man,' with interest limited to his business, 'the missus' and the kids. He hasn't even a hobby for his un-
used libido, but lays a good deal of store by his success rating in
the two-dimensional world of home and trade, with their strictly
conventional social interests. Once in a while he looks into a shop
window where pretty lingerie is on display and his phantasy fills
the blue silk nighties or lacy chemisettes with softly rounded
flesh. At such times he thinks of sending 'the missus' a big box of
Schrafft's chocolates!

"But it isn't an amusing picture, as his dream makes all too
clear, and at fifty-one his unconscious presents him with the fact
that he can't stand up to his one-sidedness any longer. In the dream
his business stronghold crashes, and when it's gone he sees a
desert about him, with his unconscious libido (*the black horse*)
roaming about in an effort to find *its natural master, the shadow,*
which it eventually comes upon in the nearly buried Arab. The
dreamer is an intuitive who knows nothing of his sensation side,
as impersonated by the strong, dark, desert man whom he has
never encouraged to live. The dream demonstrates that he has no
knowledge of how to revive the shadow and that without him the
dreamer is in a very dangerous position when mounted on the
Arabian steed. The animal libido goes wild when he tries to ride

it (because he isn't its master) and the desert castle (which under other circumstances might have come to mean his house of individuality) turns instead into the family home which breaks asunder when his black horse dashes into its walls.

"The dream portrays the dilemma of this extraverted man who knows nothing of his dark shadow side which is native to the desert, and whose anima has been projected into the wife. Her adequate feeling has taken over for him in every domestic situation. And his own persona has always performed his business and social duties in its own field. What then could have caused so great a psychological debacle? We'll consider this question after the next dream.

"Now for the dream of the introverted man. There is a short 'curtain raiser' which precedes the second dream by six or seven years and which I find significant enough to give you first.

DREAM TWO

"The dreamer is seated at a dining room table with two puddings placed before him. He is to have a portion of one of these and expects to be permitted a choice. Both puddings belong to his childhood, one a deliciously rich concoction filled with nuts and fruit and chocolate, topped with cream. The other is a tasteless dry mass—'straw pudding,' he calls it—which as a boy he always hated. But it was poor man's food, and he got it often. In the dream the two puddings are placed before him and as he reaches out for the tasty one, suddenly a thin, sharp-faced woman pulls it away. He knows this female to be Mrs. Grundy, 'who has always taken my most tempting food away,' he says.

"As a young boy this dreamer had already begun to carry a man's load of responsibility. He had to go to work while other boys were taking school for granted. He snatched his own 'book learning' wherever he could—across the street from his place of work, for example, where he ate his sandwich at noon, he was allowed to read anything he could find in a second-hand book shop. So the rich pudding was seldom available to him then, nor, psychologically now, at forty-nine. Now we come to the second dream.

"This man finds himself in Hitler's Germany. Incidentally, he is of Anglo-Saxon ancestry and has never lived in Germany. But in the dream he is there and unable to get a passport to leave. He experiences a terrifying sense of being trapped. Then he sees an old friend (a kind of double, much like himself). The friend is carrying an ancient tome which the dreamer recognizes as the Old Testament. He, the dreamer, places his hand on the Book, and to his horror knows that in touching it he has contracted syphilis. That is the whole dream.

"We have to recognize that the Old Testament lays great stress on obedience to the Law; not the law of a man's own being, but the Law of Jehovah, to be obeyed by all alike. It proclaims a social code which, in a regimented society like Nazi Germany, would infect everybody and so rule out individual freedom. The unconscious uses syphilis as its symbol of the so-called 'social disease' of Nazi regimentation. The Mrs. Grundy pattern likewise creates a social infection of 'respectability' as opposed to genuine reality, in man's attitude to life. Our dreamer is held without passport because of Mrs. Grundy in a world where the social goose-step is his life rhythm and threatens his destruction. His own association with syphilis is this: 'Decay and ruin; mental and moral and physical.' This is a terrible prognosis for his future.

"To my knowledge, neither of these two men whose dreams I have given you had ever had an hour of analysis. These are not the dreams of analyzed individuals. Quite the opposite, they show the deadly effect of one-sidedness and each dream states its unresolved moral unconsciousness of his introverted side, especially of sensation, as embodied in the Arab. It takes the unconscious libido (the black horse) to find his neglected master who would have loved to ride over the desert sands unimpeded. But the conscious side of the dreamer is unaware that anything in him wants to ride beyond the confines of his city office or family

home. But the Arab's libido is unbridled. The horse will acknowledge no master but his own. The wild ride into the tower-house
discloses explosive psychic material in the hysterical neurosis of
an extraverted man. This man's major problem is his failure to
recognize the inner claim of his introverted side, his problem of
the shadow.

"Our introvert presents a different picture, brought about
through his widely separated opposites. Tensions between intellect and emotion, between the lure of social glamor and the longing of the spirit to rove and be free, the great tug-of-war between the persona demands to propitiate Mrs. Grundy, and his
moody, ungracious anima. He tries to obliterate his extraverted
feeling shadow and in the end is nowhere master in his own
house. Ill, uncreative, childish—a highly gifted man destroyed as
his dream foretold." [1]

DREAM THREE

This dreamer had reached, in conscious life, a situation which
seemed utterly hopeless. He was a homosexual; he had fought
against the realization for years, but now that he recognized his
basic conflict, he could neither accept it as something to live with
nor envision how to overcome the problem. He had reached the
point of wondering whether it was worth continuing to live.
Then he had the following dream:

"I am in a desert. I think how wonderful it would be to discover a place where no one had ever walked before. Then I wonder: How strange! Heretofore I have always been interested in
historical places where people have already been."

Dr. Whitmont, whom I have quoted elsewhere, was counselor
to this man, of whom he says, "His association to a place of this
kind, never touched by human foot, was that it would be quite
unique and individual, that it would have an awe-inspiring quality, like original creation. For further amplification and to con-
cretize the experience, he was asked to paint this scene. Next time

he brought a painting of a man, himself, kneeling in the sand with extended hands. Asked for associations, he said: 'Prayer'; rather sheepishly adding that in the army, in combat, he himself had used to pray."

Interpreting the dream and the associated painting fantasy, Dr. Whitmont points out how the imagery depicts the dreamer's situation in life "in the sterile desert, in the hopeless waste land of his existence. There he is shown that the need is not for finding a way 'out' of it; rather, he has to discover a value 'within' the seeming confinement of his situation. This value is something most unique and individual, never before touched by any other person. It is therefore what can perhaps be best described as the central core of uniqueness in his being, which is to replace his habitual concern with traditional values (the historic places). This new attitude of search in the desert, he equates (by association) with prayer in the foxhole: that is, in the face of a destiny beyond his personal control.

"Thus, the meaning of his impasse is pointed out to him: the answer is to be found within the desert of his own life yet is not the product of his own making; it is a part of original creation, something never beheld, having an awesome and ultimate quality to be addressed in prayer, yet existing within his own life and personality." [2]

That this man was puzzled as much as deeply touched may be taken for granted. Fear is the inevitable reaction when you are confronted by some dreams, the message of which can only be construed as an intent to give new meaning and direction to the dreamer's life. Jung has formulated what the experience meant to his many patients: ". . . nothing less than a revelation when from the hidden depths of the psyche something arises to confront him —something strange that is not the 'I' and is therefore beyond the realm of personal caprice. He has gained access to the sources of psychic life . . ." The religious minded would say: guidance has come from God.

DREAM FOUR

The following dream, taken from a series discussed by Dr. James Kirsch of Beverly Hills, California, is an enlightening example of a Prospective dream late in a series when the dreamer had already won considerable insight into himself.

First, the conscious situation of the dreamer: He was a Hollywood writer who, before he went to Hollywood, had been a fine writer. Over the years he had written many screen plays and achieved success—but as Dr. Kirsch says, "his words to characterize his work for the movie industry were unprintable." He despised what he was doing and to boot, he could no longer write a good story, one that he believed was worth while. He was stuck, and barren, nor could he understand the impasse in his creativity.

After many long, involved dreams concerned with railroads, tunnels, elevators and airplanes, which showed tremendous confusion in the structure of his unconscious, began the dreams that "are a contribution of his unconscious to the understanding of our time," says Dr. Kirsch.

The Saga of the Uniform and the Dog [3]

"It is night.

"Two friends have played a joke on me. They have rigged me up in a soldier's khaki uniform. But after putting the uniform on, it ceases to be a joke. It turns out to be a grave and real problem: I am compelled to wear the uniform and not my own shirt and trousers.

"But how and where am I to get the uniform on and my own trousers and shirt off? I can not simply undress anywhere with people looking on. I must find a place where the act can be done.

"The uniform has been rolled into a small bundle which I carry under my arm. My wife appears for the first time. She joins me in the search for a place where I can change from my shirt and trousers into the uniform. We hurry everywhere. We go to various houses. To various cities. Night becomes day and passes again to night. But wherever I go, there are people too near for me to take off my clothes and put on the uniform.

"I go to a house in Middletown, scene of my childhood. I go at night into the men's room of a railroad station. I stealthily trespass in the honey-combed ramshackle house of strangers in a country home. But there is always someone close by refusing to allow me to change; or too many people nearby so that I can't take off my clothes.

"I go down a street, quiet and still. About to change, I see a Jewish lady across the street with her baby and I run away for fear she will observe me. At last my wife and I go into a New York department store. It caters exclusively to women. It is well-lighted; modern; chic. Will I be able to take off my trousers here and change into the uniform? My wife acts as watch-out while I go into a phone booth to make the change. But women are opening the door of the booth and I give up the attempt. Embarrassing episodes follow one another; wherever I go I cannot make the change. I go down into the cellar of the store. I walk out on the scaffolding of a new addition to the store. To no avail. Now we are out of the store. We drive away in a taxi. When we are miles from the store we realize my dog is missing. We grow hysterical. Hurry, cabbie, hurry back to the store! Our beloved dog is there! We must find him! As we approach the store I see people on the sidewalk with dogs but to my grief, my dog is not among them.

"I see a clock. Its hands point to nine-thirty in the morning. I realize that everything has occurred since dawn—a few hours. I rush into the store—it is broad daylight—hurrying up wide marble steps, up, up, up. On either side of the marble stairs are monstrous, fantastic mad dogs leashed to the wall with chains of steel. Foam pours from their mouths. Their eyes are red with madness. They growl and lunge at me. I run between this passageway of wild dogs . . . I must find my dog. . . . Floor after floor. . . . And on another staircase landing there are beautiful wild deer heads stuffed and set into the wall. Suddenly the heads lunge and snap at me. I hurry on. I find many dogs but not my dog.

"My wife and I arrive at a woman friend's. It is night. She lives in a city apartment. There is the familiar crowd of guests which I know so well. The woman friend is tense. The guests begin to leave. We presume only a few of us will stay on. My wife orders the friend to relax and says she will prepare ham and eggs for the few remaining people. But when we are ready to relax and eat, we discover that only four people have left—the rest stayed on.

"I look out the window into the street below. It is night. Then I see a middle-aged Jew and his family with my dog on a leash. My dog jumps into a black automobile with them. My dog is lost again and I do not know how to get him from this family. . . ."

Dr. Kirsch interprets as follows:

"The theme of the dream is clearly indicated in the first few sentences. Two friends have played a joke on the dreamer. These friends are two men of the world, successful and extraverted, with excellently functioning *personas*. They rig up the dreamer in the soldier's khaki *uniform*; that is, they put him into something which deprives him of his present *persona*. This gives him uniformity and the appearance of a fighter. Nevertheless, the situation is perplexing, since it is first stated in one way and then in another. To begin with, he says they have forced the uniform upon him and he complains that he has to wear it. Then, in the second paragraph of the dream, it appears that he has to get this uniform on and his own shirt and trousers off. At first he considers it a joke to accept in himself the uniformity of man. He is afraid that wearing this uniform will make him a completely undistinguished person. On the other hand, he also realizes that he is a human being and, as such, that he must share the weaknesses and strengths of mankind. To put on a uniform would mean that he accepted these universal human qualities only from the outside. He does not see at this point that to accept the common man is a much deeper problem, that it entails also meeting his soul and accepting his human instincts. The inwardness of the process that is necessary is expressed by the fact that he is joined on his quest by the *Anima* in the shape of his *wife*, and that later on he meets the *dogs*. That the *dogs* appear as *mad dogs* has partly to do with the fact that he attempts to accept the ordinary human being (whom he calls Mr. Smith) only from the outside; and partly with other aspects . . . which I cannot go into here.

"At first it appears to him as only a joke to give up his own ideas and attitudes to the collective—to take on the ideas of other people and outside groups, but once having accepted uniformity and conformity, he works hard at keeping it up. This urge to accept the common man on the outside only is what pushes him into such strong conflict. It is against human nature to extinguish the spark of individuality and to accept one's common humanity only in the form of external uniformity and conformity. (This is the vital problem of our time, which expresses itself in Fascist and Communist ideologies.) Man can only be Man if he truly expresses himself; and society should function in such a way as to help him. If society tries to force identical attitudes and convictions upon every individual human nature, with its indestructible individual needs, and if he attempts to conform to collective opinions and attitudes, the unconscious in him will rebel and produce a neurosis. In a case like this, a man fears nothing so much as to be aware of his true Self. Yet in the various scenes of the dream we see the unconscious trying to help him to do exactly that, first in the figure of the Anima and later in the form of the dogs. Here the fear of inner conflict with the Self appears toned down to an affect which seems no more than embarrassment. However, the embarrassment is strong enough to cause him difficulty in looking for a place where he can change from an individual who can call himself his own master to one who would be simply a mass-man.

"Everywhere he goes there is always someone or something to remind him of his true Self. In one place it is his own childhood,

when he experienced himself in his totality and abounded in inexhaustible imagination. (N.B. As a boy of ten this dreamer had
written his first published story.) In another place he meets his
Jewish *Anima* (the dreamer is a Jew) with her child. (This is an
important aspect of the dream and reappears again in the last
dream. Unfortunately, I can not go into it here for lack of space,
but can only suggest that in this way he is confronted with the
sacred mythology of his people.) Meeting her, of course, makes
his change of clothing impossible too. So he comes to a New
York *department store*, a store which '*caters exclusively to
women*' and that seems to be a modernized variation of the
Tiamat world, or 'the world of the Mothers.' [4] This is, of course,
the most unsuitable place for an attempt at becoming one of the
many, because these women represent the living mythology of
the unconscious.

"At this point we can see clearly the tragic conflict of this
man: on the one hand he attempts to wear the uniform of the
conscripted writer, and on the other hand, the Mother World is
alive and active in him, even if he is at this time in a department
store. In other words, he tries to write in a way that satisfies the
needs of the masses, he tries to act as an entertainer; but in doing
so he necessarily contacts the world of his unconscious. That he
should don the uniformity of the writing mass-man started as a
joke. But he soon feels actually compelled to change into such a
personality, though his rich and original imagination, and contact
with the Mothers, makes this situation embarrassing and ridicu-
lous.

"So he leaves the world of the women, trying to solve the
problem by his *will*, expressed in the dream as a *taxi*. But as soon
as he uses his will he becomes separated from his instinct. The
dream expresses this by stating that his *dog* is missing, the *instinct*
that accompanies man. His dog is a male, and interestingly
enough, he has given him a very masculine name—the word for
'master' in another language. He realizes that to lose his instinct
and the spiritual intensity of his unconscious means a terrible loss;

and now he no longer tries to change his uniform, but looks for his instinctual creativity. At this point, the time is indicated—not the actual astronomical time, but the symbolic time. The psychological time is between nine and ten. *Numbers* frequently have a symbolic meaning in dreams, *nine* being the number of the Mothers (on account of the nine months of pregnancy) while *ten* represents a higher octave of *one*, the unity . . . So to be between nine and ten represents a midway point between the Mothers and the establishment of a higher unity.

"The dreamer goes back to the store but because he is without his instinct the unconscious has taken on a threatening aspect. There are no women here, with their gentleness and their busy activity; they have changed into monstrous and fantastic *mad dogs* who have to be leashed to the wall with *chains of steel*, with *strong rationalizations*. The *spiritual forces* are reduced to stuffed deer heads which occasionally snap at him. He does not realize at this point of the dream that the world of the archetypes changes into wild and ferocious affects if the instinct that should accompany man is not with him.

"So in this last part of the dream he goes again to the familiar crowd of the writers, hoping to get his bourgeois needs satisfied. Of course he cannot find his instinct within that writers' crowd; but looking out from there he sees his *dog* again, held by a middle-aged Jew and his family. His dog is lost once more because he cannot relate himself to the rich and specific mythology of his Jewish ancestry. The fact that he had lost contact with his Jewish heritage is a very important factor. Awareness of (it) is for him an indispensable milestone to the world of the human spirit."

Summing up this beautiful dream, the dreamer was made to realize he cannot be a mass-man, yet he must accept the collective aspect. He has first to find out who he really is and in this dream, though he does not quite find out, he does get a glimpse of his true nature.

The prospective function of the dream is "an anticipation in the unconscious of future conscious achievements, something like a preliminary exercise or sketch, or a plan roughed out in advance," Jung informs, but adds they must on no account be called prophetic, because they are "no more prophetic than a medical diagnosis or a weather forecast." [5]

1. Eugene Henley, "A Man's World," *Spring*, 1951.

2. Whitmont, "The Religious Aspects of Life Problems in Analysis," pp. 56–57.

3. James Kirsch, "Dreams of a Movie-Maker," *Spring*, 1950, 59–62.

4. N.B. "The world of the Mothers" and "Mother" refer to the Collective Unconscious, the source of creative imagination. See Faust II, Act 1.

5. Jung, *The Structure and Dynamics of the Psyche*, pp. 255–56.

CHAPTER SIXTEEN

Somatic Dreams

DREAM ONE

This dream, personally experienced, is classified as Somatic but it is also Prospective. Here is how it was recorded at the time it was dreamt:

I am driving my car home after visiting Alicia (a dearly-beloved friend). The night is stormy; it is very cold; the snow is falling heavily. The roads are glazed with ice and the driving is treacherous. I realize I'm in for it, so I hunch my shoulders, tighten my grip on the steering wheel, and concentrate on the road ahead, what patches of it I am able to see through the swirling snow as the windshield wiper swings back and forth and the headlights pierce the gloom blindly. Although I know it is dangerous driving, I feel confident, I know I can make it home all right. Of course, it would take a little longer than usual, but it would eventually be all over. Then, my glance fell on the water-gauge. The needle pointed very close to "empty." And suddenly I knew I was in trouble. If the water level were that low, would I have enough in the radiator to be able to drive home under my own power?

That was how the question presented itself in the dream.

Subsequent events proved the warning of real danger contained in that dream. After a series of jolting mishaps, a serious illness began which lasted several months.

A strange question is raised by warning dreams and by premonitions of accidents and disasters: can you alter fate by your foreknowledge? Speaking personally, so far as the warning related above was concerned, there was nothing that could have been done under the circumstances surrounding that time. Nevertheless, there was a decided psychological advantage in having the advance notice. Although the trouble came about, the blow was softened, and the message of the dream was heeded: we took good care not to venture too much. The dream warned: illness could have dire consequences, i.e., the motor of a car is irreparably damaged if the water runs out of the radiator and the car is kept running.

In "Precognition and Intervention," [1] an article by Louisa E. Rhine, co-worker with her husband J. B. Rhine in the research on ESP (Extra-Sensory Perception) one hundred and ninety-one cases are cited where a conscious attempt was made to work against the precognition. Prevention of the foreseen event was possible in only nine cases. Observations such as the Rhines', based on nearly thirty years of investigation of telepathic, prophetic and other psychic phenomena, offer some basis for speculating that the future does not happen by chance but exists already, in some form. If so, what then of the ancient arguments about the freedom of the will?

DREAM TWO

Jung tells [2] about a Somatic dream that contained a Prospective quality in a case he handled during his early medical practice.

"I was once consulted in the case of a seventeen-year-old girl. One specialist had suggested that she might be in the first stages of progressive muscular atrophy, while another thought it was a case of hysteria. In view of the second opinion, I was called in.

The clinical picture made me suspect an organic disease, but there were signs of hysteria as well. I asked for dreams. The patient answered at once: 'Yes, I have terrible dreams. Only recently I dreamt, I was coming home at night. Everything is as quiet as death. The door into the living room is half open, and I see my mother hanging from the chandelier, swinging to and fro in the cold wind that blows in through the open windows. Another time I dreamt that a terrible noise broke out in the house at night. I get up and discover that a frightened horse is tearing through the rooms. At last it finds the door into the hall, and jumps through the hall window from the fourth floor into the street below. I was terrified when I saw it lying there, all mangled.' "

As Jung explains, the gruesome character of the dreams alone makes one pause. However, all dreamers have anxiety dreams now and then. Therefore, let us look more closely into the meaning of the two main symbols, "mother" and "horse." "They must be equivalents, for they both do the same thing: they commit suicide. 'Mother' is an archetype and refers to the place of origin, to nature. . . . It also means the unconscious, our natural and instinctive life, the physiological realm, the body in which we dwell, or are contained . . . and it thus stands psychologically for the foundations of consciousness. . . . The word 'mother' which sounds so familiar, apparently refers to the best-known, the individual mother, to 'my mother.' But the mother-symbol points to a darker background which eludes conceptual formulation and can only be vaguely apprehended as the hidden, nature-bound life of the body. Yet even this is too narrow and excludes too many vital subsidiary meanings. The underlying primary psychic reality is so inconceivably complex that it can be grasped only at the farthest reach of intuition, and then but very dimly. That is why it needs symbols."

If we apply our findings to the dream, its interpretation will be: The unconscious life is destroying itself. That is the dream's message to the conscious mind of the dreamer and to anybody who has ears to hear.

"'Horse' is an archetype . . . widely current in mythology and folklore. As an animal it represents the non-human psyche, the subhuman, animal side, the unconscious. . . . It is evident, then, that 'horse' is an equivalent of 'mother' with a slight shift of meaning. The mother stands for life at its origin, the horse for the merely animal life of the body. If we apply this meaning to the text of our dream, its interpretation will be: The animal life is destroying itself.

"The two dreams make nearly identical statements, but, as is usually the case, the second is the more specific. . . . Note . . . there is no mention of the death of the individual. It is notorious that one often dreams of one's own death, but that is no serious matter. When it is really a question of death, the dream speaks another language.

"Both dreams point to a grave organic disease with a fatal outcome. This prognosis was soon confirmed." [3]

DREAM THREE

A Somatic dream demonstrating Compensation and Reaction as well, is the following, taken from a collection of dreams [4] which were compiled by a Berlin analyst during the years of Hitler's reign. During this period she worked at the neurological clinic at the University of Berlin. In an endeavor to trace what the unconscious of those consulting her might be revealing, as a sense of guilt, or participation, she kept a careful record. Of course, all of her patients were "somatically" affected; in a sense, that was the reason she was consulted. But the following example did not show an obvious pathological bias, at first, excepting as the curious symptom described hinted at it.

A German fighter pilot, twenty-two years old, an enthusiastic aviator, suddenly lost his ability to differentiate colors. Everything was either black or white. Aside from incapacitating him for his work, this proved to be a torture to him in private life. He felt as though he were looking at a never-ending movie in which all the colors were replaced by shades of black and white. A clinical examination did not reveal any organic disturbance and he was referred to a psychologist. At first he was cooperative, but entirely uncomprehending. His philosophy of life had no room for dynamics hidden behind simple facts. Everything that was useful to Germany, Hitler, and victory was good, everything else was bad. It was as simple as all that—black and white. During the first six weeks of his consultations with the psychologist he was unable to report a single dream. Then at last he arrived with one, rather, a fragment of a dream. He had seen his brother crossing the street. That was all.

"How was your brother dressed?" asked the psychologist.

He was taken aback, and then said, rather puzzled, "He was wearing his SS dress uniform, but everything was the wrong way. The uniform was white instead of black, and—yes—his face was entirely black." And he repeated once more, "Just the opposite of life."

At the next session, he exclaimed vehemently even before sitting down, "These dreams make a fool of me! I see everything the wrong way. Last night I saw my sister, you know, the one I never mention because she is a traitor." (The patient had previously told me that his sister was active in the underground movement and therefore had been separated from her family for years.) In the dream the sister was dressed in black prison garb and her face was shining white. He said, "I could have understood if the face had been black, for that would have shown her guilt."

The psychologist pointed out that in his other dream the much adored SS brother had had a black face. The patient was stunned and then said, "So the dreams do change everything around. They make the good appear black and the bad white."

Asked whether a prison garb was good and a uniform bad, he

answered, "Oh, the outside appearance does not matter. It's the face that is important."

Unknown to himself, the dreamer had already started to differentiate between outside and inside—between the persona, expressing the outside reality, and the face, the expression of the inside reality.

He still could not see clearly, but a crack of light had penetrated his darkness, and he no longer felt one hundred per cent secure. Many dreams followed, all of them undermining his black-and-white philosophy, planting doubts of his righteousness and opening the way to consciousness for him. But the psychic breakthrough did not materialize because he did not yet really want to see. The influence of his party faith was too strong.

Then something happened during a gay get-together when his adored SS brother began describing his experiences in a concentration camp. Apparently wine had made him talk and helped him to release the terrible pressure under which he also had unconsciously been suffering. That night the young flier dreamed as follows: A long column of concentration camp inmates with radiant white faces marched past Hitler. Hitler's face was black and he raised his hand, the color deep red blood. The dreamer wrote and mailed the dream to the psychologist, adding in his letter, "Now I have to find out for myself. I've got a pass to visit a concentration camp." Shortly afterward another letter arrived, saying, "I believed too long that black was white. Now the many colors of the world won't help me any more." He had committed suicide.

1. Louisa E. Rhine, "Precognition and Intervention," *The Journal of Parapsychology*, l.c., XIX: 1.

2. Jung, *The Practise of Psychotherapy*, pp. 158–160.

3. The horse as archetypal symbol is richly amplified in Jung's *Symbols of Transformation*, pp. 275–280.

4. Annaliese Aumuller, "Jungian Psychology in Wartime Germany," *Spring*, 1950, 17.

CHAPTER SEVENTEEN

Telepathic Dreams

Of the Telepathic dream, Jung states: "The authenticity of this phenomenon can no longer be disputed today. I have found by experience that telepathy does, in fact, influence dreams, as has been asserted since ancient times. . . . I would not, of course, assert that the law behind them is anything 'supernatural,' but merely something which we cannot get at with our present knowledge. Thus even questionable telepathic contents possess a reality character that mocks all expectations of probability. Although I would not presume to a theoretical opinion on these matters, I nevertheless consider it right to recognize and emphasize their reality. This standpoint brings an enrichment to dream analysis." [1]

DREAM ONE

Dr. Meier relates this dream of a man who had once been in analysis with him but had long departed Zurich. Suddenly he reappeared "in my consulting room," says Dr. Meier, "because he had had a series of dreams within a week's time which interested him tremendously. . . . I had to tell the man that he was obviously being reminded of the fact that he was going to die before long. He was shocked by this interpretation—he was at that time 64 years of age—but eventually he faced it with equanimity. Exactly nine months later he died quietly of a stroke after having attended to all his worldly affairs in view of his approaching death. He reported his last dream as follows:

" 'At the base of a high rocky wall a huge fire of wood was burning. The flames rose high up into the air and there was much smoke. The place was lonely and romantic. High in the air a number of big black birds dove deliberately into the fire and as each died its color was changed into white.' "

"In this case," Dr. Meier states, "the unconscious produced most impressive symbolic images, the last of which most clearly gives the dreamer the certainty of rebirth or, as you would call it in Christian terms, the resurrection of the soul." [2]

DREAM TWO

Another telepathic dream, one of a great many that came to the notice of Jung, occurred to an American woman visiting Zurich. The dream came with surprising suddenness and made a tremendous impression upon the woman because it opened up recollections of an aunt's home in America which she had not visited in more than twenty years. In fact, relations between these members of the family had been disrupted, which made the dream all the more incomprehensible. Its meaning became clear only subsequently.

The woman dreamed she was alone in a house and it was evening. She began to close all the windows. Then she went to lock the back porch door but there was no lock to the door. She tried to push pieces of furniture against the door in order to block it against intruders. Without question, a feeling of uneasiness possessed her but she could not tell from what it arose. The night grew darker and darker and more and more uncanny. All of a sudden the back porch door was flung open. A black sphere came in and moved forward until it had penetrated her body. She awakened, frightened and totally unable to understand the meaning of this harrowing dream.

Ten days later she received a letter from America informing her that the aunt in question, whose house she had been in in the dream, had died at exactly the time of the dream.[3]

Mrs. Aniela Jaffe, for many years confidential secretary to Dr. Jung and executive secretary of the C. G. Jung Institut in Zurich, published a book in 1958 titled *Geistererscheinungen und Vorzeichen* ("Ghostly Apparitions and Omens").[4] It records instance after instance of paranormal perception, substantiated by more than a thousand personal testaments of persons who were most emphatically not of the type considered to be "mediumistic" or "psychic" in the sense of being visionaries, but on the contrary, just ordinary people whose main concerns are the typical ones of getting on with their work and daily life. All of them had extraordinary experiences; some had such strong premonitions of danger, an inner warning so intense, as to cause them to change their plans. The first instance is not a dream but a "feeling" which may be just as much a warning as a dream in the night.

DREAM THREE

"It was on February 22, 1948, when I was getting ready early in the morning to set out on a long-anticipated skiing expedition with my seven-year-old boy. We had everything all ready and were about to leave the house when a strange feeling came over me—hard to describe, but increasingly strong, that I should not travel. At first I did not want to give in to it, but then, in spite of the good weather reports, I decided to stay home. That evening we heard on the radio that there had been a bad accident (on the train). . . . We surely would have come back on that train and it might have been our death."

DREAM FOUR (A PREMONITION)

The foregoing instance of a strong premonition of danger, such as is often presaged in dreams, was especially meaningful to me for it corroborated in almost identical detail the experience of a younger brother of mine who was, several years ago, living in Heidelberg, Germany. He had been planning a skiing trip over the New Year's holidays for months and had written me in great detail about the anticipated pleasures of this holiday party; he is a teacher and several other young teachers and their wives would comprise the group. On his way to the train ready to depart for the Swiss mountain resort where the rest of the party would meet, since they were arriving from different parts of Germany, he was overwhelmed by a sense of danger, a feeling that he must not go on this expedition. He tried to overcome the feeling, so irrational and without foundation so far as reason could make out. He was at the train steps; his skis were on his shoulders and his overnight kit in hand—and he found that he was simply unable to mount the steps, so overwhelming was the sense of prohibition against this journey.

He turned back and telegraphed to his friends that unexpected difficulties prevented his joining them. Baffled, uneasy, unable to account for the morbid feeling of depression which hovered about him or the inexplicable prevention of his holiday outing, he moped about for the week following, at a complete loss to understand why he was in Heidelberg instead of skiing as he had long planned. Seven days later he heard on the radio the news of an avalanche sliding down upon the ski resort where he would have been. All of his friends had perished. Only one survivor, the wife of one of the young men, who had remained at the inn, returned from that sad holiday outing.

The courage to follow vague and indefinite feelings that warn speaks volumes for that person's closeness to his own instincts which always serve, as an animal's instinctive awareness of potential danger, to protect and preserve individual life, or to guide it exactly as if there were actually a "Guardian Angel" protecting the person.

Many dreams and premonitions deal with trivialities but there are just as many, more in fact, which are deeply meaningful in the sense of being fateful.

DREAM FIVE

"My son was serving at the recruit school in Basel. There he dreamed of his dead father. He only saw his face and an uplifted hand and heard him say: 'You may not go over the bridge.' In the morning he forgot the dream but the next night he saw the same apparition, and the words were repeated too. Just then he was assigned to kitchen duty where he over-ate so thoroughly that he woke up with thirty-nine degrees [C.] of temperature and had to stay in bed, while his comrades went on a march and on maneuvers. Three hours later the report reached the barracks that a bridge had collapsed and that half a train was buried under it. There was one dead, several were fatally wounded; the others escaped with bruises and lacerations. My son was well enough to participate in the funeral services; not a trace of his fever was left." [5]

The final example offered in this category is one which raises uneasy questions about the unavoidability of fate; at least in this instance the impression is definitely one that elements we know nothing whatever about can be at work in our lives. To outwit them is virtually impossible, but here is one such uncommon instance in which Fate appears to have been worsted.

DREAM SIX

"I was making use of a lovely spring day to transplant some raspberry bushes and tie them up. We went to the garden with both children. The smallest one went right off to the sandpile and we, to the berries. When I looked at the bushes I suddenly felt a heaviness in my chest which can hardly be expressed in words. I started to work, but was overcome with restlessness. I told my wife how queerly I felt, yet that very moment the question came to my mind: 'Why this restlessness? Yes, that's it. I've already done this work in the raspberries once before in a dream, and there was something unpleasant about it that I can't remember.' Now I knew that I must watch out for my little one—she is two years old—and every few minutes I looked in her direction. Suddenly, when I look again, she is gone. I send my older child to see if the gate is closed, too. She runs off, she passes the water trough, stops, looks into it, bends over it—a heart-rending scream: 'Mama!' and she pulls the little one out of the trough. Her face was already blue and she no longer breathed—but I took her to the doctor anyway, and he was able to save her."

The above are a random few examples of psychical experiences known to many; there are today ample records of Psi phenomena and Extra-Sensory Perception investigations which tell their own eloquent story in full detail. Published late in 1961, Louise E. Rhine's *Hidden Channels of the Mind* is crammed with instances of telepathic dreams recorded through years of investigations conducted with her husband, J. B. Rhine, at Duke University's world-renowned Parapsychological Laboratory, to which we unhesitatingly refer you.

1. Jung, *The Structure and Dynamics of the Psyche*, pp. 261–62.
2. Meier, *op. cit.*
3. Meier, *op. cit.*
4. Zurich and Stuttgart: Rascher Verlag, 1958.
5. Aniela Jaffe, *Spring*, 1959, pp. 34–36.

CHAPTER EIGHTEEN

Archetypal Dreams

*Whenever something turns up in a dream
that has little or no connection with
ordinary life, in which there are no
railroads or street-cars or houses, no parents
or relations, but where there are dragons
or temples or something that does not exist
in one's usual surroundings, then you can
be sure that the unconscious is tending to
convey the idea of something extraordinary,
something uncommon, and it depends upon
the nature of the symbolism to tell us
what particular kind of extraordinary
thing it is. . . . When such an archetypal
pattern comes to the foreground, you can
be sure that fate is on the way. And fate is
power, an instinctive power in man,
because he creates his own fate.*
　　C. G. JUNG [1]

DREAM ONE

A dream with many archetypal images and motifs is the following from the records of Dr. Gerhard Adler, London, England. (Extract from a series.)

"A quiet lake in a forest. A black horse is grazing in a meadow
alongside. After a time it becomes restless, pricks up its ears and
seems to be waiting for its master. It approaches the lake in order
to drink. The image reflected in the water, however, is not that
of a horse but of a horseman, that is to say of a man in the posi-

tion and action of riding, but without a horse, This figure is that of a handsome man in a purple cloak. The horse enters the water in order to reach the rider, whose image, however, recedes before it. The animal waits irresolutely and then trots away."

The dreamer was a woman of forty, deeply depressed and in a general state of anxiety but with nothing in particular to account for these symptoms. She was a handsome widow who looked considerably younger than her years, the mother of two gifted and attractive children. Her husband had died a few years previously. According to her account, she had lived on the happiest terms with him; he had been a distinguished doctor and scientist, also a most devoted and kindly human being. Her financial circumstances were assured. The only external cause of her depression was, apparently, the loss of her husband five years previously but this, oddly enough, she strenuously denied, admitting willingly that she had suffered and still suffered from his loss, but this was not the cause.

I will give you Dr. Adler's analysis of this dream. "The first thing that strikes one is that the *horse* appears to be seeking its master. The *horse*, as a symbol, appears constantly in myth and folklore. It is, as we should say, an 'archetype,' that is, a figure emanating from the levels of the collective unconscious. As Jung says, the horse as an animal represents the non-human psyche, the sub-human, biological sphere, or in psychological parlance, the unconscious, and that is why in folklore horses are frequently represented as clairvoyant and clairaudient and why they sometimes even speak. The horse is also an animal that not only carries man but brings him forward, and is thus the symbol of vehicular force possessing dynamic power. 'The horse carries one forward just as do the instincts, but like them is subject to panic, because being an animal it lacks the higher gifts of consciousness.' Wotan on Sleipneir, or, considered from another aspect, those hybrid creatures the centaurs, are just two examples, chosen from among countless instances, of the role played by the horse in mythology and folklore. The horse represents the biological libido, natural energy, or in its widest sense, the unconscious instinctual sphere. The *black color* connotes the chthonic earthly side—or to use a term of Chinese philosophy, the 'Yin'-side.

"This primitive energy, the unconscious, requires conscious direction if it is to become productive in the human and spiritual sense. *Conscious leadership* is naturally represented by *the rider*. And that is why, in a dream, the horse is seeking its master. But it is significant that in the dream the rider is represented as the reflection of the horse itself. This indicates a truly magical relation between horse and rider. They represent a fundamental unity, but nevertheless they are separated.

"The *lake in the forest* is also an archetype in mythology and folklore; it is the place of mystery in the sacred grove where the great transformations occur; it is the fountain of youth, the place of re-birth, of spiritual baptism, the place of initiation: it represents the unconscious fraught with magic power. In this magic field of force, the horse appears transformed into its master, representing at one and the same time both its own reflection and its completion on a higher level. In the dream the rider appears in the position and attitude of riding, that is, as belonging to the horse and connected with him in the closest possible manner. The rider's proud bearing and *mantle of royal purple* indicate his exalted and dominant character, but it is clear that the horse is unable, as yet, to reach its master.

"In order to understand this fact fully, we must keep in mind that the dream is dreamed by a woman. That gives the figure of the rider—a male figure—its special significance. To a woman the symbol of the man means spirit in its widest sense; he represents the principle of Logos, as the woman in the psychology of a man represents the principle of Eros. Therefore the dream indicates to the woman that the merely instinctual, chthonic side, the unconscious, must be directed by the principle of spirit. The unconscious as the 'objective psyche' must be led by the subjective Ego-consciousness. The rider, as representative of the spiritual principle, is still hidden in the magic waters of the lake; he is only

an immaterialized reflection, that is, an unrealized idea, and must
first be born from the deep waters of the unconscious, teeming
with life. At present the horse is unable to reach the rider, and
the closer it comes the further its master's image recedes. A
mysterious power prevents these two components of what is,
after all, an essential unity from meeting.

"This dream proceeds from the deepest levels of the unconscious. The unconscious psyche has not yet been sufficiently prepared and the higher level of consciousness represented by the
unity of rider and horse cannot, therefore, as yet be attained."

This striking dream presents to the dreamer the mid-life problem of developing the other-half, with the aid of the Animus, a
not uncommon demand upon women who have lived entirely the
instinctual, feminine side of themselves up to that time. "It stands
to reason that if an intelligent and gifted woman of forty is entirely sunk in memories of the past and the care of her children,
she is seriously neglecting the duty of developing her own spiritual personality. Her development has been arrested by becoming fixed in a typically feminine and passive attitude toward life
and she must learn to compensate for this by adopting a more
masculine attitude," Dr. Adler relates. He adds, however, "It is
essential to avoid the mistaken assumption that the masculine
principle is in itself superior to the feminine. Each is compensatory to the other. Thus, a man who has lived a too one-sided,
masculine life—e.g., 'an intellectual and active one—needs to
compensate by developing a more 'feminine' attitude, e.g.,
through a development of his *feeling* side. Equally, a too-
feminine woman needs to develop her intellectual side. . . ." [2]

DREAM TWO (SERIES)

The series of dreams following are a most impressive example of
inner psychical activity, archetypal in character, compressing in
their imagery the elements of Compensation, the Prospective
function, involving something of the Somatic and Reactive principles as well. The series, a short one of only seven dreams, five

of which are recorded here, is analyzed by Dr. Meier, who describes the circumstances of the dreamer thus: [8]

"The dreamer had been a very successful American businessman—a banker—of 56 years of age. When he came to me he had been in a very serious melancholic depression for over three years and had been in various excellent American mental institutions where all possible efforts had been made to cure him. He was without any hope, he was completely paralysed and could not really speak or listen. He was literally dragged into the consulting room by his wife and he was quite unable to answer any questions. He was seen once a day for perhaps twenty minutes or so and in the monologue—for he never answered any questions and appeared completely unimpressed by what was said—the effort was made to impress him with the fact that such depressions may have some deeper meaning and that it would be particularly helpful if he would tell of his dreams. After about one week of this rather one-sided conversation his wife said that he had had a dream and that she had written it down for him. From then on the patient had one dream each night for more than a week at the end of which time he was cured and remained cured for the rest of his life."

Dream #1.

"I was fishing for trout, not in an ordinary stream or lake but in a reservoir divided into compartments. For a time I fished with the usual equipment of flies, etc., but I caught nothing. Becoming exasperated, I took up a three-pronged spear, which was lying nearby, and immediately I succeeded is spearing a fine fish."

Dream #2.

"The dream began as I dropped my eyeglasses and broke them. I immediately got into a Ford car which was standing close at hand and drove off towards the optician's office. (I never drive automobiles myself in conscious life.) On the way I saw an old man, a respected friend and advisor of mine. I asked him to come with me which he did. On the journey to see the optician

I told the old man of my worries and difficulties and received from him much good advice."

Dream #3.
"In this dream I went to the railway station . . . to receive a large amount of money, which had to be taken from the station to one of the banks. I made several trips but before doing so I arranged for a guard to follow me on the street, keeping a little way behind me. After one or two trips I glanced around and I could not see the guard, so I quickly turned around and went back to the station. Then I found the guard sitting down on a comfortable bench in a small park. I accused him of neglecting his duty; I was quite bitter in my remarks to him. His only reply was that the arrangement was foolish since there was no danger of anyone in Zurich attacking me."

Dream #4.
"I was standing on Fifth Avenue, New York City, watching the return of the Rainbow Division from the Great War. I saw many old friends in the marching troops. After the parade had ended several of us met for dinner. Among the party was a very humorous officer who made prophecies about our future. Some of his remarks were very funny—but he did not get to prophesy my future before the dream ended."

Dream #5:
(The final one of the series of seven.) "I went to the home of the great male eels somewhere in the South Atlantic. I watched billions of eels starting home and could see them in the water as far as the horizon."

The principle of Compensation is demonstrated from the first dream which, in contrast with outer passivity, depicts autonomous activity within: he goes fishing. Says Dr. Meier, 'I want to say a few things about other elements in the dream. Fishing had been the patient's hobby, but the hobby no longer seemed satisfactory as he did not succeed in catching any fish; the reservoir

divided into compartments was a peculiar place, not only because
it was not a usual arrangement but also because the water was
stagnant. The *stagnation* was a very apt description of his paralysis. The various *compartments* meant that everything in life was
neatly divided up and concealed; that is an illustration of what we
are used to call 'compartment psychology.' But then something
unusual happened, unusual for his present state of mind. He got
exasperated. This was an emotional reaction which took place
spontaneously; it was connected with a faint realization of his in-
adequacy in respect to his situation. The literal meaning of the
word 'emotion' means 'to be moved out of' something, namely, in
that case, I would say, out of his paralysis. When he got emotional, exasperated, as he put it, there was a connection with his
perception of the *three-pronged spear*. This was the culmination
of the dream which brought in an entirely new element. The in-
ference was that the spear had always been there but he had not
seen it. Immediately after he became excited he did see it and the
lysis followed as a matter of course in the spearing of the fine
specimen of trout.

"Now, I consider the *three-pronged spear* to be the famous
trident of Poseidon, or Neptune. The trident, Poseidon's spear, is
the main attribute of this Greek God. In other words, it is this
God himself. Who is this God, then? . . . Poseidon is Zeus'
brother and the brother of Hades and the brother of Hera. When
they divided the world up among themselves Poseidon got the
Sea, Zeus the Heaven and Hades the Underworld. They are
equals, inasmuch as all three of them have the whole Cosmos and
rule the Cosmos. Poseidon, more particularly, is the God of
Earthquakes; he produces earthquakes by driving his trident into
the earth. With such an act the whole globe shakes. But Poseidon
is not only destructive, he is creative inasmuch as each time he
uses his trident, something creative like the welling up of a spring
(e.g., the Hippokrene) or the opening up of a valley (e.g., the
Hellespont and the Bosporus or the Peneus in Thessaly) happens. Besides this, Poseidon is the god of storms. He, also, is a

stormy lover, has affairs with all sorts of creatures producing many offspring, so that he is creative also in this sense. He is the god of the earth and as such is responsible for fertility, in particular plant-fertility. . . . Then he is a horseman par excellence and has created the first horse by using his trident. Then he is called . . . the father of men, particularly by the Ionians and as such the father of the tribe and its protector. He has a number of other qualities of minor importance; he is an oracle god in Delphi; he is a doctor, the father of the two famous doctors in the Iliad, Machaon and Podaleirios. Now from all these attributes we can see that he is a creative god and the trident is his main creative instrument. As such it has a typically phallic connotation. I want to point out in this connection that the Phallos in the Greek sense is never conceived of as being a symbol in the Freudian sense meaning only a sema for the male organ but that it means a real symbol in the Jungian sense, pointing at the power of creation in nature which is far from being understood, appearing to possess a mystical quality. . . ."

We include Dr. Meier's comments on the symbol of the trident with very little condensation, in order that you may see how the amplification of dream imagery proceeds, in actual practice. But as previously indicated, a single dream can seldom be analyzed correctly, so we proceed to the subsequent dreams to see whether there will be confirmation of what appears to be a healing dream, very much on the order of the *somnia a deo missa*, "dreams sent by God," that heralded cures in the ancient Aesculapia of Greece.

Dr. Meier continues, "Now I should like to compare the two dreams in respect to motifs. The dropping and breaking of his eyeglasses represents a conflict; it is to be likened to his unsuccessful fishing in the first dream. The glasses, in this case, were broken and that created a tension of some sort or an impasse, comparable to the emotion appearing in the first dream. At the impasse in this dream he got into a Ford car which was standing close at hand. So the Ford car had a similar function to the trident in the first dream, it came to his help, to his rescue. He began to be astonishingly active, compared to the absolute passivity he displayed in his depression; this was shown by the remark he made that in conscious life he never drove automobiles himself—he always used to have a chauffeur. Thus we can say that he got into motion, he became emotional as it were. Yet while the automobile was driven by him, the automobile is something that moves autonomously, not by conscious forces but by forces of a different sort. I noted that Poseidon was a great horseman and charioteer; the automobile can, therefore, be compared to Neptune's chariot which is driven by his horses. The man the dreamer wants to see, namely the optician who is to mend his broken glasses, is in some way an allegory of the doctor, whereas the old friend he met and whom he called a respected friend and advisor would be like the 'Wise Old Man.' The friend and advisor, however, corresponds to the fish he caught in the first dream, inasmuch as the fish was the solution, the lysis, of the dream and in the second dream the lysis was the good advice he received from his friend. Now, with regard to this advisor I should like to come back to Poseidon who is the . . . 'old man of the sea,' and who interestingly enough has many of the qualities of the advisor in the old myths.

"As I said, Poseidon was an oracle god and a doctor and he was also related to the fish. From these two qualities of Poseidon I arrived at the conclusion that the old-man advisor the dreamer met was closely connected with the Poseidon figure, thus closely connected with the fish in the first dream. Again I should say that the fish as well as the old friend both come to him spontaneously; in the first dream he seized upon the possibility given to him by Poseidon, and that in such a way that something was achieved, or came to him, or came back to him, which had hitherto been lost. I think we have to interpret the fish in the first dream as a typical libido symbol and from the epicrisis of the case we know that this libido actually did come back to him shortly after he had the first dream. . . .The return of energy in the psychological sense was indicated over and over again in the series of dreams. . . . With regard to the last dream I should like to make only one remark. The homing of the eels is one of the most astonishing phenomena in nature—as you may know some individuals among the eels stop feeding in the autumn and become silvery; then these silver eels descend to the sea and travel across the Atlantic to breed in an area southeast of Bermuda; they die after breeding. Larvae called *Leptocephali*, which are transparent, travel back to Europe in the course of two and half years' time. It has been proved that these larvae find their way back to the same waters from which their long-dead parents came when they started on their honeymoon trip to the Bermudas. In view of this fact I think we may safely draw the conclusion from these dreams that the instinct is infallible and energy will find its way back to the dreamer in due course."

1. C. G. Jung, *Spring*, 1960, 131–33.
2. Gerhard Adler, Ph.D., Guild Lecture #5, Guild of Pastoral Psychology, London, England.
3. Meier, *op. cit.*

CHAPTER NINETEEN

Conclusion

I do not address myself to nations
but only to those few people amongst whom
it is taken for granted that our civilisation
("Kultur") does not drop from heaven
but is, in the end, produced by individuals.
If the great cause fails it is because the
individuals fail, because I fail. So I must
first put myself right. And as authority
has lost its spell I need for this
purpose knowledge and experience of the
most intimate and intrinsic foundations of
my subjective being so as to build my base
upon the eternal factors of the human
soul.
    C. G. JUNG [1]

Jung's remarks, above, might have been directed to those individuals concerned with widening the range of their consciousness by learning to interpret the information contained in their dreams, so aptly put are the essentials. To "put yourself right" with "knowledge and experience of the most intimate and intrinsic foundations of your subjective being" is precisely the aim of the venture. The work really amounts to research which, as the contents of this book will have disclosed, is extremely varied. During its course you are sustained and encouraged to discern with increasing clarity the personality emerging out of your dreams, of which you previously had been more-or-less unconscious. In short, you have been *individuating*.

While the work is necessarily solitary, you are not alone. Rather, as you go deeper with your research the more plainly do you see the connections linking you to specialists in other studies. You recognize that you have taken your place in the *avant garde* of that evolutionary stream surging powerfully through our present era, as exhibited in the fantastic convergence of mental, psychological and physical achievements already here: the release of nuclear energy, the manipulation of genes and chromosomes for the control of heredity and sex, the liberation of the human spirit from psychic bondage through the knowledge of psychoanalysis and understanding of depth psychology, the recognition that words-in-use are symbols and its concomitant, that we have not yet learned to use our minds properly, all these achievements amount to breakthroughs to new plateaus in human history from which the future advances will be launched.

The aggregate of these accomplishments has created a new climate in which is emerging a new genus, called *Homo progressivus* by the late distinguished paleontologist, Pierre Teilhard de Chardin,[2] the scientist whose acquaintance with man has extended all the way back to *Sinanthropus*, which he helped to identify. De Chardin has struck perhaps the most hopeful note of any scientist of eminence as to the future prospects of mankind. I shall not digress here into an account of his views but I do want to mention a quality he singled out in particular as one distinguishing mark of the new breed, and that is, a mysterious sense of the future.

Leaving to posterity the question of whether the hermeneut truly represents *Homo progressivus*, there is no question but that you are unmistakably gripped by a sense of the future. More accurately, you perceive a curiously *immediate* participation in it, possibly the more intensified when it is deliberate, conscious choice that impels you to take on the task of *lessening the collective unconsciousness by as much as one individual's quanta*, your very own portion, in your lifetime. Such action becomes, as Jung remarks of the psyche,[3] "intervention in the existing natural order [and] no one can say with certainty where this intervention will finally end." But your own heightened consciousness will detect that such intervention is of a cosmic order, capable of effecting an alteration of principle, through transmutation, in precisely the manner of the observer in physics, the science complementary to depth psychology, as described by the Nobel physicist, Wolfgang Pauli:

"Every observation (by the observer, i.e., an individual) interferes on an indeterminable scale both with the instruments of observation and with the system observed and interrupts the causal connection of the phenomena preceding it with those following it. . . . [The resulting selective observation] may be compared to a creation in the microcosm or even to a transmutation, the results of which are, however, unpredictable and beyond human control."[4]

Profoundly, the individual counts; though the full meaning of your individual efforts to bring to consciousness what is in your own unconscious may not be revealed to you, you can know that you are going in the only progressive direction of the future evolution of man on this earth. But that is not all. Something far more personal, intimate and immediate, will come about. As Jung says:

"Whoever nurtures this contact between conscious and unconscious will, in time, experience a great spiritual and moral release of tension, his inner oppositions will be lessened; he will take root in his instincts and gain that sense of security and support which is beyond the reach of the intellect and will with its oscillating relations. At the same time there will develop in him an undreamed-of fullness of life that expands rather than shrinks with age because the instincts and values are being truly lived."[5]

1. Quoted by H. Westmann in "The Old Testament and Analytical Psychology," Guild Lecture No. 10, The Guild of Pastoral Psychology, London, England.

2. Of *Homo progressivus* de Chardin says, "When we come to look for them, men of this sort are easily recognizable. They are scientists, thinkers, airmen and so on—all possessed by the demon (or the Angel) of Research. . . . This new human type will be found to be scattered more or less all over the thinking face of the globe. . . . You have only to take two men, in any gathering, endowed with this mysterious sense of the future. They will gravitate instinctively towards one another in the crowd; they will know one another. . . . No racial, social or religious barrier seems to be effective against this force of attraction. I myself have experienced this a hundred times, and anyone who chooses can do the same. . . ." Pierre Teilhard de Chardin, *The Future of Man* (New York: Harper & Row, 1964), pp. 137-8.

3. See Chapter Three, The Psyche.

4. Pauli, *op. cit.*, p. 211. Pauli further elaborates his thesis by pointing to the fact that the emotional aspect of the observer's experience (in experimental physics) stands in vital relationship not only to contemporary knowledge but also to the actual process of cognition.

5. C. G. Jung, *Spring*, 1960.

INDEX

Abaton, 82, 88n.
Across the Plains (Stevenson), 115n.
Adams, Henry, 45, 167, 168
Adler, Alfred, views of, 24, 28
Adler, Dr. Gerhard, 230–233, 239n.
Adlerian school: Individual Psychology, 25
Aesculapia, 237
Aiken, Conrad, 158
Airplanes, in dream imagery, 211
All's Well That Ends Well, (Shakespeare), 115n.
Aloneness, as dream image, 185
Ambivalence, of close relationships, 84, 129
See also "Participation mystique"; Projections
Amplification, 145–146, 161–162, 169, 173, 237
Analysis, 141, 175–176; of dreams (*example*), 150–152; true end of, 177

"Analysis of Patients Who Meet the Problems of the First Half of Life in the Second" (Dunn), 178n.
Analytical Psychology (Jungian), 25, 36 ff., 51n.
Anima, as archetypal image, 35, 54–55; as feminine image in man, 125–139 *passim,* 139nn., 172, 190, 207; as projection of the unconscious, 125 ff.
See also Animus
Animals, 75–76
See also *names of animals*
Animus, 54, 124–130, 133–134; images of, 135, 136, 137, 139nn., 190; as masculine image in woman, 125–139 *passim,* 139nn.
Apperception, 166
See also Communication; Mercury
Arab, as dream image, 205

244